P9-EAY-559

Contents

 JEWISH
PHILOSOPHY IN
MODERN TIMES:

From Mendelssohn to Rosenzweig

NATHAN ROTENSTREICH

HOLT, RINEHART AND WINSTON

NEW YORK · CHICAGO · SAN FRANCISCO

For Binah once again

\

# Introduction

The present volume contains an analysis of the main currents of Jewish thought from the time of Moses Mendelssohn to Rosenzweig, Gordon and Kook. The substance of the view under consideration leads to a close examination of those elements that stress the ethical content of Judaism, identifying the claims of its moral code as the vital center of the religion of the Spirit. Such an emphasis is based on Jewish tradition but is prepared to take advantage of philosophical analysis and to employ concepts which are historically and systematically philosophical. Thus, for instance, the transfer of the philosophical idea of first cause to the concept of God as understood in the book of Genesis represents the use of a philosophical concept in the articulation of a biblical notion. This instance taken from the philosophy of the Middle Ages is paralleled in modern philosophy by the transfer of the concept of obeying commandments and fulfilling duties, which, again, is an employment of a philosophical concept for the sake of an articulation of a traditional and hence less defined, or even ambiguous, notion.[1]

In this respect—as in many others—modern philosophy has followed the example of the philosophy of Judaism in the Middle Ages. The very transfer of philosophical concepts to traditional religious discourse is a symptom of a "climate of opinion" characterized by the encounter between traditional currents and philosophical systems. In the Middle Ages, philosophy took advantage of the Aristotelian concept of the first cause or of the neo-Platonic concept of the One. In modern times, the philosophy of Judaism took advantage of the ethical meaning of the idea of God as implied in Kant, or of the idea of Spirit as put forward in post-Kantian systems; or again of some ideas of the human predicament and its possible religious interpretation as visible in philosophical trends whose point of departure is very often the criticism of philosophic idealism.

We may thus say that such an encounter is a constant feature of the religious situation in a world which is composed of ingredients whose nature is not exclusively religious. Although the over-all situation, and more specifically the character of the philosophical trends encountered, has changed, the philosophies of Judaism, as in the Middle Ages, have the combined objective of articulation and justification.[2] This task of justification is twofold: on the one hand, it addresses itself to different historical religions; and on the other, to the very character of philosophy. To be sure, the general climate of opinion is vastly changed from that of the Middle Ages: the criticism of Christianity—possibly, the most significant example—is now far more pronounced. There is, to say the least, less fear of suppression by ecclesiastic or political authorities. Philosophers outside the Jewish realm have themselves been engaged in a criticism and reformulation of Christianity, as was the case with Kant and Hegel, let alone Nietzsche. The extraphilosophical encounter with the Christian world tends to encourage the modern Jew to disregard historical differences between historical religions in the name of humanity and human rights. He may even be tempted to formulate a Religion of Reason, along the lines suggested either by Auguste Comte or Hermann Cohen.

The task of articulation undertaken by the philosophers of Judaism was to preserve the distinct character of Judaism as they understood it; this may explain why modern Jewish philosophy became a preoccupation of German Jewry from the beginning of the modern era until the Nazi catastrophe.

But the task of justification, as we observed before, is important not only in terms of other religions, but also in terms of philosophy. The very fact that one can employ philosophical concepts as equivalent with the innate notions implied in a tradition is in itself a kind of justification. It may be taken to indicate the fundamental affinity between the over-all view implied in a tradition and a philosophical world-outlook whose sources are non-traditional, or even, in terms of their origin, anti-traditional. On the other hand, this justification may only represent an adjustment of religion to philosophy. The other approach, represented by Pascal and not unknown in the Middle Ages, is one in which philosophy as such is criticized philosophically, and stress is laid on the fundamental limitations of philosophy as an attitude and a body of presuppositions. In the present book, we find this trend represented to some extent by S. D. Luzzatto, and especially by S. L. Stenheim and Franz Rosenzweig. But even Hermann Cohen, steeped as he was in Kantian philosophy, comes close to indicating the difference between philosophical ethics—that is, the ethics of mankind—and religious ethics, which is the ethics of every single individual who discovers himself as an individual in his relation with God. Here again the difference between the emphasis placed on the totality of mankind as against the irreducibility of individuals is neither accidental nor simply historical; ultimately it is an essential difference between the domain of philosophy and religion.

No analysis of the modern interpretations of Judaism can be unaware that its ethical core is strongly emphasized. This is most probably due to the changing character of philosophy since Kant. The critique of metaphysics brought about the critique of *religious* metaphysics. The continued recognition of ethics as a value unchallenged by achievements of empirical knowledge brought about the emphasis on religious ethics (whatever the meaning of "religious" in this context) as the essence of Judaism. In a different interpretation, it was seen as the residual content of Judaism whose validity can be safeguarded even after religious metaphysics has been demolished by Kant. To be sure, there are nuances here; the philosophical anti-philosophies are naturally less prone to an ethical orientation than the philosophies which take philosophy positively. But even the former could not escape the earth-shaking effect of the Kantian critique.

The significance of the ethical interpretations of Judaism can be clearly discerned from another point of view. As man's attachment to God, religion retains its identity in spite of all the stress placed on the ethical character of God. Ethics, however, can be understood as having sources in a religious world-outlook; but eventually goes beyond it. The ethical interpretation of Judaism makes possible a further, more radical interpretation, that the ethical teaching of Judaism may be meaningful and binding apart from religious attachment. Thus the ethical interpretation can be placed historically on the borderline of the religious attitude and the secular transformation of Judaism. This transformation is prompted not by the inner logic of the religious world-outlook, but by the dilemma of the modern Jew who, while being modern, attempts to adhere to Jewish tradition. The ethical core of this tradition can be interpreted as meeting his need or as solving his dilemma.

Obviously, it is no easy matter to distinguish between essential and peripheral aspects of this tradition as it unfolds within the process of history. At one period, religion includes both ethical commandments and an over-all understanding of the universe as it is described in Genesis. Later, the idea that man has to act in a certain way and give preference to spirit over his animal drives is seen as fundamental, while myths pertaining to the structure of the universe are no longer regarded as having intrinsic religious relevance.

The ethical trend has an additional and most important aspect which, philosophically speaking, only brings to the foreground the dialectical character of the development to which we are pointing. The ethical trend obviously highlights the personal character of human conduct—man is understood as a thinking and rational being endowed with a capacity for reflection on his endurance in different times and places. In what sense, it should now be asked, can we still speak about a personal God, assuming that we retain the ethico-religious attitude at all? As long as "person" carries with it the distinction between subjects and things, the concept of person and personality can be applied to God, since God is not a thing. Yet in what sense is God a person as a being referring to himself, capable of being answerable for his deeds? The ethical trend is bound to be concerned with the meaning of God, not simply as an idea but as person, within the boundaries delineated by this very trend. Here again one may wonder whether the superimposition of the ethical concept of the person on God is just an articulation of a meaning implied in the traditional scriptures, or rather a transformation of a concept, or both.

For the sake of systematic unity, the problems dealt with in this study have not been treated chronologically, but as a whole. I hoped, in this way, to do greater justice to the baffling variety of questions and proffered solutions, and to indicate significant lines of connection with, or points of divergence from, other systems of thought without losing sight of historical continuity. My aim is an objective presentation of the various manifestations of Jewish thought in the last century. A critical evaluation however, is implicit in the exposition of the problems which, I hope, may serve as an aid and incentive to further study.

This volume presents the fruit of an intensive study of Jewish problems that has occupied me since the years of World War II and the fate of European Jewry. I have attempted to trace the progress and development of ideas and of ideals in a generation that has lost its belief in the authority of religion. Obviously, the problems discussed, which have their roots in man's nature and practical experience, will not be solved in this book. But one may hope to shed some light on the underlying issues, indicate their relevancy for modern man and thus deepen his understanding. The world must be understood before it can be changed.

It remains for me to express my gratitude to Beryl Katznelson, of blessed memory, who encouraged me to write this book. Dr. N. Jacobs was good enough to prepare this version of the book and I am much obliged to him and to his help and insight.

The former President of the Hebrew University of Jerusalem, Mr. Eliahu Elath, extended his friendly help. Professor M. Davis, Head of the Institute of Contemporary Jewry at the Hebrew University, has shown his faithful interest in this book. Rabbi Benjamin Kahn, National Director of the Hillel Foundations, encouraged its publication in the United States.

Mrs. Rita Sapir has again undertaken the burden of preparation and proofreading. I am grateful to her, and to Mr. Joseph Cunneen, who acted as editor on this book at Holt, Rinehart and Winston.

Jerusalem, 1968   N. R.

The Rule of Ethics

MOSES MENDELSSOHN

A. ROOTS

Jewish thought in recent times has been characterized by the prominence given to the ethical values of Judaism. This interpretation is not altogether novel, since Judaism was never divorced from moral values, and human conduct in the light of moral imperatives is an inseparable part of the religious world of the Jew. What strikes us as new is the insistence on the primacy of ethics in the sphere of faith; traditional religion is divested of its beliefs in transcendence, and pressed into the service of morality.

The dominant position of ethics is not foreign to the development of traditional Judaism. Through the ages the daily conduct of its adherents has been regulated by moral imperatives and guided by law. The religious world of Judaism is distinguished by the fact that it combines faith in God with reliance on the Torah. The principle of morality, submission to the imperative of conduct, is inseparable from the first principle of religion, which is the love of God. The opinion of Elijah Delmedigo (ca. 1460–1497), one of the teachers of Pico della Mirandola, that religion consists of moral conduct not dependent on syllogisms or rational demonstration, expresses a deep-rooted Jewish religious sentiment.

The prominence given to ethical values in Judaism is reflected in this practical aspect of Jewish life. Ethics is implicit in human action, constituting the end of social intercourse and the norm that guides it. It lifts the prosaic deeds of the phenomenal world of accident and caprice into the realm of meaning. The spiritual tendencies in modern Judaism were indeed governed by this dominant phase of human conduct to which law and justice imparted the authority of the moral imperative. Mendelssohn's significance lies precisely in this emphasis on human conduct as the essence of religion and on law as the guiding principle of Judaism. The reasons that underlie Mendelssohn's attitude and the vexing problem of the relation of law to the moral imperative, which he left unresolved, will concern us later.

If the problem of ethics looms large in modern Jewish thought, it is not only because of internal developments within Judaism, but also from general philosophic considerations. Modern religious philosophy, for example, was concerned with defining the limits of religion with respect to the other disciplines, in order to establish a sovereign sphere where it might reign undisputed, with its own criteria of content and form. This task of demarcation was felt to be necessary not only because of the expanding spiritual horizon and the development of methical instruments of criticism but also because of the growing conflict between theoretical reason and its application in the sciences on the one hand, and religion as a system of doctrines and beliefs on the other. The question which engaged the thought of the Middle Ages, namely, the relation between reason and faith, science and religion, the revelations of the intellect and divine revelation, became increasingly acute with the rapid development of the modern sciences. One solution was to divorce faith from reason and sever all relations between the religious and the theoretical spheres. A religion with no claims to revealed speculative truths is unable to dislodge reason from its pre-eminent position or disprove its revelations. Religion, as a system of imperatives forced upon us by the nature of our practical lives, is invested with ethical meaning and relegated to an independent sphere where it is immune to the arguments of metaphysics or epistemology. In this way two closely related currents, the speculative-critical and the polemic-apologetic, have come together in modern European thought: the first designed to define the limits of religion and science and their respective spheres of influence, and the second to defend religion from apathy and skepticism.

As a system of imperatives directed towards human action, however, religion may be viewed in a different light. It may be regarded as a realm in which the ethical imperative is so formulated as to erase all distinctions between what is called religion in traditional terminology and what is simply called ethics or morality. Every imperative that embodies an ethical value thus becomes a religious imperative and religion assumes the function of regulating the basis of man's ethical life. This represents the extreme view of those who felt called upon to defend religion against the renewed attacks of the Enlightenment. In other more conciliatory solutions a fundamental distinction is made between religion and ethics and religion is assigned definite tasks not subsumed under ethics, or the ethical realm is made independent and given authority to forge its own imperatives and to advocate their imperious claims. This progressive emancipation of ethics towards autonomy is a process which has not reached its final stage; until it does, positive religion (and this applies also to Christianity) need not forfeit its position as the highest development of ethical consciousness. The province of ethics is not identical with that of religion but exists in its own right. Take from religion its doctrinal basis and the autonomy of ethics is established. The difference between the two realms is not in the *content* of the ethical imperative, but depends rather on its doctrinal foundation. This view, which was held by various circles in the eighteenth century, revived a medieval idea, found also in Jewish philosophical literature, which denied that there was any difference in *content* between philosophy and religion or between science and Torah as the fruit of divine revelation. The difference is only one of *form*; in other words, in the last analysis the autonomous intellectual truth is also a religious truth that stems from divine revelation. When religion is transferred from the speculative sphere to that of practical ethics, the question arises concerning the relation between an autonomous ethics and one founded on the imperatives of positive religion. Here, too, the relation between the two spheres is conceived as one in which the content is identical and the bases different.

Another interpretation conceives of religion as being not identical with ethics but *supplementary* to it. The imperatives that guide human action are not restricted to the sphere of man's social life and his relations with other men but also include man's relations to his Maker, the region where religion holds sway. Religion is not a system of beliefs and doctrines in a metaphysical sense but an adjunct of the ethical domain of deeds. One of the most enduring aspects of the influence of religion in human society lies precisely here, where religion provides ethics with rewards and punishments to spur conduct to greater moral perfection. The various expressions of this view will concern us later.

In the world of religious concepts itself it is also possible to discover evidence of interaction with ethics and the progressive approximation of the two spheres. The reality of sin is the cross-road where religion and ethics meet. Sin may be conceived as a perversion of an ethical imperative, a transgression of a divine command, or a denial of man's relation to his Maker. Sin has two faces: It is an objective bridge between religion and ethics in their limited sense and may also be, as expressed by Hermann Cohen, a bolt or latch that connects these two spheres.

This shift of the center of religious life from the sphere of speculative beliefs and doctrines to that of practical ethics resulted, at least partially from the indifference to metaphysics that characterized influential currents of thought in modern times—especially the criticism of Kant. Even in Christian theology ethics was sometimes made the basis of religion, as in the Ritschlian school of theology and its illustrious exponent Wilhelm Herrmann, who was a professor of theology in Marburg where he had many friendly discussions with Hermann Cohen. The repudiation of metaphysics as an instrument for attaining objective truth formed the common background for such diverse thinkers as S. D. Luzzatto, Hermann Cohen, and Moritz Lazarus—all of whom were influenced by Kant's writings in which he removed metaphysics from cognition and confined reason to the phenomena of the sensuous world.

The removal of religion to the sphere of ethics and morals in-

not universalist in all its morality by chance (handwritten margin note)

volves still another factor which is not to be overlooked, since it
reflects hidden intellectual currents. In the eyes of modern thinkers
religion appears as a historic reality—not merely the phenomenon
of religion itself, but the various religions in their individual forms.
The sphere of ethical imperatives lays claim to general validity;
the quality of universality is involved in its authority. Religion was
transferred to the ethical sphere not only to render it more secure
against the attacks of science from without but also to strengthen
its own foundations. A religion which is fundamentally ethics is
capable of acquiring a universal validity absent in the historical
religions which consist of both theory and practice, of faith and
ethical imperatives. This universalistic ideal also animated some
modern Jewish thinkers, such as Moritz Lazarus and Hermann
Cohen, who found in ethical Judaism the seeds of universalism,
whether revealed in the Messianic concept, in the idea of holiness,
or in certain imperatives found in Judaism and shared by all men.
It is not surprising, therefore, that recent Jewish thought expounded the seven Noachian laws as evidence of the ethical universalism of Judaism. This idea occupies a prominent place in
the writings of Elijah Benamozegh (1822–1900), the famous Italian
rabbi, and is one of the arguments advanced by Hermann Cohen
to prove that Judaism is a universal *Vernunftreligion.*

The significance of the ethical problem in recent Jewish thought
is apparent from the circumstance that in all the philosophical
treatises that deal with the nature of Judaism, however different
their points of view, a prominent place is accorded to ethics. One
school of thought begins its analysis by making Judaism dependent
on a metaphysical category, such as Spirit or revelation (Hirsch,
Formstecher, Steinheim). Despite the methodological and categorical differences in their systems, they all give prominence to
the ethical aspects of Judaism (the most outstanding exception being
Krochmal), except that Hirsch and Formstecher give an ethical
content to the ethical framework of Judaism and Steinheim an
ethical content to the metaphysical framework of Judaism. In
either case the consequences that flow from these divergent presuppositions are not far removed from one another. We now turn
to a consideration of those views which regard moral values as the
Alpha and Omega of religious speculation.

B. LAW THROUGH REVELATION

Moses Mendelssohn (1729–1786) sets forth his view of Judaism in both a positive and a negative form. According to the positive version Jews have been given a divine legislation; its precepts, commandments, ordinances, regulations, and prescriptions, which guide them in the attainment of temporal and eternal felicity, were revealed to them by Moses through miracles and supernatural means. In the negative version, supernatural legislation was understood as the supernatural revelation of religion; Judaism is spoken of as a revelation prior to the religious commandments and ordinances necessary for man's happiness. Mendelssohn does not recognize eternal truths outside those that accord with human reason, that can be explained by human faculties and verified by them.[1]

Judaism is a law and a way of life ordained by a divine Legislator, not a system of beliefs and doctrines that is essentially different or contradictory to reason, or even supplementary to it either in form or content. The shift of Judaism from the speculative sphere of metaphysics to the practical sphere of ethics, which is here distinctly formulated, becomes even clearer when we examine the concept of Judaism as legislation in Mendelssohn's system. Mendelssohn distinguishes not only between *metaphysics* and Judaism, but also between *religion* and Judaism, which is understood as a system of law ordained by a divine Legislator and hence not a religion in the proper sense of the word. The sphere of religion itself is not different from that of metaphysics either in content or method. On the contrary, the truths of religion, such as the reality of God, the immortality of the soul, and so forth, are part of the province of general speculative metaphysics. Christian Garve (1742–1798), a contemporary of Mendelssohn, summed up the thought of his age when he stated that the truths which constitute the substance of our dogmatic theology are the existence of God as a rational and ethical essence, the immortality of the soul through which alone our striving for perfection attains its goal and, finally, the truth that through ethical perfection we merit the love of God and the state of bliss in the life hereafter.[2] This formulation, with its obvious Christian overtones, is a true expression of the intellectual climate of that period and reflects a view it inherited from the Middle Ages, namely, that of the two independent spheres of religion and philosophy.

The Age of the Enlightenment went a step further, and by investing religion with speculative meanings, was able to subsume it under metaphysics and make it part and parcel of a metaphysical system. There were two facets to the rationalism of that period. On the one hand, it believed in the conquering impulse of the cognitive faculty, of the ability of the human intellect to demonstrate the principles of religion by rational means and logical syllogisms. On the other hand, this rationalistic age looked upon religion as a speculative sphere whose doctrines are unsusceptible of intellectual formulation and which can be made an integral part of metaphysics, once the artificial boundaries that separate it from the other disciplines are dissolved. Mendelssohn is an uncompromising advocate of the view that religion is not a separate realm apart from metaphysics, since its basic speculative truths constitute the proper subject matter of metaphysics. Judaism, however, is a well-defined historical reality which cannot be, in fact or in theory, subsumed under metaphysics. The distinctive historical image of Judaism is not conditioned by its being a religion and has no need of such corroborative support. Judaism is in essence a nonspeculative realm distinct from that of universal metaphysics, and is hence not a religion but a legislation, a system of laws and commandments. This ambiguity in Mendelssohn's thought is expressed in J. Guttmann's observation that Mendelssohn has elaborated a philosophy of religion which is, however, not a philosophy of *Judaism*.

An intimation of a different tendency is revealed to us in a passage in Mendelssohn's reflections on Charles Bonnet's Palingenesie[3] where the religion of Israel is said to consist essentially of only three principles—God, Providence, and Legislation. The first two are substantive truths of metaphysics into which the speculative doctrines of religion have been absorbed and the nonspeculative discarded. The third principle, legislation, defines the sphere that distinguishes Judaism; but here Mendelssohn includes under the rubric of religion, which is at bottom universalistic and not metaphysical, the peculiar features of Judaism which in his view is not a religion in the strict sense of the term. It seems that Mendelssohn is searching for a common denominator between the essentially religious aspect of Judaism, which it shares with other religions and with metaphysics, and the special legislation which makes Judaism separate and distinct. The metaphysical-religious view that recognizes God as an active agent and regards the idea of Providence as a metaphysical principle constrains us to find a metaphysical explanation for the fact that God stands in a special relation to the Jews and that divine Providence, through the enactment of specific legislation, is particularly solicitous for their redemption.

Mendelssohn believed that reason can establish the basic principles of human knowledge and by means of logical deductions arrive at the truths of religion.[4] But how can reason, which is universal according to its nature, be reconciled to such a particularistic activity as the divine enactment of special laws that apply only to Israel? This question, although not explicitly formulated, is interesting in itself, and also because its answer involves significant traditional elements. The peculiar essence of Judaism lies in the laws that were revealed to Israel by God—commandments, precepts, and ordinances, which went beyond those vouchsafed to other nations and were applicable to no other people. This supplementary legislation of positive and negative commandments is not the only road that leads to felicity; how could God permit the majority of men who are non-Jews to live without the light of revelation? It was, however, by a pure act of grace that God was moved to reveal himself to Israel alone by means of special legislation that would guide Israel in attaining the common goal of all men. The Jew as a member of the human race is entitled to this felicity but *qua* Jew he must seek it in a specific manner, by keeping the commandments ordained for his benefit by divine fiat.[5] Divine Providence, which is a rational-metaphysical principle, is thus enlisted in support of a theory concerning the special character of Judaism. In his relation to Jews, God acts as a Legislator. In this way an attempt is made to reconcile the metaphysical aspect of Judaism, which is common to all religions, with its particularistic, nonrational aspect, which depends on revelation and the love of God.

This view, which is highly significant from the historical point of view, represents eventually an attempt to preserve the concept of the *chosen people* under new intellectual and historical conditions. The pursuit of felicity and the certainty of attaining it is not an exclusively Jewish matter but the prerogative of all men. The selection of Israel as a chosen people does not affect the content of faith or the nature of belief, but is merely the *way* prescribed for Israel to attain felicity, a way ordained by God Himself and identical with the laws that He revealed to His people. Since all men long for happiness and seek to attain it, relying on their own efforts and on autonomous reason, the existence of a separate road for a select people is not amenable to rational explanation. Nor is the metaphysical assumption that entertains the idea of a private Jewish road to felicity a rational one since it resides in the principle of Providence which, in turn, is a clear speculative, metaphysical principle. The way that is prescribed for Israel is outside the framework of rational experience because it contains a particularistic, supranatural element that lifts it beyond human reason.

Because of its extra-rational character, the Way is impervious to the incursions of historical changes or to the attempts at reform: Other nations can alter their laws in conformity with the changing times, conditions, and needs; but for me the Creator himself has ordained laws and how can I, a frail creature, venture to change these divine laws according to my views?[6] Accordingly, only He who first promulgated the Law can change it; just as the giving of the Law, so also its abrogation must be the product of Revelation. The essential nature of Judaism is nonspeculative and nonmetaphysical. Its specific content is nonspeculative because it consists of the Law and the act of giving the Law cannot be explained by speculative logic. Judaism is based on a system of laws that are derived from a particularistic Revelation, that is, one addressed to Israel alone. Therefore, it is not incumbent on a recipient of this Revelation to defend its content against criticism, since it simply sets forth and defines the *way* to felicity as the goal of man, not the goal itself.

In short, Mendelssohn restricted the essence of Judaism to Law in order to find a more secure place for it in the rational-metaphysical system. This condensation makes Judaism a nonspeculative—and consequently also a particularistic—system in which Revelation is assigned a specific function, although it needs no theoretical proof that it is universal. In this connection it is instructive to note that among the proofs advanced by Ibn Rushd, the famous Arabian philosopher (1126–1198), we find the argument that the laws of Islam are good for all men, whereas the laws of the other religions are good only for their respective adherents.[7] Ibn Rushd clearly seeks to demonstrate the *superiority* of Isalm and to this end stresses the universal character of its laws. Mendelssohn, a child of the Enlightenment, is not concerned with demonstrating the *superiority* but the singular *right* of Judaism, which he ascribes to its particularistic elements.[8]

The unique relationship between God, the Legislator, and Israel whom He elected to bear the yoke of the Law (which is, for Mendelssohn, the essence of Judaism) becomes clearer when we examine the distinction between man as such and man as a citizen of the State. Mendelssohn distinguishes between the realms of culture and enlightenment (*Kultur und Aufklärung*), both of which are included in education (*Bildung*). Culture is primarily concerned with the moral order in the practical life of man and its task is to foster magnanimity, refinement, and the appreciation of artistic beauty—that is, to perfect man in his visible, objective activities and in his subjective emotional life. Enlightenment, on the other hand, is concerned with perfecting the cognitive processes of the human mind and its unillumined aspects. The relation of enlightenment to culture is that of theory to practice, cognition to morality, criticism to virtuosity—a distinction that corresponds to the two sides of man's nature, man simply as man and man as a citizen of the State. Man as such is in no way dependent on the world of culture and its efforts to elevate his practical life; what he needs is education or *Bildung* and the improvement of his intellectual faculties.

The importance of this distinction, by which Mendelssohn attempted to restrict Judaism to Law and thus remove it from the realm of speculation, has not been sufficiently appreciated. Speculation is indigenous to religion, and a man who bases Judaism on ethics or on universalistic principles must inevitably expose it to the speculative enlightenment of man as man. The uniqueness of

Judaism and its separate status must therefore be sought in that realm which we defined at the outset as that of heterogeneous particulars—that is, of practical action, law, and culture. Since the law is essentially part of the world of culture which by its very nature is particularistic, the laws revealed to the Jews may well have been meant to be observed by them exclusively. Judaism is particularistic because it revolves around the observance of the Law, which is a fragmentary, cultural acquisition of only a small fraction of mankind. This fundamental distinction between the speculative and the practical, between culture and man's activities as man and citizen, served Mendelssohn as a basis for restricting Judaism to Law and removing it from the sphere of religion.

There is a threefold distinction among the truths of the Torah: a) commandments that contain eternal truths concerning God, that are measured by the same criteria as eternal truths in general and amenable to the same proofs; b) historical truths, or past events in the life of the nation; c) laws, precepts, ordinances, and rules of conduct. God did not reveal Himself as the Creator and Sustainer of the world but as a Legislator, the Rock of Israel, the King and Defender of the people He redeemed from slavery.[9] The God of the first part of the distinction above, who is the root and anchor of eternal truths, is a metaphysical God whose existence and nature can be metaphysically demonstrated. Moving within the confines of speculative truth, He is one of the subjects that engages man's intellectual powers. The third part of the distinction is an essentially particularistic (not religious) category; this God is related to Israel alone and to that exclusive area of Israel's practical life which has from the beginning been defined as separate.

But how is one to proceed from a God conceived as a human, speculative category to God, the Legislator, who acts only in the practical life of Israel? Such a distinction had stood Mendelssohn in good stead when he asked the Christian world to acknowledge Israel's right to lead a separate, discrete life in its practical affairs without jeopardizing the political status or civil rights of its adherents.[10] Civic life is by definition heterogeneous with its inevitable diversity of cultural forms. In such a pluralistic structure room can surely be found for Israel's peculiar life pattern. In other words, the fusion of the two disparate realms, the practical and the civic, and the use of enlightenment and speculation as the criteria for both, blurs and obscures their respective contents. The multiplicity of forms, like speculation, is a quality that inheres in the very definition of culture; the unity of speculation, however, flows from the very definition of enlightenment.

After making a distinction between the practical and speculative spheres—and between culture and enlightenment, Mendelssohn draws a line between Church and State. Religion is devoted to things eternal and its concern is life eternal; the State is devoted to the temporal and its concern is with the ephemeral and contingent. The concept of eternal things is used in two senses, either as an attribute of religion—that is, applied to God, or to characterize the truths of religion that are not subject to time or amenable to rational evidence. The idea of temporal things is also used in two senses, either to describe the fleeting concerns of man's brief life that change under different conditions, or to indicate those areas controlled by the State. In religion man *qua* man is related to God, the bearer of universal meaning—a relationship that is unaffected by circumstances of time and place. In the State man is related to man, and this relationship is by its very nature fragmentary, circumscribed, and without universal application.[11]

It was on this basis that developed his doctrine of separation and the respective limits of Church and State. In the case of Israel, however the fusion of the two—for which of course no explanation is found in Mendelssohn's metaphysics—is one between God as a religious and metaphysical category and God as Lawgiver. Since God has a special function as the Promulgator of Israel's laws, religion and the State were not only united but virtually identical, forming two commensurate and congruent areas with the same content.[12] The State and its laws, which in a limited sense were separate from religion, acquired religious significance in Israel. If we conceive of man as a creature of the earth whose life is regulated by the State and as a son of Heaven made in the image of God and guided by His revealed law, then under ancient Jewish rule man was equally a citizen of both.

These fundamental distinctions of Mendelssohn—between reli-

gion and Judaism, Church and State, the universal and the particular—reflect a deep struggle in his intellectual development and
raise a barrier separating the beliefs of faith and the problems of
religion from the statutory laws that regulate our practical lives.
The analysis of this distinction will appear to us in another light
when we come to examine the relation between ethics and law.

The first question we should raise regarding Mendelssohn's
ethical theory concerns the very basis of ethics, or the degree of
truth it is to be accorded. Ethical truth is by its very nature theoretical and hence demonstrative. The general principles of ethics,
according to Mendelssohn, are geometric exactitude and certainty[13]
—that is, an ethical judgment has certainty; with respect to both
validity and form it is in no way inferior to the theoretical judgment. Ethical actions are part of a well-knit, articulated system
based on certitude, each judgment being linked to higher and more
inclusive presuppositions. Implicit in every ethical act is a concealed rational syllogism, that is, given the term A, I must act in
accordance with principle B. It follows that the validity of the
ethical principle rests on self-evident truths and its certitude is
derived from the logical sequence of the syllogism.

Ethical judgments are also based on common sense and stand in
no need of logical proofs, for they can be clearly perceived by the
ordinary intellect.[14] From this point of view, the basis of ethics
is parallel to that of reflection and metaphysics. Conscience is to
ethics what the sense of truth, the *bon sens* exemplified by ordinary
minds, is to reflection. It is the faculty that distinguishes between
good and evil, just as the sense of truth is the faculty that distinguishes between truth and falsehood by means of its own immediate,
rudimentary reasoning. The perception of truth by conscience is no
less valid or credible than the truth based on evidential proof, the
only difference being that the former arrives at the truth un-
consciously and spontaneously, guided by the *instinctus naturalis*,
whereas the latter proceeds step by step according to the rigorous
laws of logic. Hence, every judgment that is based on common
sense is effected without mediation of prior discussion. Ordinary
sense, *recta ratio*, is the general faculty in which both ethical and
speculative certainty are found together, just as exact logical rea-

soning is the comprehensive form of cognition that prevails in the theoretical and ethical realms.

Furthermore, Mendelssohn established a complete identity between reason, with its proofs and syllogisms, and plain common sense, the *sensus communis* of Scholastic philosophy, with its spontaneous judgments and certainties. The difference between these two forms of cognition is to be found only in the tempo of execution. Common sense arrives at its judgments with the speed of intuition without deviating from its original course; reason pursues its inflexible cognitive process with circumspection, qualms, and toil.[15] It follows that the difference between reason and common sense is not to be found in the content of their respective judgments or even in the degree of certainty they achieve but merely in the *way* in which they seek this content and its manifestations: Reason follows the beckoning goal along a winding path of logical twists and turns, whereas common sense appropriates its object in one swift move, without the intervention of a *tertium quid* between subject and object.

It may be said that Mendelssohn sought to unite the two disparate currents of thought in modern philosophy—the critical stream that flowed from Descartes to Leibnitz, and the one that stems from the Scottish School and its doctrine of common sense. Looked at from a broader historical perspective, it appears that Mendelssohn's concept of common sense usurps the place held by revelation in medieval philosophy where, besides being an intellectual concept, it also served as the source of cognition and knowledge. In some important intellectual circles of that era, Jewish thinkers along with others accepted revelation and common sense as identical modes of thought. The only difference between intellectual cognition and knowledge based on revelation was in the *way* in which they led to the attainment of knowledge. Revelation presents the intellect with immediate truths without laborious, methodical inquiry—the very truths that will eventually be discovered independently by the discursive intellect. Since Mendelssohn made revelation the concern of reason, it was no longer necessary to postulate divine revelation as the source of cognition. Within autonomous cognition itself, however, Mendelssohn distinguished between common sense, a kind of revelation of reasonable truths that belong to man's original constitution prior to all inquiry, and reason as the sum total of principles and methods that consummate the cognitive act by means of syllogisms. The same rule holds for metaphysics as for ethics, and the process by which the latter is subsumed under the former is demonstrated in Mendelssohn's monograph, *Über die Evidenz der metaphysischen Wissenschaften* (1763), which received the prize of the Berlin Academy of Sciences in preference to an essay submitted at the same time by Kant.

Ethics and speculation are also on the same plane when looked at from another point of view. The end of our existence is happiness,[16] that is, the perfection of man through the development of his latent powers and hidden resources. This view of happiness as the goal of human existence comes down to us through Gottfried Leibnitz's theory of the monads or entelechies, in which the theoretical and practical aspects are indistinguishable. Leibnitz's *Monadology* rests on the assumption that every existing object is independent and self-sufficient and the difference between these isolated objects lies only in the degree to which their latent powers have been developed. Perfection, then, is the criterion by which levels of existence are to be measured. The hierarchy among the monads is determined by the extent to which the individual monad develops its latent content. According to this theory, development is tantamount to perfection. Whereas Leibnitz stressed the speculative phase of this process, those who followed him stressed its practical, ethical aspect by asserting that *perfection* is the end of human existence and happiness the *summum bonum* of ethical conduct, a view that can be described as intellectual eudemonism.

This view, which elevates ethics to the level of metaphysics, by a comparison of their origins or their ends, also finds support in Mendelssohn's attempt to press ethics into the service of speculation as an equal partner or ally, without becoming identified with it. We have already described this view as *intellectual* eudemonism and we now turn to a consideration of the meaning of the first part of this phrase. It is apparent by now that the highest value has been attached to metaphysics which, as the realm of speculation, is the sphere of general human activity (enlightenment), whereas

ethics, the practical sphere, is characterized by its diverse, detached
and fragmentary activity (culture). This relation of ethics to metaphysics is expressly emphasized by Mendelssohn—ethics provides
us with the means by which we may bring the lower faculties of
the soul into harmony with reason.[17] Ethics, as the sphere of
precepts and rules of conduct to regulate action, is not an independent sphere capable of sustaining itself without the prop of
metaphysics but essentially a middle region comprising means designed for a specific goal, the perfection of man's rational faculties
and the elevation of the non-rational powers of the human soul to
the level of reason. Ethics is the instrument to promote within man's
rational life, the harmony which is the goal of human existence.
We can thus say that there is no ethical good in life except one
that is rooted in our perfection[18] which, essentially, is a speculative
category. But from another point of view Mendelssohn emphasized
the practical values of metaphysical truths (properly called pragmatic values by E. Cassirer) when he observed that he is prepared
to stake his faith on the assumption that metaphysical statements
about God and the good life, since they are so useful to society, are
also true judgments. Ultimately, the relation between ethics and
metaphysics was not sufficiently examined by Mendelssohn; in
addition to placing them on the same level he also attempted to
elevate the latter over the former by stressing the ethical and
practical importance of metaphysical propositions.

The relation of ethics to religion and to law are two other areas
that need to be examined. From the ethical point of view, the good
is an attribute only of those actions that proceed from good intentions, the ethical end itself being the motive force that prompts
the act and inspires its execution.[19] Other actions are not divided
into these two phases, that is, the objective meaning of the act and
the subjective springs of conduct. In other words, the focal point
of the action resides in the circumstance that the ethical good, being
dependent on good intentions, is from the outset also an intellectual
good—the *bonum morale* is the *bonum mentale*. The ethical good
is an expression that refers to the inner powers of the doer and
not to the external manifestation of these powers. Action as such
tends to fall within the sphere of the ethical good, but its visible

effects, being part of the physical world and corporeal existence, are not regarded as within that sphere.[20] The basic principle of an ethical act is, therefore, the intention behind it and not its ostensible manifestation: The very execution of an act removes it from the ethical and intellectual sphere and places it in that of external, physical existence. The deed itself is nothing more than a kind of symbol or expression of an inner sentiment (*Gesinnung*).

The origin of the ethical act in good intention is also the essence of religion. Mendelssohn argued that religion only recognized those actions that are prompted by the emotions of the heart or are a product of the spirit.[21] The religion of God is based upon the spirit and the heart,[22] by contrast, the State insists on compliance with its law, while indifferent to whether the motive that prompts compliance is fear, obedience, or constraint. With respect to religion, Mendelssohn also stresses the absence of compulsion. This is but the obverse side of good will, or the voluntary nature of an act, and is obviously emphasized by Mendelssohn to underline the distinction between religion and the State.

In summing up, we may say that Mendelssohn identifies religion with metaphysics by including the truths of the former among the certified, verifiable truths of the latter, thus erasing the differences between the two spheres. At the same time, however, he finds a common ground for religion and ethics (not with respect to speculative content, since ethics, in contradistinction to religion, is a practical and not a theoretical realm) in which an act is judged by the motives of genuine sentiment and good will that prompt it. Insofar as ethics is part of metaphysics it coincides with religion, which is also part of metaphysics; and insofar as ethics is not part of metaphysics (a theme that is not absent in Mendelssohn's philosophy) religion bursts the metaphysical frame and becomes one with ethics in the practical sphere of human conduct, a separate sphere or, at least, one that is not included in the speculative realm.

Since the essence of both religion and ethics is to be found in the indispensable element of good will, to follow medieval thinkers, identifying Judaism with religion would mean that Judaism is identical with ethics. Mendelssohn, however, transfers Judaism from the speculative to the practical sphere where ethics is based on law alone. Although his analysis of the relation between ethics and law is open to a grave objection, let us first inquire into the views of some of his predecessors and contemporaries who dealt with this subject.

Although the relation of law to ethics is not explicitly mentioned by the founders of natural law philosophy, it is nevertheless implicit in their thought. When Hugo Grotius maintained that the validity of natural law is not dependent on the existence or non-existence of God, he was not referring to law as the product of decisions or provisional legislation but to that which is inherent in the very essence of man's nature. Natural law is the sphere in which the concept of the ethical imperative comes face to face with positive law. The product neither of legislation nor convention, based neither on constraint nor on man's brute nature, the concept of natural law may best express the inner relationship between ethics and law.[23] In the course of time, however, more elaborate distinctions between the various forms of law and ethics were developed, until the concept of ethics acquired an independent status with a content of its own.

The purpose of the law, according to Melanchthon, Luther's famous associate in the German Reformation, is to restore man to the natural state of innocence that was his before his first sin alienated him from God. By means of imperatives designed to regulate human conduct, law seeks to remedy the flaw that makes man prone to evil and to lift him to the ethical plane he occupied before the Fall. Human nature is basically ethical, but the corruption that set in after man's first sin prevents him from returning to his original state. Hence, law is not a product of human nature but a gift of divine revelation that comes to repair man's damaged soul, cleanse him of his pollution and restore him to prelapsarian bliss.

Exponents of the theory of natural law, however, make no qualitative distinction between human nature and brute nature and hence do not feel obliged to base ethical imperative on divine revelation. Samuel Pufendorf (1632–1694) touched on this subject when he defined law as the autonomous sphere of man's ethical nature, but it was Leibnitz who distinguished three stages in the domain of natural law and thus helped to clarify the distinction between law and ethics. The first, which is law in its most stringent sense, is based on a negative principle—that is, the purpose of law is to maintain peace, to prevent man from maltreating and doing severe injury to his fellow man. In the second and more advanced stage, which is that of equity or integrity, the law seeks not only to prevent and redress injury but enjoins positive actions that serve the interests of the entire community; here the ethical act is no longer in the negative realm of mere prohibition but is at work in the service of the general welfare. *Pietas* or the fear of Heaven, is the third stage in which man is commanded to act in conformity with the divine law. Leibnitz has here expressed the distinctions among the various types of law, from the standpoint of both form and content, until law becomes the common denominator of diverse types of action. Mendelssohn's conception of Judaism as the divine law corresponds to the third stage, but he does not view the development of law from the standpoint of stages or the nature of its content.

These stages or levels in the development of law are particularly conspicuous in the philosophy of Christian Thomasius (1655–1728), who makes a clear distinction between law and ethics in the restricted sense of these terms. There are, in his opinion, three levels of human action. The first, *iustum* or probity, which we also found in Leibnitz's classification, is basically negative, although differently formulated; we are to refrain from doing to others what we do not wish others to do to us: as Hillel said "What is hateful to thee, do not unto thy fellow man." On the second level, that of *decorum*, we are positively enjoined to do unto others as we would have them do unto us (the Golden Rule). The third level, *honestum* or honorable conduct, has a positive content that refers to the agent himself: We are required to do for ourselves what we would desire our fellow man to do for himself, provided we believe the action to be praiseworthy.

The difference between these stages of development can be formulated in another way which, although not explicitly stated is more in keeping with Thomasius' intention. The first stage of the law is thereby seen as preserving the *external* peace of society;

in the second stage the members of society actively promote this peace by positive actions that flow from their common social life; the third stage seeks to *unify* man's active personality aiding him in his efforts towards perfection and the attainment of inner peace. The differences between the various stages are not determined by the nature of a deed, whether it proceeds from sincere motives or from compulsion, but by its direction; that is, whether it basically concerns the relationship between man and his neighbor or whether it is directed towards the doer himself. The fundamental distinction then lies in whether the goal of the ethical act is negative or positive. The three spheres of man's active life are based on these three levels: a) natural law arises from the first stage, which restrains us from doing injury to our fellow man; b) the second stage gives rise to politics, a sphere of activity that comprises positive acts, since it is primarily concerned with the men's relations to one another; c) the third stage, the ground of ethics in its strict sense, is concerned with enhancing man's active personality and developing his latent powers towards the goal which Leibnitz defined as perfection.[24]

Such gradations in man's practical and ethical activity are not found in Mendelssohn, who emphasizes the distinction between an act prompted by good will and one dictated by other factors, such as coercion on the part of the State. Mendelssohn established a fundamental distinction between Church and State when he defined religion as the sphere that is concerned with man's relation to God, and that requires good will, whereas the State, which governs man's relation to man, demands nothing more than the act as such, devoid of all intention, motive, or inner convictions.[25] This distinction is fundamental in the sense that Mendelssohn does not ascribe differences to man's inability to act at all times out of avowedly good intentions but to the distinctive nature of the two spheres; in addition, Mendelssohn sometimes raises a technical distinction between the State and religion, namely, that the State is primarily concerned with the acts and not the thoughts of its subjects; its interests are served when the act is carried out in conformity to the law whether from good will or from coercion. Religion, however, cannot rest content with the mere execution of the act but insists that it proceed along an ethical detour in conformity with the highest ideals which it befits a man to cherish.[26]

The disparity between the two spheres is not fundamental but stems from man's difficulty in living up to the religious (or ethical) ideal of perfection; finite man has no authoritative guide to define and harmonize the conflicting duties of his practical life which is based on the minimum requirement represented by the act. The State is thus chiefly concerned with the accommodation of the act to law and with the executive power to enforce its decisions, not because it finds it expedient or because man's unruly nature makes coercion indispensable but simply because the State is based on law which, in the parlance of modern jurisprudence, is called *minimum ethics*. Hence, this distinction made by Mendelssohn between religion (or ethics, if we consider the practical aspect of religion) and law is one of degree and not of principle. A similar distinction was made by Kant (and Fichte) between morality and legality. An act is ethical if it is regarded as a duty or a self-imposed obligation; an act is legal if it is carried out only in *conformity* with an obligation but not prompted by a free and responsible sense of duty insofar as it is an imperative. Kant formulated this principle, which is an integral part of his moral philosophy, by emphasizing the element of duty, whereas Mendelssohn insisted on the element of good will or inner conviction; however, the underlying thought in both is the same—that man's powers must be exercised not merely as a means to some good but as good in themselves.

Mendelssohn's postulate that the ecclesiastical and civil power in ancient Israel were one (the State being concerned with the outward act and religion with the inner motives) means that the boundary between the two spheres had become indistinct—that is, law was on an equal plane with religion and ethics. Mendelssohn himself was not aware of the grave consequences that this identification of religion with law entailed.

The function of law, according to Mendelssohn, is to define the limits of man's field of ethical activity and to determine the scope of the spiritual powers immanent in his nature. The law comes to reconcile man to the limitations of the historically real as he seeks to modify, penetrate, and transform the world around him. What latitude is to be permitted to the imperious demands of man's ethical nature? The determining principle lies in the very nature of ethical activity, which must be made to conform to the precepts of wisdom and of the highest Good.[27] Ethics recruits the law to help it determine human behavior by removing it from the intellectual sphere, *bonum mentale*, to the sphere of physical existence. The law is not extrinsic to ethics but ancillary to it in assessing human conduct. It may be described as a kind of latch or bolt between ethics and the physical world, defining for the ethical imperative the limits within which the ethical good can assert its sovereignty. This intimate relation between ethics and law gives Judaism its specific character. The purpose of law in Judaism, especially the law that defines the other of the divine service, is to bring man face to face with religious and ethical truths. The heathen gods were worshiped in the form of images and idols; the religious truths of Judaism were fashioned by law which is the bearer of symbolic truth.[28] Even here the law is in the service of religious and ethical truth, not by determining the limits for the exercise of man's faculties and by transferring the ethical imperative to the physical world but by converting its speculative inner content into a visible symbol. The highest expression of Israel's uniqueness is precisely that in it the law appears as a symbol and incentive to ethical action.

Mendelssohn's purpose was to separate the three spheres of metaphysics, religion, and Judaism, but he ended only in attenuating their boundaries and blurring their outlines. It is precisely this failure, however, that gives us a deeper insight into the problems that arise when one seeks to make Judaism co-extensive with ethics and synonymous with the performance of the divine commandments. In such an attempt ethics must be defined from the standpoint of both method and content. Mendelssohn, however, seldom resorts to methodical elaboration; for him the content of ethics consists in the exhortation to perfect our inner and outer lives and those of our fellow men to the best of our ability.[29] But he did not assert that this ethical principle constituted the content of Judaism, conceived as law or ethics, but only that Judaism was *one* of the many ways to reach the goal of human striving, from which we may infer that Judaism is one of the ways of establishing the ethical principle outlined above.

In the development of nineteenth-century Jewish thought the problem that had been inadequately treated by Mendelssohn, namely, the content and the basic principle of Jewish ethics, was seen with greater clarity. Two divergent evaluations of Mendelssohn's contribution emerged. S. L. Steinheim (1789–1866) points out that Mendelssohn sought God outside the Holy Scriptures and that he deprived Judaism of everything except its divine commandments and ritual practices. His identification of Judaism with the law drained Judaism of its belief and faith;[30] an infidel in mind and a Jew body. Z. Jawitz (the writer and orthodox historian 1847–1924), on the other hand, maintained that Mendelssohn endeavored to understand the Torah from *within* instead of reducing it to a bare catechism which every man can interpret according to his own lights; he believed in religion as the Law of life whose vital center is both in the heart, in the home, and in the people.[31] This identification of law and religion, which constitutes the essential core of Judaism from the orthodox point of view, became the chief target for the critical barbs of the Hebrew writer P. Smolenskin (1842–1885), who refuted Mendelssohn's theory that Judaism is only a religious confession, contending that it is primarily a people. Judaism conceived as law is by definition a way of life, a bridge between the Law or Torah and the life of Israel, the covenanted people.

To understand the background of Mendelssohn's conception of Judaism we must consider his indebtedness to the thought of his age, particularly to the influential theological movement of deism in the eighteenth century.[32] In the field of the philosophy of religion in Mendelssohn's generation three basic currents of thoughts can be distinguished: a) the first (chiefly represented in Protestantism) accepts the tenets of traditional religion but reserves the right to subject the sacred text to a critical examination; b) the second interprets Revelation as a historical, religious fact but does not regard the Bible as the private possession of the Church or its interpretation as necessarily authoritative; c) the third repudiates

Revelation either because it is devoid of truths or because the evidence adduced in support of the historical reality of Revelation cannot stand up against historical, rationalistic criticism.[33] Mendelssohn agreed with the third group in holding that the resolute exercise of reason is sufficient to give us religious truths without concurring or competing with a supernatural Revelation. With respect to Judaism, he agreed with the second group that Revelation is a reality; however, its content was restricted to law.

It is thus evident that Mendelssohn was influenced by the teachings of deism, the English counterpart of the Enlightenment, in resenting the intrusion of metaphysical principles into the constitutive meaning of those axioms asserted by faith, in transferring the seat of religion to the sphere of ethics, and in testing religion not by the truths it proclaims but by its utility and social benefits, by its *ethical* consequences in the regulation of practical affairs and in the perceptible realm of legislation. By subsuming religion under law and ethics Mendelssohn reduced Judaism to dimensions that satisfy the moral mind but not the religious temper.[34] If Judaism defines only what is right and wrong in action but not what is true and false in beliefs, and if the laws of the Torah are not indispensable to salvation, why should Jews continue to abide by them? People do not revere what they can dispense with, and moral enthusiasm alone is poor fare for the afflicted and those who seek God's pardon.

2

The Religion of Morality

S. D. LUZZATTO

In his Introduction to the *Lezioni di Teologia Dogmatica Israelitica* (§4) S. D. Luzzatto (1800–1865) sums up Mendelssohn's conception of Judaism as being a religion that rests on the performance of the positive commandments and not on articles of faith; and in a letter to Moratara in 1855 he points out that the basic idea of Mendelssohn's *Jerusalem* is that belief or dogma is not prescribed in the Mosaic Code. These direct references to Mendelssohn indicate the continuing importance of the problem of the relation of religious principles to practical morality or ethics. Unlike Mendelssohn, however, Luzzatto relegated religion unreservedly to the sphere of ethics and at the same time stressed the ethical content of the commandments over against their ceremonial and legalistic character. The imputation of ethical meaning to the commandments was a direct result of the criticism leveled against the rationalistic view and the rigorous distinction that was made between ethics and rationalism. The ethical interpretation of the commandments, according to Luzzatto, stemmed from the desire to understand Judaism from within.

The Torah sets forth no doctrine of beliefs; Israel's faith goes back to the days of Abraham. If Israel had been without faith, a commandment to elicit it would have been to no avail.[1] The Torah

[30]

contains no articles of faith, first, because the historical Israel's acceptance of the Torah and its commandments already implies a prior voluntary act of faith. The second reason is one of *principle*: Faith cannot be enjoined, for it is not amenable to commandments. This basic reason is derived, in a formal sense, from Mendelssohn, who held that faith belongs to a sphere in which the imperative has no jurisdiction. But whereas Mendelssohn based the essence of religion, which has nothing in common with the imperative, on rationalistic proofs and intellectual considerations, Luzzatto perceived the inadequacy of the imperative as an *emotional* component of belief. Beliefs and imperatives move in different spheres and adhere to diverse allegiances. The imperatives guide the ethical activity which constitutes the essence of Judaism; the purpose of the divine Torah is not to impart wisdom and knowledge to the people, but to lead them in the paths of righteousness.[2] From the standpoint of content, belief is concerned with the concept of God; from the standpoint of the emotions, with the heart of man. Belief or faith has its roots in faculties that are removed from the influences of the imperative. Ethics, on the other hand, consists of imperatives which prescribe the actions that govern moral conduct by removing action from man's arbitrary whims and the insistent claims of the flesh. Since ethics consists of imperatives that serve as a guide to action, we can determine the inner relationship between it and the commandments that appear in the Torah as imperatives.

For Luzzatto, human conduct is the heart of religion, where ethical man comes face to face with the moral imperative. In Judaism the moral ideal of human life is apprehended and embodied in its practical teachings; the Jew is judged not by his acceptance or rejection of metaphysical tenets or theological dogmas but by his moral activity.[3] Luzzatto puts his reliance on the social, historical, and psychological aspects of the living Jewish community rather than on literary documents.

The shift from speculative belief to moral action is nowhere seen more clearly than in Luzzatto's interpretation of the pragmatic value of religion and its complete rejection of the objective criteria of speculation and discursive truth—Religion is dear to God, he says, not because of its truths but because of its usefulness for morality. All its words may not be true but we do not need to deny its divine origin or attribute untruths to God, for it is not possible to communicate the works of creation to finite man of flesh and blood. Without illusion, society could not exist nor its members thrive. Nature, no doubt in accordance with God's will, deceives us in many things—entangling us, for example in coils of love in order to preserve the species; if a young man knew beforehand the toil involved in raising children, not one in a thousand would marry.[4]

The pragmatic nature of religion thus has a double aspect. Its primary purpose is not to reveal truths but to serve the interests of morality, which is used by religion for its own ends. The speculative truths of religion are divorced from moral activity, which is valued in proportion to its usefulness for society; it is sometimes identified with illusory aspects of religion that may be devoid of all truth but are nevertheless beneficial to morality. Religion is not measured by the criterion of truth; it may even employ error and falsehood for its own ends. The pragmatic value of religion here appears in contradistinction to its speculative value, which is governed by the sole criterion of truth. Luzzatto's chief argument in support of the supernatural character of religion is that since morality has recourse to illusion, it is not fundamentally rational. As we have seen, Mendelssohn also emphasized the pragmatic aspect of metaphysical judgments, considering it as valid as the speculative, whereas Luzzatto places these two aspects in opposition to each other.

The conjunction of the speculative and the pragmatic reappears in Luzzatto's teaching in another connection. In the passage summarized above, Luzzatto asserts that religion does not depend on its truth-value, for it is not possible to communicate the works of creation to finite man of flesh and blood; again, in his booklet against Benedict Spinoza, he says that the essence of the Creator and the essence of creation are things concealed from our understanding.[5] Here the agnostic tinge in Luzzatto's religious conception is clearly apparent. Religion does not prescribe faith or belief, not only because there is no *need* for such a commandment (since Israel had faith before it accepted the Torah) and no *possibility* for enforcing it (since belief is not amenable to imperatives), but because there is *nothing* to command since the cosmological and theological elements of religion are beyond the scope of cognitive apprehension. Luzzatto's supernaturalism is composed of the moral act, which occupies a central position in religion; ethical activity and speculation, which are placed in direct opposition to each other; and the rejection of speculation in general as a competent guide and authority.

Ethics, then, is the essence of Judaism and speculative judgments do not apply to it. For Luzzatto, it is an autonomous, nonspeculative realm that requires no further proof; either he felt there was no need to dwell on the obvious or he lacked the metaphysical vigor to marshal the evidence. Since ethical enthusiasm springs from the heart,[6] it is free of cognitive elements and requires no methodical justification. Luzzatto finds the source of ethical activity in compassion and in righteousness: compassion is the desire to alleviate the burden of pain and sorrow in our fellow man; righteousness is the desire to be a true judge in the rival claims between man and man.[7] The lack of clarity in the elaboration of this question stems from Luzzatto's determination to base ethical feelings on the two qualities of honor and compassion.[8] The relation between honor and the ethical activity that flows from righteousness is not sufficiently analyzed by Luzzatto, but it seems that compassion refers to the emotional element in ethics, whereas honor and its derivative righteousness refer to the objective ethical judgment. Compassion is the incentive to the ethical act, and righteousness, in the sense of law, its social expression; but the ethical and juridical implications of this distinction are not adequately developed. From the standpoint of the history of this problem in Judaism it is interesting to note that these same two elements—honor as an ethical quality and pity as an ethical element in religion—reappear in the ethical philosophy of Hermann Cohen.

In Luzzatto's *Yesode ha-Torah* (Foundations of the Torah), a treatise on Jewish principles published in 1880, only the emotion of pity is given as the basis of ethical activity, and honor (or righteousness) plays an unimportant part. Pity is explicitly defined as the root of love, mercy, and uprightness,[9] and as that quality in the religion of Israel whose sole aim is the improvement of morality. The opposition between ethics and metaphysics—or rationalism, as it is understood by Luzzatto—is clearly reflected in this view. Pity is an unadulterated emotional quality, an affection that is disparaged in Spinoza's *Ethics*, and this probably led Luzzatto to make a clear distinction between the ethical emotion of pity and the discursive—that is, rational—faculty of metaphysics. Luzzatto makes no attempt to analyze pity, regarding it as a natural endowment of the human heart. Ethics does not rest on imperatives but on pity and cognate emotions. Here we see a basic difference between Luzzatto and Hermann Cohen, who scorned to base ethics on a natural emotion, an unlawful concession to sensibility and a usurpation of the original prerogatives of the understanding. Luzzatto's theory also differs from that of Schopenhauer, who derives the emotion of pity from a metaphysical root inherent within it—that is, the knowledge that it is identical in all men—and who assumes that the basis of ethics is to be found in metaphysics.[10] Pity arises when my will is identified with that of my fellow man and the barriers between us are removed. Luzzatto, however, erects ethics on the slender basis of natural psychologism alone, and in this respect reminds us of Jean Jacques Rousseau.

Although Luzzatto places the root of ethics in the emotion of pity, that is, in a feeling that inclines us to our fellow man, he does not share the optimism of the Enlightenment concerning man's nature. On the contrary, he regards man as incurably evil and, as he says in one of his letters, incapable of improvement. Luzzatto considers pity a strong emotion at the root of man's good impulses, but not strong enough to subdue his raw appetites. To help man accommodate his vile nature to his good impulses the Torah appends an auxiliary principle—reward and punishment—to aid morality.[11] The pragmatic character of Luzzatto's conception of religion is here unmistakably clear. The principle of reward and punishment is not an absolute corollary of ethical consciousness that requires the righteous to be rewarded and the sinners punished; it is an educational discipline designed to habituate man to moral acts in conformity with his good impulses. The will is provided with an additional incentive and man is spurred on to greater moral excellence. The third principle in the Torah, the doctrine of election, or the belief that Israel was chosen by God to be His people,[12] also serves a higher morality, falling within the category of *noblesse oblige*: It is incumbent upon those God has elected to devote themselves to the pursuit of the highest ideals and practice the strictest virtue.

In short, of the three principles in the Torah, the first, the sentiment of pity, is the *root* of ethics; the other two, the principle of reward and punishment and the election of Israel, serve as a kind of *support* or *prop* for ethics. This distinction is not explicitly formulated by Luzzatto but can be inferred from his writings on the subject.

Whether the principles of the Torah serve as a root or support of ethical acts or as a vehicle for their realization is not made clear by Luzzatto. The emotion of pity is a purely ethical principle, whereas the other two principles—reward and punishment and the election of Israel—constitute the permanent element in religion, which must not be abandoned for the customs of other nations.[13] From this point of view the preservation of religion itself becomes a religious dogma, although it depends on elements which of themselves are not necessarily ethical but which promote morality while preserving religion.[14] The principles of the Torah here serve a double purpose—to preserve the religion, and to isolate Israel from the surrounding nations. This is particularly true of the third principle, the election of Israel, and also of the many precepts and ordinances in the Mosaic Code designed to safeguard the religion; it is only in this way that Israel could be kept apart from the idolatrous nations.[15] The very guardianship over Israel is a function that acquires religious significance since Israel's preservation is itself a religious value. A commandment assumes a religious aspect whenever it proceeds from the imperative to preserve Israel's uniqueness—that is, its separate existence apart from the other nations. Luzzatto is following Mendelssohn when he says that the only purpose of the rules that govern divine worship is to fortify us before God, so that righteousness will be the possession of our souls forever; to awaken in our minds the idea of God and his Providence; to teach us to subdue the impulses of our heart.[16] The purpose of the commandments, then, is to arouse the mind and quicken the memory, and in regard to the speculative aspect of the religious idea, to awaken in our minds the idea of God. We can thus say that for Luzzatto the commandments have a dual religious function: to serve as a vehicle for the idea of God and to safeguard Israel's separate existence. The common ground of these two functions is to be found in the circumstance that the commandments are only the *means* to preserve these independent religious values. Luzzatto epitomizes this phase of his thought when he asserts that the true philosophy that is destined to endure will make God's commandments the firm foundation of its speculative part and the emotions of pity and mercy of its practical part.[17]

The conception of Israel's unique existence as an independent religious value leads to the question of Israel's opposition to the outside world, a problem formulated in the well-known antithesis between Abrahamism, the original culture of Israel, and Athecism (derived from Athens), the culture of the non-Jewish world. This antithesis may be viewed from several aspects:

a) A clear-cut distinction is made by Luzzatto between the creativity whose goal is ethics and the one whose highest value is expressed in the manifestation of beauty and its embodiment in art.

b) There is a clear opposition between lack of faith (rationalism) and the belief in religion as such (supernaturalism).[18]

c) Luzzatto identifies philosophy with supernaturalism and supernaturalism with ethics; the aim of philosophy is to seek the truth and the aim of religion is to seek the ethical good.[19]

d) Rationalism imperils Israel and endangers its existence, for, as he writes in a letter to Leopold Zunz, it is a philosophy that leads to assimilation and eventually to the disappearance of Israel. In a letter to Abraham Geiger (1810–1874), he points out that all who give aid and comfort to rationalists contribute to the destruction of Jews and Judaism. Rationalism endangers the existence of Israel from two points of view: It denies the historical character of Judaism, which is based on supernaturalism and religion and not on rationalism or philosophy, and to ignore or minimize this fact is tantamount to denying the unique existence of Israel. Furthermore, rationalism is based on intellectual speculation, which is the common possession of all men; it is thus, by its very nature, opposed to all claims of particularity and singularity—including the separate and unique existence of Israel.

Supernaturalism is closely related to faith in revelation. It affirms that Jewish creativity is not rooted in human faculties but transcends them, whereas rationalism insists on the autonomy of man in his capacity as man. It is necessary, Luzzatto says, to know the history of this unique nation and its singular vicissitudes, to understand at all times the significance of its historical past, its successive conditions and fortunes, the incessant war between the divine spirit, which is its heritage, and the human spirit that comes to it from without. This is a war in which the former has always been victorious; indeed, if the latter should ever gain the upper hand in Israel, as it is now beginning to, the nation would disappear.[20] In this view the divine spirit is identical with the roots of Jewish original creativity and the historical forces that determine Israel's history. To understand the history of Israel means to understand the tensions that exist among the various principles and to recognize the supremacy of the divine element. Luzzatto's historical studies and his polemical writings against Abraham Ibn Ezra and Moses Maimonides doubtlessly arise from his interpretation of the rationalistic tendency in Jewish thought as a denial of its supernatural origin, and hence of the spiritual nature of Jewish history. Throughout his writings Luzzatto constantly stresses the supernaturalistic element in Judaism, which he commends as the indispensable criterion or compass for contemporary Jewish creativity, since this alone can provide the modern Jew with the original values that shaped the life and thought of Israel throughout the ages.

This sharp distinction between supernaturalism and rationalism, with its consequent emphasis on the ethical character of Judaism, dispenses with external criteria and helps us to understand Judaism from within. Luzzatto reproaches some of his contemporaries for their failure to grasp the essence of Judaism on the basis of its original sources. This generation, he says, has lost the feeling of Judaism. Enamoured of the wisdom of the Greeks, they withdraw from the knowledge of the Holy Books, and their thoughts stray more and more from their heritage. Those who sit in high places were the first to transgress, like Maimonides and his followers. But, Luzzatto continues, the lily of Sharon will be cleansed of the idols of the Greeks and the sin of Samaria. And like a fool, he will cling to the ways of his forefathers.[21]

Luzzatto regards Judaism as a moral discipline embracing all of life, a system of imperatives designed to regulate man's conduct, and he raises this conception to the level of an absolute criterion for Jewish life and its creations. But he does not close his eyes to the changing fortunes and conditions of the nation in the course of its development; we should not judge our forefathers by our thoughts, he says, but by their own thoughts. All the ancient peoples, and not only Israel, were inclined to ascribe historical happenings to the will of God.[22] This historical view, however, did not lead him to relativize Jewish values and creations or to ignore the distinction between what is important in Jewish history and what is trivial. One who affirms that there is but one God, even though he errs in his understanding of the nature of this unity and imagines God as his parents described Him when he was a child, if he acknowledges the prophecy of Moses and the truth of his miracles and his Law and keeps the seven Noachian commandments, such a man surely finds more favor in the eyes of God and his fellow men than a Jew who has a pure conception of God's unity, but does not acknowledge the truth of divine revelation of the Torah. The latter considers Moses fictitious and the Law an invention, and says to those who observe the Torah, "What are these commandments that you perform?" By saying *you* and not *I*, Luzzatto says, he withdraws from the congregation; he is an infidel, having denied the fundamental principle.[23] The criterion here is plain and unambiguous: Israel's religion and existence depend on the purity of its conception of God as One, its faith in the existence of God and in the basic principles that constitute the foundation of Jewish ethics. The revealed Law is the basis of moral life, to which are attached principles of faith from the ethical realm itself, such as reward and punishment and the election of Israel.

The ethical nature of religion may also be seen from another point of view: to know God is to know that He is good and that He performs good deeds in accordance with His mercy and abundant kindness, and that His will is that we cling to His attributes all our lives.[24] Two examples illustrate Luzzatto's thinking in this area. First, his interpretation of the nature of the sin committed by the generation of the Flood: the earth in the days of Noah was corrupt, he argues, not because it began to call God by the names of the pagan Gods, but because it was filled with violence and evil.[25] The generation of the Flood was not led astray by dogmatic or speculative errors but by its wicked deeds, and it was for these that it was punished. The second example is more instructive, for it concerns the focal point of Israel's religion, the unity of God. Here again Luzzatto tends to minimize the speculative aspect and stresses the ethical consequences: Those who believe in many powers deny to infinite perfection each of them. When we think of one of the gods as being perfect—that is, omnipotent, omniscient, etc., without end or limit—then no room is left for the existence of a rival god ... each god is lacking in some respect and limited in some attribute; only he who believes in one God and thinks of Him and His attributes as perfect.[26] The polytheistic view implies a lack of perfection among the gods, and deities with imperfect attributes cannot serve as patterns of ethical conduct for a man's whole life. Only monotheism, which attributes to God the sum total of all virtues and ultimate perfection, provides a basis for ethical imperatives.

In his study of the role of ethics in the life of religion, we have seen that Luzzatto introduced a speculative, theological factor: the existence of God. Although this principle is directly concerned with human conduct and practical morality, it is not included by Luzzatto among the principles of the Torah. The postulate of the existence of God may have served him as a *terminus a quo* for all discussions of questions relating to Israel's religious principles, the existence of God being the ultimate Idea, the last logical antecedent at the end of the epistemological process. But despite the shadow of agnosticism that accompanies Luzzatto's views, his work contains some speculations on the question of God's existence, either from the standpoint of cognition or of being. It seems that Luzzatto made a distinction between the *existence* of God, which can be the subject of intellectual speculation, and the *nature* of God, which belongs to the realm of those matters that are closed to our understanding. With reference to God's nature, therefore, he advanced a number of opinions, but the principle of God's existence he took to be beyond all dispute.

The cognitive element implicit in the above view is based on the assumption that all human knowledge is *a posteriori*—that is, derived from experience. All knowledge that comes to a man through his intellect reaches him only by means of other knowledge previously acquired; all intellectual knowledge is hence based on knowledge for which there is no proof, else there would be no end to the process. There is no escape from this. Yet, all our knowledge is based on fundamentals which, although not subject to proof, cannot be disproved for we tend to believe them intuitively. These fundamentals are the five senses, inner perception, and memory.[27] Luzzatto assumes that all knowledge is, in the last analysis, based on ultimate facts which defy further investigation and for which further proofs cannot be adduced, facts that are different from the judgments and knowledge based upon them. Luzzatto concludes that this ultimate element is neither deduced from nor confined to speculative discussion but lies in the sphere of perception, the most elementary level of cognition whose certainty rests on intuitive conviction derived from the senses.[28]

This cognitive element in the acquisition of knowledge supports the religious view. Since knowledge is based on the *fact* of sense perception, which is devoid of the certainty and verifiability incident to intellectual proof, the objection can again be raised that the sensory system is indispensable; that is, logically derived. The fact as such is accidental, for we could have been endowed with a different sensory system that would bring us knowledge differently organized and thus change the order, force, and disposition of our thoughts. Luzzatto borrowed this idea from the history of religious thought, where it is known as "the contingency of the natural world," but he transferred it from the objective cosmological sphere to the subjective cognitive sphere, so that he does not speak of the contingency of the *world* but the contingency of *cognition*. This indeterminacy of the basis of cognition leads to the inevitable conclusion that He who created the world as it is could have created it differently, could have renewed it and organized it according to His will, for who could tell Him what to do?[29] The philosophers who deny this may be compared to ignorant folk who believe that the customs of their native land prevail in all countries of the world.[30]

In the objective, cosmological sphere Luzzatto also depends on Kant's physico-theological proof for the existence of God, which rests on the nature of the physical structure of the world. There are three aspects to this proof:[31]

a) It is *a posteriori*, that is, it rests on facts given in nature and not on conceptual data that require ontological proof to derive God's existence logically from the concept, or cosmological proof to demonstrate God's existence by means of the principle of causality.

b) This *a posteriori* element does not confer certainty on the physico-theological proof, but provides it with a sufficiently solid base to make it plausible.

c) This proof cannot be used to demonstrate the existence of the Creator of the world, for it is based on *design* and *orderly sequence* in the phenomenal world and not on the emergence of *novelty*. It can apply only to the Organizer or Governor of the world.[32] Explicitly relying on Kant, Luzzatto argues that true philosophy will place God on a firm foundation in its speculative part, and pity and charity in its practical part; to demonstrate the existence of God, it will take its proofs not from what is beyond nature (metaphysics), but from nature that is manifest to the eye in the created world. This is the proof which Kant calls *physico-theological*, which he commends as being of ancient origin and acceptable to the human intellect. . . . The nature of creation will never be understood, but the marks of wisdom in creation are manifest to all.[33] Luzzatto disregards the fact that the restriction implicit in his view applies to the existence of an Organizer of the world, not to its Creator.

Besides being used to demonstrate the orderly nature of the world, the physicotheological proof is also used to demonstrate the existence of *one God*. The design and order in nature can be explained only by the existence of *one* power; therefore, in addition to the ethical argument against polytheism (the idea of the perfection of morality), we have a speculative proof against the plurality of gods, which is but another version of the physicotheological proof.

Luzzatto's place in the development of subsequent Jewish thought depends on the prominence that was given to the ethical in contradistinction to the legal aspect of Judaism. Side by side with this strong emphasis on ethics, we find in Luzzatto some reservations about the rationalistic aspect of religion, reservations that border on agnosticism. The *a posteriori* proof that he advances for the existence of God represents his attempt to set limits to agnosticism in the speculative sphere. It is interesting to note that Luzzatto's opposition to rationalism does not lead him to adopt an irrational conception of God and the world (and consequently he does not accept the Kabbalah). The concept of God as the Organizer of the rational world compels Luzzatto to introduce a definite order and structure in the ethical world of moral precepts and principles to vie with the well-ordered world of speculative thought.[34]

3

The Inner Imperative and Holiness

MORITZ LAZARUS

In Luzzatto's conception ethics with its divine imperatives constitutes the content of the religion of Israel, comparable to the Law based on divine Revelation in Mendelssohn's philosophy. With its imperatives and heterogeneous roots, ethics does not have the status of an independent philosophical problem in Luzzatto's system, but constantly raises the question of how to bring the life of religion into closer accord with ethical imperatives.

The step taken by Moritz Lazarus (1824–1903)—if we look at his teachings from the standpoint of the development of the religion of Israel as ethics—was to reverse the relation between these two spheres. Ethics, now an independent sphere in its own right, no longer constitutes the content of religion; religion is the arena for ethical activity and its most conspicuous expression.

"The purpose of ethics," Lazarus writes, "is to assign definite boundaries to all instincts clamoring for satisfaction, to establish order among contradictory demands, and harmonize the opposing claims that arise in social intercourse."[1] Its basic function is to promote man's unity and his integration into society. The unification of man's personality—that is, the regulation and harmonious development of his instincts—is the common denominator that makes for social cohesion. This is the negative or restrictive task

[43]

of ethics. At the same time, however, it has a positive function that seeks to uncover the springs of elevated moral action in man's heart. Ethics lifts man's turbulent passions to another dimension where they are nourished by imperatives and made to conform to the fitness or rightness of things.[2] Hence, the ethical imperative and its content cannot be derived from nature, for nature is the soil in which the instincts strike root and flourish. The ethical ideal seeks to transform nature and press it into the service of the imperative.[3] Ethics does not address itself to man's natural, given powers and the instincts that nourish them but to the goal of human development, the ideal; insofar as man responds to this ideal he lifts himself above nature to the level of freedom. Freedom and ethical purpose are the two sides of the same coin.

The law of which ethics treats is not law in the political sense of the term, but the outer garb of the ethical imperative. It is nothing but the norm directed to the ideals of life or to the fashioning of these ideals.[4] Ethics, therefore, has a threefold task: to curb man's instincts; to harness them to nobler, more elevated actions; and to channelize these actions to the end of regulating human conduct in conformity to the norm.

On what is ethics based? Are its imperatives innate? Lazarus attempts to make ethics an independent sphere, following Kant's doctrine of the autonomy of ethics but giving it, as Julius Guttmann observed, a vague psychological direction. Kant's doctrine of ethical autonomy rests largely on two elements: a) The active will is subject only to its own imperatives, which are at the same time, general imperatives; hence, while following its own laws, it is also subject to public legislation; b) the will is set in motion by imperatives alone and is not dependent on the nature of the objects it directs, for the will depends on itself and not on matter. These two aspects of Kant's doctrine of ethical autonomy are closely related. The independence of the will and its sovereign position within its own sphere as the lawgiver of ethics is seen most clearly in the fact that the will is not actuated by matter or by outside forces.

Lazarus places ethics on an autonomous basis, but selects from the concept of autonomy only its independent and self-sufficient phase, thus attenuating and even somewhat blurring the objective meaning of Kant's ethics. He uses psychological concepts to define the autonomous will, whereas ethics in Kant's system is autonomous in the sense that it does not depend on emotions or sentiments. Lazarus speaks of the emotion of duty, which also contains the idea (or semblance) of the content of duty, and in this he includes the emotion of obligation, that is, the inner acknowledgment of the content of the ethical imperative.[5] These two phases inherent in the feeling of duty must not be underestimated. Although seeming to follow Kant's doctrine, Lazarus deviates from it or changes it in two important respects. The imperative, in his view, is based on feeling and this consists of both obligation, that is, the inner acknowledgment of the imperative, and the contents of the imperative. Autonomous ethics has psychological roots *and* constitutive meaning, and the union of these two elements makes it significant for Jewish ethics. By and large, Jewish ethics is social ethics—that is to say, the content of the ethical imperatives deals with relations among men and the regulation of public affairs—a theme to which Lazarus devoted the second part of his posthumous work, *The Ethics of Judaism*. With the psychologism (the feeling of obligation) and the supplementary content (social ethics) that Lazarus introduced into Kant's doctrine, the categorical, ethical imperative ceased to be a methodical basis for objective ethics and became a constitutive imperative designed to regulate social life. It was justly observed by H. Steinthal that in Lazarus' conception the "I" is understood only in its function as "we." The objectivity of ethics in Kant's system is completely socialized by Lazarus.

The autonomy of ethics means that the ethical spirit contains within itself the roots of ethical principles and is of necessity independent of laws and ordinances from without. A methodological difficulty arises at this point, a difficulty unnoticed by Lazarus himself, that of defining the spirit which is the source of ethics. The true meaning of the autonomy of ethical law is not that man bestowed it on himself but that *ethical* man, or the ethical element within him, produced the law.[6] The basis of ethics does not reside in man *qua* man but in man as an ethical being. But how can we distinguish the one from the other except with the help of concepts derived from ethics, that is, concepts whose roots are to be found

in ethical man? This methodological difficulty lends prominence
to the psychologism which Lazarus injected into the concept of
autonomy, according to which ethical man is the source of ethics.
The ethical element in man is a psychological fact of interest to
students of psychology; the root and source of ethical autonomy is
the feeling of obligation,[7] and the essence of ethics (obligation) is
to be found in the psychological fact of feeling.

The question then arises regarding the nature of Jewish ethics.
"In its origin Jewish ethics is theologic. For the Jewish mind the
theistic reason looms up in the foreground of all speculations on
morality. The whole Jewish conception of life is as little think-
able without God as is our physical world without the sun."[8] It
is thus evident that Jewish ethics has a heteronomous structure—
that is, its roots are not in the human sentiment of obligation but
in the divine imperative or in divine revelation. Ethics is thereby
automatically given a specific content, since the divine imperative
needs no methodological basis but only a content to order and
direct. If the autonomous nature of ethics is invalidated, ethics
itself disappears. The philosophical problem dealt with in Lazarus'
book on the ethics of Judaism is that of reconciling the autonomous
nature of ethics with the divine basis of Jewish ethics. This problem leads him to a distinct formulation of Jewish ethics from
which he removes all specifically religious characteristics, especially
the religious quality inherent in the concept of God.

For Lazarus the conflict between theistic and autonomous ethics
is resolved by making God the Author and Founder of ethics.
Even God is subject to the ethical imperatives He Himself revealed, because He is *ethical*. The formal laws of logic (the Law of
Contradiction), as Leibnitz expressed it, also apply to God's
thoughts. "Morality was not created by the Sinaitic code; it springs
from its own and from man's peculiar nature."[9] "Moral laws . . .
are not laws because they are written; they are written because they
are laws."[10] "Not because God ordained it is a law moral, but
because it is moral, therefore God has ordained it."[11] Its relation to
God, therefore, does not deprive ethics of its autonomous nature,
for ethics is not dependent on any heteronomous basis and hence
needs no theistic moorings.[12]

The scope of ethics and the validity of its imperatives, then, do not derive their force from their dependence on God, their Author and Promulgator. God is now assigned a definite function *within* the autonomous sphere of ethics, and man's allegiance is directed to both God *and* His imperatives. This dual allegiance is the patent mark of the integrated ethical personality, giving man depth, volume, and a new source of power.[13] Man as a creature of nature, when he is not impelled by moral endeavor, is without inner force, harmony or consistency, and in his wretched condition seeks to cast his burden on God, who becomes the perfect embodiment, the Archetype of ethical ideals. The ethical principle resides within itself, but precisely because of this it also resides in God, the Archetype of ethics.[14] The relation of man to God finds no expression in feeling, experience, or reflection outside the sphere of ethics. Man no longer looks upon himself as dust and ashes in the face of an implacable, transcendent God who can trample him down. Both are now subject to the inner logic of ethics. An *objective* relationship, that is, a relationship based on the ethical imperative, now obtains between God and man within the bounds of ethical experience.

Lazarus uses the Judaic principle that man is made in God's image and should therefore strive to imitate His attributes (just as He is merciful, be ye merciful, etc.) in order to support this conception. In Jewish tradition God's attributes were not only objects of imitation but were also the root of ethics. The God whose attributes were imitated was also the one who revealed their content and planted in man the very idea of imitation—the desire to embody God's attributes in the finite world. Lazarus himself does not seem to be aware that this conception removes God from the sphere of being to that of ethics, nor does he realize its far-reaching consequences. God performs His function, as the Archetype of ethics not because He established the concept of the Archetype, but because He is the Pattern of right conduct and the Paragon of ethical perfection. He has no existence in His own right and no religious function of His own. Lazarus must have been aware of this distinction between the ethical and the religious when he said that religion, or more accurately, the ethical ground of all religion, is "to be with God, the Highest among all essences," "to fill the soul with the Most Perfect among all ideas."[15] Nevertheless, he did not define the essence of the religious area that lies beyond ethics. The religion of Israel was for him synonymous with the ethics of Judaism.

Lazarus arrives at his understanding of God as the Archetype of ethical attributes through his concept of holiness. For this, too, he was indebted to Kant, but he failed to realize the import of the change that he introduced into Kant's idea. The nature of the "holy will," which for Kant is the good will *par excellence*, lies in the fact that its rules of conduct necessarily include the laws of autonomy,[16]—that is, the subjective rules that guide the will are at the same time the objective principles of ethics. Here instinct and imperative are not divorced, since such a will has no need of any imperative at all.[17] What is proper and fitting for ethics is immanent in this will, which is not realizable in the finite world of senses where a distinction is made between the sensible and the intelligible, between instincts and imperatives. The holy will is a postulate of ethics and necessarily implies the corollary of immortality—that is, the permanent existence of the soul beyond the sensible world and the ultimate realization of the imperative beyond the visible world of appearances. In the intelligible world, beyond the confused world of particulars, the will is elevated to the level of the holy will.

In his conception of holiness Lazarus introduces several modifications, chiefly with respect to the relation of this concept to God. It is evident that Lazarus has in mind the text, "Be ye holy for I am the Lord your God," but he gives this commandment a purely ethical interpretation. Nothing of the irrational or the esoteric is left in this understanding of holiness, and nothing of the transcendence of existence of which holiness is one of the manifestations. To Lazarus, holiness has only ethical meaning since the ethical idea is autonomous—that is, has validity and regulative value even if it is not embodied in God.[18] The concept of holiness is, therefore, not fundamentally related to God and does not apply to God's existence as a religious principle. Holiness is one of the categories of ethics and in the realm of ethics there is a correlation between holiness and God. From the standpoint of ethics, holiness is nothing more than ethical perfection,[19] identical with the Archetype of ethics and with the principle of unity inherent in the ethical ideal. Ethical holiness is an attribute that is not irrational and has none of the sublimity that comes from the consciousness of the deep gulf that separates man from his Creator.

The relation between man and holy God is an immanent relation in the ethical world and has no meaning beyond this sphere. God as holy—that is, God as the Archetype of all the good attributes—is the embodiment of practical ethics,[20] which is the stage of holiness that man has not yet reached. The sanctification of life means the penetration of ethics into life or the elevation of life to the level of ethics.[21] Life as such is not opposed to holiness; it merely has not *as yet* reached that stage.[22] The idea of holiness does not bring with it a consciousness of the absolute separation between man and the God of holiness. On the contrary, holiness has an immanent meaning within the confines of man's existence; by obliging man to pursue ethical ideals and embody them in his practical life, it serves as a bridge between man and God. Furthermore, holiness is *the* bearer of ethical meaning; it is the striving towards a state of ethical perfection which is synonymous with God. The concept of God is deprived of all existential meaning, the gulf between God and His creation is bridged, and the tension between the finite and the infinite removed.

This aspect of holiness, which constitutes its essence, is most clearly expressed by the explanation given to its content. The realization of ethical ideals signifies the elevation of society and humanity to an ethical level. The sanctification of life means the unity of mankind, or the harmonious relations between the individual and society.[23] Holiness, the highest ethical value, is not attainable in practical life among men. It is an idea in the Kantian sense of the term, an ever-receding goal at the end of a process towards which life moves. This process is understood by Lazarus in an exclusively social sense and thus acquires universal validity. Ethical law is basically universal; it applies to all men and is binding on them. The category "all" emerges from the nature of the ethical law, and within its confines ethics and holiness grow and develop. Just as the purpose of ethics is the cultivation of the harmonious individual, so the purpose of holiness, the highest ethical value, is the cultivation of a harmonious society. Holiness, which finds its perfect realization in God, is the ideal to which society strives. Lazarus does not seem to be aware that by resorting to Kantian concepts he approaches the Fichtean idea which identifies God with the ethical order of the world.[24] The messianic goal envisaged by Lazarus is the perfection of the human race.[25] This conception of God as a purely ethical category lies at the root of Liberalism, which regards the growth of society as the product of evolutionary ethics and the realization of the divine ethical attributes. The difference between God as an ethical category and society as a historical category is the difference between ethics as already exemplified in action and ethics in the making.

Lazarus distinguishes between ethical holiness, the highest ethical value rooted in the autonomous nature of ethics, and the holiness of worship which has no inner reason and whose source is not the nature or concept of holiness but divine legislation.[26] This goes back to Saadia Gaon's distinction between the intellectual commandments derived from cognition and the commandments of obedience derived from divine will or revelation. Lazarus combines this distinction with Mendelssohn's view, according to which the positive commandments of worship and ritual are the symbols of eternal verities. Mendelssohn regarded these commandments chiefly as *symbols of speculative truths*, but Lazarus, who had transferred the concept of God to the ethical realm completely, saw them as the *symbols of ethical imperatives*. Commandments relating to the holiness of worship have the sole purpose of orienting man ethically.[27]

By equating Judaism with ethics, Lazarus deprives it of its religious and doctrinal elements. God the Creator ceases to be the cornerstone of reality and becomes the crown of ethics. He is the sum total of ethical attributes and the goal of social progress, not God the Father who hears the prayers of the penitent.

This point of view is open to two grave objections. David Neumark (1866–1924) argued that it is basically foreign to Judaism "where God's commandments are derived from Creation and

Providence." Far from being autonomous, ethics is related to the religious categories of creation and providence; to make it with a foreign Kantian element is to vitiate and debase the original Jewish element. Hermann Cohen also objected to the mechanical union of the two elements in Lazarus' conception (which, on the one hand, has God as the basis of ethics, and on the other hand, insists on the autonomy of ethics) with the consequent confusion resulting from the identification of the concept of God with that of man. However, Cohen's methodological proof that the autonomy of ethics is a *cognitive* principle indicates that this concept was part of his systematic thought. In his ethical philosophy God appears as an Idea, the Guarantor that the good will ultimately be realized, but in some important respects he eventually arrived at an opposite view, and gave the concept of God a meaning in terms of reality. Hermann Cohen begins with ethics and ends with ontology, a development that requires a closer examination.

From the Ethical Idea to the True Being

HERMANN COHEN

A. ETHICS AS THE END OF RELIGION

The transition in Hermann Cohen's treatment of the nature of religion in general and Judaism in particular is from a conception that subsumed religion under ethics to one that tried to impart to religion an independent character of its own, based either on its intrinsic ethical principles or its innate concept of God. This transition reflects the problems that Cohen had to deal with when he came to compare the ethical with the religious aspect in his system.

The problem of ethics, Cohen maintains, is to place the individual in correlation to the general order and to effect the integration of man within it.[1] Ethics is the realm of the imperative and of the good and its task is to deliver man from the bonds of nature. The ethical imperative, like the imperative of the ideal good, finds its most perfect expression in man's emergence from the narrow confines of his individual self into the larger world of society. This social world is not given in nature; it is built by the ethical activity of man and the imperatives that guide it. Ethics, as the realm of acts directed to the realization of the ideal good, binds man to the community and to the entire human race. The ethical relations between men are not based on given elements,

[52]

either the instinctive drives or the biological interdependence of men, but derive their inspiration from the ought. Society here performs an important ethical task for it serves as the arena of moral endeavor and is itself the highest ethical value. Ethics leaves man only his identification with the whole human race.[2] Correlation between individuals is not the only relation on which ethics is built; the active ethical realm is brought into being not only by the relations among men but also by man's identification with the larger society and his dependence upon it.

The most pregnant expression of the general social order is equality among men. Since all men are members of society, which in its comprehensive form represents the highest ethical value, the differences among men have no ethical significance. We shall later have occasion to consider these differences, which arise because of various conditions and circumstances, and which constitute the subject matter of those sciences that deal with the data of experience. These empirical facts, however, are to some extent influenced by the high ideals that are shared by all men as members of society, for it is these ideals which have raised man to the social level of mutual co-operation.[3] Virtue mediates between the ethical task and the isolated individual art.[4] It responds to the ethical task which urges man to identify himself with society, and is expressed in the respect that one man bestows on another. Respect is the emotion of virtue.[5] He who shows respect to his fellow man does so because he regards him as a member of society as a whole. The relations among men, then, are not based on elements derived from nature, such as the instinct of attraction or the desire to share things, but from the ideals of the ought that man seeks to incorporate in society and the elementary ethical insight that regards all men as members of one common humanity. Humanity, conceived as one large social family, is the embodiment of the concept Man.

The general order of society is not a concept of nature—that is, it does not exist in nature as does a table or the stars. The social order bursts the bonds of the given. It is the goal of ethical endeavor, the criterion of practical morality and of the good impulse. The very nature of the social order, furthermore, is such that we fail to see it as a reality, as an example of a natural phenomenon. Ethics has its own concept of reality and this is the concept of the *ideal*; the ethical ideal has no corresponding reality.[6] This does not impair its power or disparage its authority. On the contrary, by its very nature ethics *seeks* to embody its ideals in practical life but never wholly attains them. This sets ethics apart from reality and from the given in nature. To discover the essence of ethics we must separate it from reality and place it in the goal of our ethical striving. The distance between natural reality and ethical endeavor is the distance between the actual and the ideal and is the reflection of the irremediable gap between the two.

The ever-receding ideal, then, is the goal of ethics and, consequently, ethics must adopt as one of its basic principles "the eternality of ethical progress."[7] Progress is the mediating process between the is and the ought, the never-ceasing attempt to realize the ideal. It is the inevitable consequence of the assumption that the good is an ideal to which no given reality corresponds. Progress is the bridge between the irreconcilable realms of the actual and the ideal, but since the ideal is not realizable in practice (for then it would no longer be the goal or task but part of the given world of facts), true ethics is identified with the never-ending advance of progress. Here, as in other parts of Cohen's system, we plainly see the shift from truth in *reality* to truth in *progress*, from the goal to the pursuit, from the victory to the struggle. For him, the *search* for the truth is the truth; truth is not the quarry but the labor of extraction.[8] It may be said that the two realms of science and ethics are concerned with nothing but progress: progress towards the truth in the former, and progress towards the ideal good in the latter. In science progress is made by proceeding from one concept to another or from one category to another, as from substance to causality; ethics progresses as it struggles towards a future good. The teleological structure of ethics, therefore, assigns an important role to the concept of the future which expresses in *time* the distance between the actual present and the far-off ideal. Progress presses on towards the ever-receding ideal hidden in the inexhaustible depths of the future. To attain the ideal is to embody it in action and thus convert the future into the past, the empire of facts and phenomena, which is the principal concern of the sciences.

Science and ethics are not co-extensive. Ethics needs nature not as an arsenal to provide it with its values and imperatives, but as an arena in which it can realize itself. Ethics is an autonomous domain with respect to its content and its categories, which serve it as a pattern, but it needs nature for the *embodiment* of these categories. What would ethics and its principles be without the reality of nature or if the natural world were destroyed?[9] The teleological dependence of ethics on nature serves as a bridge between these two spheres. Ethics needs nature, to be sure, but we have no proof that there is a corresponding fulfillment of its needs on the part of nature nor can we forsee *how* the fulfillment actually occurs in practice. Nature is permanent, Cohen insists; its permanence coincides with ethical permanence, and this truth we call God.[10] The meaning of God is that nature is real in the same degree of certainty that ethics is eternal.[11]

This aspect of Cohen's philosophy, however, does not appear to be altogether unambiguous. The question that needs further clarification is whether the Idea of God is identified with the relation between ethics and nature or whether this Idea is nothing more than a *guarantee* for the reality of this relationship—that is, the assurance that the reality of nature will continue to correspond to the eternality of ethics. The difficulty here emerges more clearly when we examine the specific formulation that Cohen gives to the relation between nature and ethics. The connection between logic and ethics, he says, corresponds to the principle of truth.[12] Truth means the connection and correspondence between the theoretical and the ethical spheres.[13] The question now arises whether God means *Truth* in the sense indicated above—that is, the correspondence between the theoretical sphere which is the cognitive element in progress, and the ethical sphere which is the activity concerned with the embodiment of the ideal—or whether God is the *Guarantor* of this correspondence. In the first case God means the Postulate of the correspondence and in the second case the Guarantor of its actualization. It sometimes seems that Cohen is inclined to identify God with the element of certainty in the correspondence between nature and ethics. In the philosophical system which places its main emphasis on the process rather than on the goal, God is assigned a more modest function—he becomes the name for the correspondence between the two spheres of nature and ethics, without the guarantee that this postulate is actually fulfilled.

Whether God is conceived as the Truth—that is, as the correspondence between nature and ethics—or as the Guarantee for the reality of this correspondence, it is clear that in Cohen's philosophical system God is not *Reality*. The concept of reality is found both in nature and in ethics, appearing in the former as the *goal* of progress and in the latter as the *path* of progress. God is an Idea, not a Reality,[14] posited as a methodological concept between ethics and nature in order to help solve the relation between them and to lend coherence to Cohen's system. God is not prior to this system and its problems, temporally or logically. He is not reality but the Guarantee of reality, that is, reality as the anvil of ethics. Since all reality according to Cohen's idealistic conception is conditioned and posited by the concept, it is not surprising that the reality of nature should be conditioned by the concept God. God cannot be conceived as the cause of the reality of nature, as it is in religion, because He is not reality but an Idea—that is, the logical condition of all reality.

From this basic notion of God as an Idea and the condition of reality, in contradistinction to God as reality, Cohen draws conclusions with respect to other attributes generally ascribed by the religious consciousness to God—for example, God as a personality, and God as living. Being an Idea, God cannot be either; only the idea, the concept and the truth of ethical knowledge, can be applied to God.[15] In mythology, God is conceived as an active, living personality, since myths conceive God as reality; in pure religion, however, God as Idea dispenses with these attributes.

The common religious consciousness and sentiment looks upon God as transcendent—that is, as a reality separate from the world or from nature. Reality, however, cannot be separated from nature, for it is a concept of nature formulated by natural science. Reality is also a concept of morality and has meaning insofar as it contributes to the progress of ethics towards the ideal. Cohen seeks to establish a distinct separation between the human and the divine by emphasizing the difference between God and each of the two spheres. God is transcendent over against ethics as well as nature, because He is between them and not in them.[16] But this does not make God transcendent over against the system wherein the two spheres coincide. God, as the Correspondence between the two spheres and its Guarantor, is transcendent with respect to each of the spheres, but He is immanent within the system wherein they correspond.[17] It follows, then, that God has two aspects: From the standpoint of each of the sovereign spheres of nature and ethics, He is separate; but from the standpoint of the sum total of the spheres, He is not separate. Even God's transcendence has a relative-methodical character and not one of absolute reality.

The concept of God, then, is posited between the two spheres: ethics and nature. Although it serves as a bridge between them, its fundamental allegiance is to the sphere of ethics, which determines its problems and its systematic function. Since the problem of the correspondence between ethics and nature stems from the needs of the former, it is necessary at the very outset that God, who occupies an intermediate position between the two, should be assigned a function principally directed to ethics. We deprive ethics of its soul and reduce the force of religion if we ascribe value to God beyond the domain of ethics. Whatever religious value is to be found in the divine essence of Judaism is in the domain of ethics. Its essence is in its attributes alone; and the attributes are concerned only with the love of God and his righteousness.[18] (The attributes refer to the verse in Exodus 34:6, "merciful and gracious, long suffering, and abundant in goodness and truth, keeping mercy unto the thousandth generation, forgiving iniquity and trangressions and sin, and that will by no means clear the guilty, visiting the iniquity of the fathers upon the children and upon the children's children, unto the third and the fourth generation.")

This inclination to give the divine essence an ethical content is also to be found in Maimonides. Just as Kant opposed proofs for the reality of God so did Maimonides oppose positive attributes;

and just as Kant agreed to but one religious-ethical proof, so Maimonides accepted only the practical attributes. The ways of God are the ways He conducts Himself with man—that is, His ethical attributes.[19] Cohen finds in Judaism an inclination to give unreserved ethical meaning to the concept of God. The thirteen attributes of God are not attributes that determine God's essence with respect to His active, living personality; they have no meaning except in the moral realm. In this respect Cohen found parallel views in the teachings of Maimonides and Kant. Only the attributes of action are ascribed by Maimonides to God—that is, those attributes in which God appears as active in His relations to man and to human conduct. Cohen describes this as seeing God in the mirror of ethics, and finds it a confirmation of Kant's physico-theological proof as the only possible proof for the existence of God. This is a basic notion of modern Jewish thought; those who seek to give Judaism ethical meaning always turn for support to Maimonides' understanding of the attributes of God as attributes of action. Of those thinkers who subscribed to the ethical view, Luzzatto was the only one who failed to look to Maimonides for support, seeing only the metaphysical aspect of his teachings—which, as we have seen, he calls Athecism—and not the practical-ethical aspect. We are not concerned, however, with the interpretations given to Maimonides' philosophy, for they reveal more about the attitude and intent of the expositors than of the subject discussed.

The view that imparts meaning to God's relation to man's ethical conduct is closely related to the conception of God as the pattern or archetype of ethical activity. Cohen himself was not aware of how closely he approached Lazarus' views in this matter despite his severe criticism of the latter's book on Jewish ethics.[20] The concept of the Jewish God is co-extensive with its ethical meaning—that is, God is the *Urbild* and *Vorbild*, the pattern and example of ethical human conduct. Ethics can become our reality only and exclusively by our own conduct. Hence, God means, as it were, only the possibility of being a pattern or *schema*.[21] The phrase "as it were" (*gleichsam*) tends to vitiate the absolute character of the relationship between God and man's ethical conduct. Actually,

Cohen has no other theory concerning God's nature except that which sees Him as the pattern of ethical conduct. The philosophers of the Middle Ages deprived God of all the attributes not directly related to human activity or capable of serving as patterns for such activity.[22] It seemed to Cohen that the prophetic-Jewish conception reformulated the negative theology of the Middle Ages. In his early period Cohen saw in this negative theology only the negation of God's real attributes in order to affirm His attributes of action. In his second period, which we shall discuss below, Cohen found in this negative theology and its concepts the means for imparting real meaning to God and identifying Him with the *only* true reality. At any rate, it is clear that Cohen saw the relation between God and man as existing within the sphere of ethics —that is, as a relation that touches man's conduct and the pattern it strives to emulate. God was, and in Judaism He will continue to be, the ethical Paragon and its Guarantor.[23] But God's imperatives and the divine Law are only other expressions for this essence of God as archetype and pattern of human ethical conduct.[24]

When Cohen formulated his basic views concerning God as an Idea within the ethical sphere, he did not intend to have them apply exclusively or primarily to Judaism. His basic consideration was the claim of ethics and the demands of his philosophical system which rests on the correspondence between ethics and nature. But even in this systematic formulation emphasis is placed on the tendency in Judaism to form ethical concepts. The three fundamental concepts discussed above are concepts that appear in prophetic Judaism:

a) Universalism. Ethics is basically the correlation between man and humanity—and it was the prophets who discovered this ethical category which is called humanity. This belief in humanity is the faith of Israel.[25] Cohen follows the Jewish theologians of the period of Religious Reform in his emphasis on prophetic universalism as the principal concept of systematic ethics that breaks through the confines of historic Judaism.

b) The Future. The concept of the reality in ethics is identical with our progressive advance into the future. This concept of the future was also renewed by the prophets, who stressed it in distinction to all past time.[26] The prophetic interpretation of this concept reveals an original feature of Judaism; in contradistinction to the pagan conception which placed the ethical ideal of the golden age in the past, the Hebrew prophets transferred it to the future. Messianism was born at the moment when man's gaze was directed to the future.[27] The past and present vanish in the messianic idea and the consciousness of time is directed to the future and its revelation.[28]

Here Cohen draws a parallel between the messianic idea in its pure form and monotheism. The future is never experienced and is beyond our sense perception. Hence, Cohen says that just as the monotheistic idea revealed the suprasensible God, so also did it reveal the dimension of suprasensible time.[29] The removal of God from sense-perception and the transformation of future time as the principal dimension of ethics reflect the abstract character of the Jewish idea. The revelation of future time is also the revelation of the coming of historical events which are directed to the future; it constitutes the idea of progress which characterizes the concept of reality in the ethical sphere. The messianic idea became the idea of world history;[30] Judaism provided ethics with its concept of reality—that is, the idea of progress towards the future.

c) God and Ethics. Furthermore, the ethical nature of God was first revealed in Judaism. From the historical standpoint and from the standpoint of the history of religious doctrines we here find a clear expression of the distinction between Judaism and mythology. Mythology conceives of God as a real, living personality whereas prophetic Judaism sees Him in His relation to ethics.

Cohen needs the concept of God as a mediating concept of religion, not to preserve religion but to promote the realization of ethical ideals. Theology must eventually be transformed into ethico-theology,[31] the goal to which it constantly aspires.[32] Religious concepts do not have an independent existence of their own, nor, do they constitute an independent realm known as religion, but serve ethics as auxiliary concepts. Nor does ethics draw its concepts from religion but rather from the inexhaustible source of the understand-

ing. The connections between ethics and Judaism are merely historical—that is, the basic notions of ethics were first revealed in
Judaism, but are disclosed by the understanding through its own
independent efforts. Ethics coincides with religion neither in content nor in the formation of its concepts, but only at the point
where the ethical imperative and the ideal good are about to be
realized and consummated. It is only at the end of the ethical
process, and not at the beginning, that morality seeks the aid of
religion.[33] This dependence of ethics on religious concepts does
not make ethics inferior to religion. Ethics encroaches upon religious territory merely to usurp it and inflict upon it ethical meaning. Religious concepts are thus not only devoid of intrinsic
meaning, but the whole sphere of religion forfeits its sovereignty
to the conquering impulse of ethics.

The dependence of ethics on religious concepts is viewed by
Cohen from the standpoint of ethics alone. In the province of
morality the individual is left nothing but his identification with
humanity. The problem of God is confined to the limits of morality
as the problem of the guarantee or the embodiment of ethical
principles here on earth.[34] Cohen's original contribution to the nature of religion and the unique place occupied by Judaism within
it, made during the second period of his creative work, will be
examined below.

B. THE BREACH FROM BELOW AND THE BREACH FROM ABOVE

Ethics places the individual in a material relationship to society
and transfers the ideal good to the social realm. The individual as
such, isolated and cut off from society, is without ethical significance
and does not constitute an ethical category. This is the most basic
distinction between ethics and logic. In his Logic Cohen includes
uniqueness (*Einzelheit*) among the critical categories and then
examines the relation between uniqueness and sensation. Uniqueness is the category that gives expression to what sensation dumbly
feels but cannot articulate;[35] in it the claims of sensation are
acknowledged but not its independence of the conceptual framework in which it is embedded.[36] Furthermore, Cohen recognizes

the relation between reality and sensation and takes uniqueness as the concept that serves as a bridge between the two. Only the individual can be known as real. The category of reality, however, does not isolate the object from its conceptual framework. Logic rejects the independence of sensation, but the category of reality in no way disrupts unity. The category of uniqueness seeks to preserve the individual object within an articulated, comprehensive system. Ethics, however, as formulated by Cohen in his first period, places the ideal good within society and defines the ethical imperative as that which identifies the individual with society. The concept of ethics does not apply to the individual but to society and its progressive development. In terms of logic and the theory of knowledge, reality means the relationship, or even the tension, between the individual and the general social order; in the sphere of ethics, reality applies exclusively to the general social order. Cohen aptly describes this ethical point of view: Because of its methodological opposition to all sensational and empirical elements in man, ethics is constrained to take the fateful step of totally depriving the "I" of individuality; ethics converts the "I" of man into the "I" of mankind.[37] Since ethics cannot abandon the concept of ought, it must transfer its postulates from the "I" as an existing individual to the ideal good as mankind.

Here the breach in Cohen's later conception emerges. But even in the formulation of his revised view he continues to stress the relation between religion and ethics: Religion itself is morality or it is not religion.[38] Cohen repeatedly emphasizes that religion is not an independent sphere like science, ethics, and art. Religion has specific characteristics which distinguish it from ethics, but this does not give it absolute independence with respect to ethics.[39] When religion is separated from ethics, it is reduced to a philosophical system interested in all phases of culture and also in the differences between them. Even in his revised view Cohen sought to establish the validity of ethics with respect to religion, a validity such as ethics already has with respect to the disciplines founded on practical activity—politics, law, and the philosophy of history.[40]

Cohen himself did not realize to what extent he had removed religion from its dependence on ethics and attached it to logic.

The concept of God that he had formulated in his earlier view as the correspondence between logic and nature, on the one hand, and the ideal good and the sphere of ethics or its guarantee, on the other, was completely conceived in relation to ethics, since it was only for the sake of ethics that Cohen found it necessary to posit the idea of God. God was placed between nature and ethics, but only in the interests of ethics; in the later conception this prominence given to the special character of religion over against ethics reappears in order to establish the relationship between the concept of God and the province of logic. To this relationship Cohen relegates all that concerns the concept of God, which he now identifies not with the ethical idea but with true Being.[41] We shall return to this subject, but it is worth noting now that there are two poles to this relationship between religion and logic—one that relates to God, another that relates to man.

The methodological difference between these two periods in the development of Cohen's conception of religion may be stated as follows: In the first, religion was relegated to ethics, religion being the means and ethics the end; in the second, Cohen established a much closer relationship between religion and logic. He does not go beyond the bounds of his general system, therefore, but merely arranges the relationships within it somewhat differently by stressing logic instead of ethics.[42] In short, with the emphasis on the relation between religion and logic in his second period, Cohen had to make use of significant, real concepts; from the standpoint of method, he had to rely on *experience* as the source of important religious concepts, such as the "I," sin, fellow man, love, suffering, etc. The realm of experience is not opposed to religion in contradistinction to ethics, as Cohen had assumed in his first period, but is an inseparable part of it. The revised understanding of religion rests on two concepts of reality—the empirical "I," which has its roots in experience, and the concept of the True Being, derived from pure perception or pure thought. In this new conception of religion (although Cohen himself did not dwell on this part of his system) the two poles of his logic meet—True Being, which is the first link of the logical process and the derivation of its principles, and the reality of the "I," the last link. The meaning of the individual is real in relation to sensation. The breach in Cohen's conception of the nature of religion is connected, from the standpoint of method, to this shift to logic, and religion is given an existential meaning. To put it more accurately, in Cohen's later interpretation, religion retains the ethical content, but is delineated by the two poles—of God as Being and man as reality, and neither are merely ethical concepts.

From this point of view we can understand Cohen's words about the incomplete nature of ethics and its material defects. The principal weakness of ethics is to be found in its concept of man. The individual has no independent status in ethics since he is an empirical concept; it is precisely because of this that he can serve as a typical example of society. The individual is a part of the general social order and cannot be understood in his isolated state in and of himself.[43] Whenever ethics comes upon the problem of sin and the consciousness of sin, it solves the problem by suspending or invalidating the "I" that deliberately sins.[44] Ethics finds the solution for the essential problems of the "I" as an individual by doing away with the substance of the "I"; but he whose existence is subject to annihilation is in no position to demand that his problems be treated seriously. Religion is born the moment the individual refuses to accept this arbitrary annihilation, the moment he becomes aware of his isolated state and the bitter taste of finitude, obedience, poverty, and worthlessness.[45] This wretched condition, however, does not exist beyond the confines of society, but is the lowest stage in the life of the individual within society.

Turning now to the opposite pole, the concept of God, Cohen shows that "ethics defines for itself its own God as the Guarantor of morality upon earth, but beyond this definition and the postulate of this idea, its means are of no avail. Through its trust in God, religion creates the ethical God-idea."[46] Ethics posits the idea of God as the Truth—that is, as the correspondence between ethics and nature, or as the Guarantor of this correspondence. The idea of God expresses the *postulate* that nature cannot express, since ethics needs nature for the realization of its imperatives. But the postulate contains no surety of realization, since it does not create out of itself a corresponding reality. When we conceive of

God, then, as the Guarantor of truth, we conceive Him as the Guarantor for the realization of the postulate. We thus find, even in the earlier view, the beginning of the conception according to which God ceases to be merely an Idea and becomes the Being that guarantees the Idea. But since Cohen by and large regards the idea of God as identical with the concept of Truth, he is able to criticize ethics from the standpoint of the God-idea inherent within it. It may be objected that the ethical ideal lacks the power to guarantee its own realization, since the guarantor within the idea itself needs a guarantee. The discussion of this point is highly interesting, since it involves the existential conception of the God-idea in Cohen's early period. God as Idea is at most the Guarantor for the progressive advance of ethics, but cannot be the Guarantor for the final consummation of the ethical process. In his second period, however, Cohen is not concerned with the process alone but also with the *end* of the process. In other words, the Idea as a concept within the system tends to be a guarantee for the dynamic nature of the ethical process, but not for its completion. Only God who is beyond the Idea—that is, God who is complete within Himself—is able to guarantee the end result of the ethical process.

Cohen sought to find support for the existential meaning of God even in his first period, when God was the Guarantor for the reality of nature, the sphere of ethical realization. But now he interprets this guarantee not only as a postulate but as an actual interdependence of nature and God. The meaning of the correlation between God and nature is, he thinks, already implicit in the preservation of nature by God, in the preservation of the reality of nature. Therefore, in the Idea of the preservation of a world God becomes the Originator of its incessant, perpetual reality.[47] God as Idea or the Guarantor keeps His pledge by having created nature, the same nature that ethics finds indispensable for the realization of its imperatives. This relation of God to nature, which exists for the sake of ethics, is given existential meaning by Cohen—that is, a meaning of interdependence between the Creator and what He has created. The creation of nature is the best assurance and the guarantee of its continuation. The idea of the inter-dependence of nature and God within the sphere of ethics serves to corroborate the concept of Creation. Preservation is re-creation and creation is at bottom nothing more than the renewal of preservation.[48] The God who has been posited in order to preserve nature performs His task as the Creator of nature, whose continued existence is but an unceasing daily re-creation. Cohen seems to believe that it is possible to adhere to his early position and use it as a basis for his later conception—that is, to supplement the concept of God as merely an Idea with that of God as Being. It is evident, however, that this interpretation was made *post factum*—that is, an existential interpretation acquired at a later stage was imposed on an early conception. At any rate, it will become apparent on closer study that the true derivation of the existential meaning does not stem from the interpretation of the first view, but is based on principles derived from logic.

"The individual constitutes a problem in which the peculiar quality of religion emerges in distinction to that of ethics."[49] Ethics demands that in the process of realizing moral principles and the ideal good we should not fail to include humanity as the bearer of ethical progress. The God of ethics, however, is unable to vouch for the interests of the "I" in the process of realizing the ideal good. The general order of society, which is identified with mankind, offers no assurances to the isolated, individual "I." Ethics advocates the concept of a universal God of all mankind, whereas the "I" demands a personal God for itself, which is the God of religion.[50] The individual feels weak and neglected by himself and fears being swallowed up by the voracious whole; he yearns, therefore, for a God that is related directly to *him*, and not simply the generality of mankind.

In this new conception, religion ceased to be subsumed under ethics; it acquired a specific character of its own the moment that man took up, as it were, a position of equality over against God.[51] Religion assumes its peculiar character the moment the individual becomes conscious of his own separate existence and seeks to relate himself to God, not through mankind but through himself and for his own sake. In ethics we have a twofold correlation: that of the "I" to mankind and that of mankind to God.

The individual does not have an independent status of his own, either from the standpoint of humanity as a whole society or from the standpoint of God as an ethical idea. The individual thinks of himself as isolated and absolute and consequently creates a new correlation which constitutes the essence of religion—not the correlation of the individual to society or humanity, but to God. In religion we have the correlation of the individual who is a reality to God who is true Being.[52] The position of religion in Cohen's system is determined by a new relationship set up between God and man, on behalf of which both have been detached from their moorings in humanity. Both poles of the axis, man no less than God, are to be regarded as equally important if the relationship is to be preserved. The equality of these two eternal foci of the theological ellipse, august God and feeble man, and the enduring struggle between them, is the deepest insight of the religious consciousness.[53]

Ethics differs from religion in still another respect. Man is the focal point of ethics and the unifying core of its problems, whereas for science man is an anonymous instance to illustrate a natural law or a member of a class deduced on the basis of common characteristics. The individual himself, however, is in his own eyes more than a mere cipher, a label, or a noun. Whenever man says "I," he sees himself as absolute and independent and not as a mere strand in a network of laws. The question concerning the difference between ethics and religion can be formulated, from the methodological point of view, as the struggle between the comprehensive network of laws which concern the general social order and the individual who refuses to be entangled in its abstract meshes.[54] Ethics, which depends on the concept of the good will, and which is removed from experience and even opposed to it, stands by the legal network and its ramifications. Religion, which depends on experience and the uniqueness of the individual, insists on the independent existence of the empirical individual. For ethics, the individual is a transitional point to be overcome in order to attain the ultimate goal of the social good, whereas, for religion, the individual has an absolute status.

The dependence of religion on experience and its concepts is further illustrated by the fact that, whereas ethics insists on the correlation of the individual to mankind as a whole, religion insists on the correlation of one individual to another. The fellow man and the "I" are the two concepts that are derived from religion.[55] Both are given realities; hence the ethical relation need not relegate the ideal good to a sphere beyond the empirical reality of human society. If Cohen still confines religion to morality, as in his first period we must now say that religion is the morality that dictates the relations between the individual and his fellow man, whereas ethics is the morality that dictates the relations between man and society as a whole. Affective changes consequently occur in both spheres. Religion bases human conduct on love and pity, emotions that unite men to one another; ethics bases human conduct on the sentiment of respect for man as man—that is, as part of the social whole and of humanity.

We can sum up the difference between religion and ethics in Cohen's system by saying that religion restricts the scope and activity of man by concentrating on the individual and his relations to his fellow man instead of on society, on the personal God of the individual instead of the God of humanity. The advantage of this restriction is that it permits religion to create more intimate relations than is possible in ethics, relations based on love and pity among men and the mutual love of God and man. These refined derivations, which determine the transition from ethics to religion and define the changing relations between them, create the need in the human soul for a more intimate relationship with God, but Cohen does not investigate the factors that foster this religious feeling.

The finest expression of the ethical element in Judaism was for Cohen the concept of humanity, the emergence of the future as a basic, temporal dimension, and the concept of God as the God of ethics. After clarifying the ethical nature of Judaism, Cohen turns to a consideration of its purely religious aspect, pointing out that the God of ethics is not the same as the God of religion. "Monotheism reaches its high point in messianism, but its center of gravity lies in the relationship between God and the individual."[56]

The prophets prior to Ezekiel laid special stress on the social aspect of morality and human conduct—that is, the relations of the individual to society. They put ethics into religion, but failed to give sufficient emphasis to the nature of religion in its relation to the individual *qua* individual. It was the prophet Ezekiel, the son of Buzi, who gave prominence to this phase of religion when he proclaimed, "What mean ye, that ye use this proverb concerning the land of Israel, saying, The fathers have eaten sour grapes and the children's teeth are set on edge? As I live, saith the Lord God, ye shall not have occasion any more to use this proverb in Israel. Behold, all souls are mine; as the soul of the father, so also the soul of the son is mine: the soul that sinneth, it shall die. (Ezekiel 18:2–4) Ezekiel revealed the individual as the bearer of ethical values and ethical responsibility, hence his correlation to God.

Were it not for Ezekiel's proclamation of this new doctrine in Judaism, it is inconceivable that the Book of Psalms, where the doctrine reaches its fullest expression, would have been shaped, as it is, in the Bible.[57] The development of biblical Judaism may be said to have taken a paradoxical turn. The prophets had created ethics but not religion proper. At the center of man's ethical conduct they placed the social community and the relation of the individual to this community. With the Book of Psalms, however, Judaism bursts the bonds of ethics to become religion, the sphere where the individual establishes intimate relations to God as True Being.[58] But even here the development of Judaism from ethics to religion took place within a historical context which could be formulated, on the one hand, as a breach from below—that is, from the direction of the individual as individual—and, on the other hand, as a breach from above—that is, related to God as the True Being.

C. THE INDIVIDUAL AND HIS STATION

Sin, Cohen declares, is man's specific characteristic,[59] guilt is and remains the attribute of the individual.[60] Guilt or sin are qualities that pertain to the individual as individual, and cannot be imputed or transferred to someone else. They are hard facts within the life of the individual that make him conscious of himself as a unique reality. The sons shall not die for the sins of the fathers; the con-

cept of sin implies the concept of the individual, the particular
man.[61] The specific nature of Cohen's system here comes to the
fore. The individual, as we have seen, is a category derived from
the sphere of logic, but appears here as the bearer of a quality
derived from the sphere of practical ethics and specifically concerned with man's conduct. The characteristic quality of the individual as a reality is sin, which is a religious-ethical category. In
other words, sin as a fact derived from the sphere of human conduct serves to enhance the individual's unique status as a reality.
This specific combination of qualities, one that applies to human
conduct and the other to reality, makes of the individual a religious
concept. If the individual, however, is confined to one of these
spheres, he is subject to the same conditions as any other concept
within that sphere—that is, in the sphere of practical conduct he is
subsumed under society and absorbed by humanity, and in the
sphere of nature he is an anonymous fact catalogued among many
others. It is the combination of an ethical and a real quality within
the individual that defines his position in religion.

A distinction must here be made between the religious and the
mythological conception, for the latter also deals with the concepts of sin and guilt. The principal difference consists in the fact
that mythology has no place for *individual* sin, since it conceives
man to be the last link in a long line of descent from ancestors
whose sins he bears. Therefore, it is impossible in mythology that
the individual should attain the status of "I."[62] It is not sin or
guilt in and of themselves that sets the individual over against
society, but rather the *consciousness* of sin and guilt that gives him
his distinctive quality. To gain a deeper insight into the difference
between the religious and mythological conceptions, we must take
notice of the distinction made by Cohen between the "I" and the
individuality, and the consequences that he draws from this distinction.

The individual as a category of reality becomes a religious category only when it emerges from its neutral sphere and presses
forward towards the realization of the imperative. Sin or guilt is
the transitional stage through which the individual must pass in
order to unfold its "I."[63] This unfolding of the "I," however, is not

the ultimate stage; the individual must also overcome sin in order to arrive at a state of inner perfection. Man can become a new man; it is the possibility of this inner transformation that makes of the individual an "I." By means of his own sin, man first becomes an individual; but through the possibility of repenting of his sin, the individual becomes a free "I."[64] In the sphere of the individual, then, we can distinguish two layers or stages of existence. In the first stage the individual appears with his specific characteristic of sin, and the "I" appears with its fundamental quality of overcoming sin. In mythology no meaning is attached to the individual; he is not subject to sin, and therefore has no possibility of overcoming it through repentance. Here lies the radical difference between mythology and religion, since religion invests the individual with meaning by summoning his insurgent energies to the task of overcoming the poignant experience of sin by an inner, spiritual transformation. Sin thus performs a teleological function in religion. It serves as a curb to help the individual overcome himself and enter into a larger freedom. The true "I" is not the anonymous individual who sins but the individual who repents. The individual became the man with a knowledge of his own guilt; he becomes an "I," however, by dint of his power to create in himself a new heart and a new spirit.[65]

Self-transformation itself does not make the "I" a religious category unless it is effected in relation to God. This gives rise to a fundamental problem in the philosophy of religion and of Judaism as Cohen saw it: The relation between man and God consists in maintaining the tension between the two. The inner transformation of man leads from the anonymous individual to the repentant "I." This conception of the independent power of man achieved through repentance is for Cohen the essence of Judaism and the point in which it differs radically from Christianity. The inner transformation of man is effected in Judaism by man himself without divine intervention, whereas in Christianity God participates in the ethical act that leads to the true "I." Christianity with its leanings to pantheism blurs the boundaries that separate God from man, depriving man of his authority and invalidating his power of personal realization. The separation (not the alienation) between God and man in Judaism means, from the standpoint of man, the power of inner transformation and self-realization by dint of his own unaided efforts; from the standpoint of a transcendent God, it is the power to overcome himself and create his own image of man.[66] In Judaism, as Cohen puts it (and before him Samuel Hirsch, as we shall observe later), every man is Jesus.

From another point of view, however, God is assigned the role of Savior and Deliverer with respect to the inner transformation. God, as a personal God, guarantees that the inner transformation will be consummated and crowned with success. The God of ethics was the Guarantor for the realization of ethical ideals within society, He who pledged that man shall not disappear from the face of the earth in order that the ethical imperatives might be fulfilled. In religion, however, God is the Guarantor for the very process of transformation within the individual himself. It is against this background that we are to view the separation between God and man and the relation between them. Man and God remain separated and are related to each other as aspiration is to attainment, as war is to victory. God, who is the goal of perfection, is also the Guarantor for the success of man's ethical striving. He appears as the Savior and Redeemer in the sense that He lends assurance and certainty to man's need for inner renewal and repentance. Redemption is the last stage of the inner renewal where the "I" blossoms into its authentic self. Redemption through God leads to man's reconciliation with himself, and eventually to the reconciliation of man with God; it is reconciliation with God that transforms the individual into a mature "I."[67] The maturity of the individual is the product of this inner renewal, but the struggle is always carried on with relation to God, the Guarantor of its successful completion. Reconciliation with God, however, is not the end but only the means for man's reconciliation with himself.[68] In this respect Cohen approaches the point of view held by some of the Jewish philosophers of the nineteenth century, such as Formstecher and Hirsch, for whom religion was primarily a problem that concerned man and not God.

The unique character of the individual becomes evident in the experience of sin and guilt, an experience that leads directly to the process of inner renewal. The reality of the individual revealed in this experience acquires a religious status through the inner renewal in man that leads to his reconciliation with God and with himself. The manifestation of the *reality* of the individual is rooted in experience—his *religious status* is derived from his striving to attain reconciliation and inner renewal and not from the goal at the end of the process.

Dependence on experience as a source of religious knowledge is also to be seen in the importance attached to Cohen's religious conception of the Other or of the fellow man. The question of the Other had also occupied Cohen during his first period in which ethics meant the identification of the "I" with society as incorporated in mankind. This conception shows some points of similarity with the problem of the Other.

Since the Other is not given in experience, we must ask the same general question that relates to all concepts arising in the sphere of ethics from the sources of pure will—namely, the question of the origin of the concept of the Other and its systematic justification. The Other may be derived from the principles of ethics where it performs a definite function.[89] In fact, it is hazardous and even harmful for ethics not to regard the concepts of man and fellow man as anything but *a priori*.[70]

How is the Other identified with the object of ethics? The pure will acts upon two subjects.[71] The concept of this activity, which is the principal concept of ethics, since it realizes the imperative of the ought, is a concept that by definition requires two subjects, the subject of the activity and the subject to which the activity is directed. The Other does not emerge from man's direct contact with his fellow man but from a legal relationship[72] implicit in their mutual negotiations. In other words, the Other is a subject because he is the ethical object.

Furthermore, the Other is the source of the discovery of the "I." Here we see how far removed Cohen's conception is from actual human experience. Ethics manifests itself in an objective activity and not in man's subjective sentiments. Ethical activity is directed to an object which is the subject and for this reason Cohen con-

cludes that the Other is not foreign to the "I" but its reciprocal
pole, its *alter ego* from whence it is derived.[73] Thus, the consciousness of the "I" is intimately connected with the consciousness
of the Other, and only in union with it can the "I" become fully
conscious of itself.[74] In short, according to Cohen's conception the
Other and the "I" are the two nonempirical concepts involved in
the ethical act, the former being prior to the latter.

The derivations of the Other and the "I" follow from the main
principles of Cohen's ethical system. Ethics rests on the correlation
of the individual to humanity and his identification with it. The
individual or the "I" is not invested with ethical significance. The
Other, being rooted in humanity and the object of the ethical act,
is logically prior to the "I." The two concepts, however, are necessarily derived from ethical principles. That this conception is far
removed from actual experience is obvious in that the "I" is in
fact derived from the general order of society as a whole. The individual acquires ethical status as the subject of negotiations that
are not limited to its own sphere but that are carried on indirectly
through society as a whole.

Since the relationship between the "I" and the Other is an objective one within society and is not nourished by the emotions, love
is not considered an element in this relationship.

This conception of the Other and the "I" as derived concepts must
be considered in conjunction with Cohen's later view according to
which they are given in experience. Natural as well as historical
experience presents man in new settings and configurations.[75] The
concept of the Other is derived from experience as is the concept
of the "I."[76] In contradistinction to the derivation of the correlatives in ethics, we are now presented with given basic realities in
the sphere of religion, namely, the "I" and the Other. The ethical
problem in the relationship between these two concepts appears as
a task imposed upon us to make of the simple Other (*Neben-
mensch*) a fellow man (*Mitmensch*) to whom the "I" is attached
with the bonds of pity and love. The "I" and the Other are empirical realities given in nature and their religious value emerges
here, as is generally the case in Cohen's second period, from the

Is not the
infant all
"I" and not
all "Other"?

combination of the realistic aspect with the ethical correlation. It now remains to explain how this combination takes place, how the Other emerges from the category of the anonymity of the "he" to become a "thou."

The Other is lifted from the impersonal realm of the "he" by the empirical fact of suffering. It is in witnessing the Other's suffering that he becomes a "thou."[77] Suffering breaks down the walls that divide men and unites them in a common fellowship. The concrete manifestation of suffering is poverty and the poor man is the natural object of human love.[78] The poor are the real bearers of human suffering,[79] for they are the most convincing specimens of human misery.[80]

By reflecting the deep-seated contradiction at the root of man's existence, suffering and poverty reveal to us the Other as our fellow man and raise him to the level of "thou." The realization that the poor man has fallen below the level of human existence creates a new dimension in which the "I" is drawn to the Other, who thus becomes his fellow man.[81] This transformation of the Other into a fellow man is also important because of the logical significance attached to it; the existential contradiction between the concept man and the fact of poverty is the active factor establishing the new relationship among men, which is no longer confined to the ethical realm but has become a religious relationship.

The stranger is another type of unfortunate man, through whom the concept of man is further revealed.[82] Whereas the affliction of the poor man is social and economic,[83] the stranger's misfortune is civil and political. The significance of monotheism is that it discovered the concept man in general, *all* men, including the stranger. This problem of the stranger, or the gentile who renounces idolatry, was already treated by Cohen in his *Ethik des reinen Willens* in order to emphasize the universalistic essence of monotheism, since one humanity is the necessary corollary of One God. In *Die Religion der Vernunft aus den Quellen des Judentums*, and in monographs connected with this book, Cohen shows that the love of men for one another is more fundamental in the phenomenon of strangeness than the idea of equality. From the stranger we have now learned that monotheism began with the love of man.[84]

Poverty and suffering excite pity; strangeness—love. Cohen, however, does not make any basic distinction between pity and love and treats them both as two human emotions of equal force. Pity is evoked as a new *Urform* of humanity, love.[85] Pity and love are not merely passive reactions but active forces that produce new relationships with the poor man and the stranger.[86] An important place is given in Cohen's ethics to the quality of respect shown by one person to another. This quality of esteem or regard is not the product of convention, but is rooted in humanity and constitutes an integral part of social life. Whereas love and pity create an inner relation between men, the quality of respect creates an intimate bond of reciprocal relations between the "I" and his fellow man.[87] Pity kindles in man the love of his fellow man, now no longer the mere Other, and binds them together in a common fellowship. What ethics had failed to do has now been accomplished by religion, which evoked in man the love of his fellow man.[88]

The dynamic character of reciprocal love is also evident from the fact that it is evoked without external aid. This relationship is the origin of man's love of man and his love of God. God created man, but this human bond of love is the work of man himself. God participates in creation by means of man whom He created.[89] The category of fellow man, therefore, is derived from the sphere of man himself. Love is the inner transformation of the understanding which turns it from a theoretical into a practical organ, creating a new dimension of existence in which the "I" sheds its egocentricity and the "thou" emerges from the confines of the "it."[90] The authentic reciprocal relationship thus created is, for Cohen, a religious phenomenon to whose seed-bearing power we owe the rise and growth of the human community.

Love, which springs from the transformation of the understanding, has its roots in man and not in God. From the love of his fellow man, however, man deduced the love of God—that is, that God loved man.[91] It is not clear whether Cohen means that man attributed to God his own experiences or that the love of man is an attribute of God as the Creator of man. Some pertinent allusions in Cohen's treatment of the subject, as well as the general tenor of his ethical system, compel us to reject the first view. God's love of man is not an anthropomorphism but an inherent trait of God's being and, as Cohen observes, more than a mere logical corollary of Creation.[92]

After God is conceived as loving man, we can understand man's love of God. The circle of love is completed in three steps—the love of man for his fellow man, which is kindled by suffering and poverty; the love of God for man; and, after the position of the fellow man has been defined, the love of man for God.

The consideration of man's love of God leads Cohen back to the ethical attitude of his first period: Man's love of God is the love of the ethical ideal.[93] Pure love is directed only to archetypes, to patterns that can serve as models for the ethical act. The archetype, which man is incapable of fashioning by himself, is identified with God, and through his love of the archetype man attains to the love of God.

As in his first period, Cohen conceives of God, the Archetype and Pattern of the virtuous life, not as a Being but rather as an Idea. The question of how it is possible to love an idea[94] is answered by Cohen with another question: How is it possible to love anything but an idea? Even in sensual love we love only the ideal person, the idea of the personality.[95] The relation of man to the ethical ideal is not merely theoretical; it is a constant striving to attain this ideal. Pressing forward to the luminous, ethical ideal which gives life its spiritual radiance—this is what Cohen calls love. God, the goal of this enduring aspiration, is not a Being but an Idea. The distance that separates man from the archetype of ethical conduct and virtue makes it impossible for man to identify himself with God, as is the case in the mystery religions and in Christianity. Man is permitted a progressive ascent to the Infinite, but he can never free himself of his finitude and remains riveted to his temporal and spatial world. The love of man for God means only the incessant reaching out for God and not, as in sensual love, the unchaste desire, to be united with Him.[96]

Cohen thus teaches that the love between God and man remains within the confines of ethics and the ethical idea. God is conceived as the ethical Idea but is not, as formulated in Cohen's first period, the Guarantor for the realization of ethical ideals within the realm of nature. An ethical idea means an archetype of human conduct and a pattern of practical virtue. But God, in Cohen's second period is also *True* Being, a conception that we shall now examine more closely.

D. TRUE BEING

The love of God entails a new conception of the nature of God and His relation to the concept of being. If God were only the object of cognition, He could not possibly be the only God, for cognition has altogether other objects and problems. The only God must therefore postulate another attitude of the human spirit. *Love* thus becomes requisite of this attitude to the only God.[97] In monotheism the love of God's being must of necessity develop as a definite *Geistesform* of religion over against which all theorizing is but a preparation. The veneration of God is thus converted into actual knowledge of God.[98] In the true relation of man to God we find an attitude of the will[99] which expresses itself in love. This assertion of Cohen sheds light on the problems that arose when he conceived of God as true Being as well as ethical Idea. Cohen derives true Being, which is identical with God's uniqueness, from the nontheoretical and noncognitive aspects of man's relation to God. The cognitive relation necessarily applies to many objects; it cannot make God a distinct object of cognition and raise it to the level of Being in the full sense. The relationship of love is by its very nature selective—that is, from the multitude of cognitive objects it chooses a special object. According to these presuppositions, then, the evidence for this new concept of God resides in the *uniqueness* of God. God is true Being because of His singularity, and He is singular because of the singular relationship that man has with Him. The method of deriving this new concept is but one of the methods found in Cohen's system, all of which deserve a separate and more detailed treatment.

The derivation of God's uniqueness as proof of God's true Being involves an internal difficulty. Cohen seeks to demonstrate that man's love of God is the love of the ethical Idea, that there could be no other love than that of the Idea, and that the ethical idea is the archetype and model of man's ethical conduct. Ideas are the archetypes (*Urbilder*) for action and archetypes have no value of their own unless they are patterns (*Musterbilder*) for the activity of reasonable creatures.[100] The inevitable corollary of this idea of the archetype is that God has no value of His own unless He is conceived as the archetype for the ethical conduct of man. And if man's love of God is a love of the archetype of ethical conduct, this does not constitute evidence of God's uniqueness as true *Being*. As a result of His uniqueness, God is no longer only an archetype but an independent Being. This gives rise to the question as to how God could be conceived as a Being with independent value, as a unique Being, if we derive the concept from the relationship of love which applies only to the Idea and not to Being. The dual nature of the love relationship is here apparent— it is selective and unique, but only within the confines of the structure of ideas. We must therefore go a step further to come to the true uniqueness of God, which is the uniqueness of Being.

To derive God's uniqueness from man's love of Him is defective from still another point of view. Love has its roots in the social life of men with one another, and from this social sphere it is then taken and applied to the relations between man and God. We must find other grounds for God's uniqueness and not base our proof on man's relationship to Him.

It is detrimental to religion to rely exclusively on noncognitive elements; to sever its inner relations to cognition is to forfeit the cultural values. Those who disdain science are, therefore, inimical to the very soul of religion.[101] The cognitive aspect of religion is acknowledged when we conceive of God as Being. Being is the central problem and common ground of both logic and religion. A fundamental distinction, however, exists with respect to the concept of Being in the two spheres. Being in logic is constantly formed and fashioned and lies at the end of the cognitive process. In religion, on the other hand, Being is a constant factor that is identified with God and is a basic concept at the beginning and not at the end of religion. Although this difference was not expressly formulated by Cohen, it can be gathered from his treatment of the subject. This distinction, however, does not obscure the fact that in both spheres, that of logic and that of religion, the problem of Being has become the central problem.[102]

The advantage of the cognitive derivation of the concept God over against the noncognitive derivation of the relation of love is evident from the idealistic conclusion that Cohen draws from it. To attribute Being to God means to remove the concept of Being from the realm of sense and perception to a supersensible realm.[103] We can sum up and say that only Being, which is rooted in thought, is not the opposite of spirit.[104] This Being, which we derive from thought and cognition, is then the source of spiritual Being; its source of derivation is he who imparts its spiritual image.

Two methods of derivation are to be found in Cohen's later system—one from the relation of love, and the other from the sources of cognition, revealing respectively two qualities of the God-concept, *uniqueness* and *being*. In Cohen's later conception these two qualities are combined: God is True Being and at the same time unique. The focal point of religion is to be found in "being," that is, in its uniqueness which constitutes the being of God.[105] But there are times when these two qualities, here combined as one, appear separately in Cohen's later conception, a kind of echo from the days of his first period, which we shall discuss later.

From the identification of True Being with God flows the corollary of His uniqueness. This identification involves several steps which require clarification.

GOD AS BEING

Only God can have being. The identification of God and being is reciprocal—that is, only God is being and being is nothing but God. The relation of being to subjects other than God leads necessarily to polytheism. Being that is related to many subjects, however, leads to its opposite. Not only is there no other God, but there are also no other beings in the sense of true being outside of God.[106] Since Cohen identifies being with uniqueness, we cannot assume that being is related to many subjects, that is, that the concept of being is more comprehensive than the one and only God. The reciprocal relation between being and God can also be formulated as follows: God is *True* Being and there is but one Truth. True Being is of necessity a concept that applies to one sole substance, that is, to God.

TRANSCENDENCE

We have thus far seen how Cohen began with being and by analogy deduced from it the concept of God and His uniqueness. It is clear that by identifying being with God and limiting its relation to God alone Cohen attempts to give logical expression to God's transcendence, a problem that already appears in his ethical system where he formulates the nature of God's transcendence over against the spheres of nature and ethics. God is a concept within the general system and is at the same time beyond these two separate spheres. By extending the God-concept beyond the sphere of ethics and by demonstrating that God is not only an ethical Idea but True Being, Cohen invests God with a wholly transcendent character. God is distinguished from all other substances in that He alone is True Being. Religion generally thinks of a transcendent God as outside of this world in a spatial sense. Cohen, whose God-concept depends on logic, gives transcendence a logical meaning, that is, God is not extramundane in a spatial sense, but is differentiated in His quality as True Being. The nature of transcendence may be defined in logical terms as follows: True Being is a concept that comprises only one substance, God; the concept of being is co-extensive with the content of the God-concept.

UNIQUENESS

This transcendence of God means a logical distinction between God and the world: The uniqueness of the Creator is totally different from any other existence.[107] The concept of God's uniqueness as true Being consists in its opposition to the *world*[108] and not to any one of the many gods. In Cohen's system the God-concept is then differently conceived than it generally is in religion, which emphasizes the opposition between God and the many gods and not between God and the world, and which considers the unity of God to be a quality within the realm of the gods, but not a quality which establishes beyond dispute God's transcendence over the world. Only when we raise the God-concept to the level of a logical class in itself and see God as True Being and hence unique can we define His true content.

ATTRIBUTES

The transcendence of God or His uniqueness as True Being means that there is none like Him among the other substances, in the words of Isaiah (40:25): "To whom then will ye liken Me, that I should be equal? Saith the Holy One." Since the concept of True Being applies to God alone, He is in a class by Himself and hence beyond comparison. Consequently, God cannot have positive qualities of any kind. In this Cohen seems to be following the negative theology of the Middle Ages and Maimonides' theory, according to which only one attribute, being, may be attributed to God, and even this is interpreted negatively to mean that God is distinct from the world and cannot be compared to it.[109]

THOU SHALT MAKE NO GRAVEN IMAGE

The absolute distinction between God and other essences vitiates at the outset all attempts to portray God's image or likeness. Every portrayal of God appeals to the senses; it thus contradicts His uniqueness and only succeeds in removing Him from us. It is the mark of the God of Truth that He does not lend Himself to any likeness or image whatsoever.[110]

THE CONFLUENCE IN RELIGION OF THE LOGICAL AND ETHICAL

The twofold character of Cohen's conception becomes apparent when he attributes uniqueness and true being to God. To the extent that God is the content of religion there is an inner relation between religion and logic. Cohen attempts to establish both a cognitive and a noncognitive relation with respect to being. On the one hand, he argues that only God is the content of thought[111] and, on the other, that only God's essence is beyond positive cognition. But God's existence is the fire of holy faith that contains a knowledge of truth, ethical knowledge.[112] God as Being is a cognitive concept, but since this Being is devoid of positive qualities that can be apprehended by cognition, the mediation between man and God is not amenable to cognition. The cognitive concept, God as Being, is the object of a noncognitive relationship—that is, of ethics—since the concept, which is at bottom negative, is inaccessible to cognition. In other words, after we have derived Being logically, we find that logic has not the adequate means for arriving at this concept. This union of ethical and logical aspects is a further illustration of the peculiar nature of religion, a peculiarity that also appears in the concept of man, where the individual as such is a concept of nature and the penitent "I" a concept of ethics. The union of these two concepts, which gives the individual his religious status, is also found at the other pole of the religious axis, in the concept of God. Here God, as Being, is a concept of logic; and as man's correlative, a concept of ethics. The combination of the ethical and the logical removes God from the sphere of ethics alone (with which in Cohen's early conception He was co-extensive) and transforms Him into a religious concept.

BEING AND EXISTENCE

The distinction between God and other entities is further emphasized by another corollary derived from this conception of God as True Being: If God is True Being, then His reality is Truth, in comparison to which the rest of existence is but a shadow and a figment of the imagination. Over against True Being, nature is devoid of the reality of truth. The distinction between True Being and illusory reality, a distinction that arises from the basic principles set forth by Cohen in his treatment of this problem, may be stated as follows: God is Being (*Sein*) and the world is existence (*Dasein*); God is Reality and the world is a state of becoming. Cohen, who always put becoming above immutable reality, here reverses the order of values—God is Being from the very beginning, a quality that differentiates and separates Him from the world. Complete Being is higher than becoming. This reversal of values emphasizes the change in Cohen's development. God is now conceived as Being, an ontological category, and is no longer chained to the concept of progress, an ethical category. The problem that occupied Cohen is the problem of the meaning of God as an ontological *and* as an ethical category and the problem of the relation between the two. In other words, the problem is that of the relation between God as Being and God as the archetype of human conduct.

PURIFICATION

From the concept of God's uniqueness Cohen drew both an ethical and a theoretical conclusion. Man's relation to God is not only theoretical but fundamentally ethical. Through his relation to God man is given the opportunity to repent. God is One, for only before Him can man be purified.[113] The idea "before God shall ye be purified" discloses the special relationship between man and God. Purification can take place only before God—it is this that reflects God's uniqueness as the object of man's endeavors.

Furthermore, God's uniqueness implies a sharp distinction between God and nature which, in turn, is a proof of the ethical conception of the God-concept. "From this metaphysics it would be possible to deduce the only God of ethics."[114] It is interesting to note in this connection that Cohen here regards *as metaphysics* the distinction he makes between God and the world, as well as the distinction between True Being and illusory existence. The God of ethics is placed in logical opposition to nature, making it possible for Him to contravene the laws of nature as conceived by the instrumentality of logic. God, who is beyond nature from the standpoint of His logical essence and transcendent to it by reason of His attributes, is the God who ordains *teleological* laws in the place of the *causal* laws of nature. Ethical laws are teleological, since all ethical activity is directed towards a goal. We may thus say that God, who as True Being is separate and distinct from nature, can be conceived from the standpoint of ethics in its relation to teleology and not from the standpoint of theory in its relation to causality. From this it is clear how Cohen is able to introduce the various aspects of the God-concept—that is, how he can conceive of God as True Being both from the standpoint of His ethical nature and His relation to the world. At any rate, the problem that faced Cohen was how to emphasize the ontological nature of God and at the same time retain His relationship to the sphere of ethics.

The uniqueness of God is as opposed to pantheism as to Christianity. The belief in the uniqueness of God is primarily directed against the belief in many gods and also against pantheism; God and the world are not one, for God is unique.[115] At the root of all pantheistic modes of thought lies the view that God and the world are identical; God is absorbed in the world and the world is comprehended in God. From this point of view there can be no compromise between monotheism, which is based on the uniqueness of God, and pantheism, which believes in the consubstantiality of God and nature and the eternal co-existence of the two.[116] Monotheism attributes Being to God alone and is astonished when His uniqueness is vitiated; the keynote of the pantheistic inspiration is God's immanence in nature and the identity between the universe and its Author. Cohen rejects pantheism in his analysis of the nature of the God-concept as well as in his analysis of the nature of man. The problem of monotheism is the problem of the relation between the perishable universe and its unchanging Creator. By obliterating the differences between the finite and infinite, the relative and absolute, the contingent and necessary, lowly man and august God, and reducing them all to one absolute essence, pantheism disrupts the foundation of all moral government and overthrows the two pillars of religion—God as True Being, who is apart from and above the world, and man who is made in the image of this Being.

The idea of mediation between God and man is another attempt to obliterate the essential difference between God and the world: The God of Israel is unique. Therefore, mediation between God and man, which a superior human being might take upon himself, is incompatible with His essence.[117] Christianity is based on the principle of compromise and this tends to curtail God's uniqueness and His absolute separation from the world. It does not abolish God's uniqueness, as does pantheism, by absorbing Him in the world, but it attenuates the distinction between God and the world by diminishing the distance between the two.

The intercession of a mediator deprives man of his independent, direct approach to God, whom he must now seek out by way of a detour: Personal ethics can make no progress as long as it fails to recognize that every man through his own moral exertion can attain the level of Jesus.[118]

We have seen how, in Cohen's ethical system, the relationship established between God as Idea and the concept of truth is capable of a dual interpretation: God is identified with Truth, which means the congruence between ethical progress and the continuity of nature, or God is conceived as the Guarantor of that congruence. In either case it is clear that the connection between God and the concept of truth emphasizes the *methodological* nature of the God-concept and necessarily implies a negation of His *ontological* nature. In his second period Cohen transferred the God-concept from the sphere of method to that of being—that is, God was identified with Being. We have seen how Cohen attempts to find proof for the ethical nature of God in the concept of being; the basic problems of his second period are related to a further investigation of this proof.

Cohen seeks to harmonize the two aspects of the God-concept, the ontological and the methodological, by relying on the concept of truth. God is True Being and all reality outside of Him is illusion. The opposition between True Being and illusion is formulated as the opposition between *truth* and illusion.[119] In any case, the meaning of truth is substantial and essential over against illusion and the workings of the imagination. Cohen sometimes interprets the God-concept ontologically as True Being in contrast to illusory existence, and sometimes cognitively as Truth in contrast to the counterfeit imagination. Just as True Being is one and indivisible, not subject to multiplicity and absolutely distinct from illusory existence, so also is Truth one and indivisible, not subject to multiplicity and absolutely distinct from the counterfeit imagination. Here ends the comparison between the ontological meaning of the concept of God and its cognitive meaning.

Cohen, however, took an additional step. "Truth is more than reality which the imagination imitates. As God is Unique Being, so is Truth . . . and is not to be characterized by criteria outside itself."[120] Truth as a cognitive aspect is here completely identified with Being. God can be viewed from the standpoint of both Being and Truth. Of these two inseparable aspects, Truth is the more decisive; it alone is Unique Being. The ontological aspect is not abolished and Truth no longer has only methodological meaning. As in Cohen's first conception, Truth is given a fundamentally idealistic meaning, that is, it is identified with Being. God as Truth has an ontological aspect, but He is the God of Truth in both its cognitive and ontological aspects. It seems that Cohen is searching for a category even higher than that of Being to describe the God-concept. At first he distinguished between the world and God, describing the world as existent and God as True Being. Then he formulated the inner truth of this Being and set it above Being in its narrow sense. Just as Plotinus was not content to demonstrate that the One who is the Author of the world is not only Being, nor only Thought, but attempted to represent Him as *One*, so Cohen was not content to characterize God only as Being, but represented Him as Truth in which Being was implicated.

The conception of God as Truth takes us back to a certain extent to Cohen's first period when he maintained that the equation of "God with Truth means that only the union of theoretical and ethical knowledge, the union of the two sources of scientific consciousness, is able to express the idea of God."[121] In similar words Cohen described Truth as Being in his first period when God signified for him the sphere of congruence between knowledge and ethics. It seems that Cohen was not consistent in his use of the concept of Truth, which had both an ontological and a methodological sense, and would often use them side by side. This duality of meaning emphasizes Cohen's fundamental problem, the relation of God as Being to ethics. Against the background of his revised conception, he formulates the problem in terms of the relation between God as Being and God as an Ethical Idea.

This relationship is seen in a broader light when we consider the distinction that Cohen makes between God as True Being and the world of illusory existence. Since Cohen is not an exponent of the Platonic conception (which is the origin of this distinction), how does he explain the relationship between these two metaphysical poles? Is the Idea as True Being present in the world or does the world participate in the Idea? Cohen investigates the relation between these two poles by considering the distinction between them. This problem lies at the root of his conception of correlation.

E. CORRELATION AND ITS EXPRESSIONS

The uniqueness of God's Being implies an absolute separation between God as True Being and the world of illusion. The problem that faced Cohen was the basic religious problem of bridging the gap between the two.[122] What is the nature of this God whose relation to the world is only negative?[123] Cohen attempted to solve this problem in several ways: a) by elaborating the content of one of his basic concepts (Creation); b) by defining the common area in which man and God participate (the spirit of holiness); c) by determining the focal point in religion where the Infinite God responds to finite man (reconciliation). These ways, all of which seek to determine the relationship between God and man, are rooted in correlation.

God is defined as True Being and as such is the opposite of the world He created. How are these two concepts logically related? The relation must first be defined negatively as one that does not obtain between Being and existence. Being did not create existence; that is, God is not the Creator of the world by *an act* of will that took place *in time*. He did not set himself to create a world at a given time; there was never a condition where there was a God and no world. The relation between God and the world is a logical-immanent and not a temporal-transcendent relation. The nature of this relationship must be examined in order to clarify the concept Being as a logical principle for the concept of creation.

God is Being and as such is not existent in itself, for all Being exists for the sake of creation.[124] Being is an aspect of substance. Relations are introduced by means of creation, so that the sphere of creation, as against the sphere of Being, is a sphere of relations. Being as substance exists for the sake of relations and is the ground for relational concepts.[125] In other words, the relation between God as Being and substance, on the one hand, and the world as creation and the realm of relations, on the other, is the concept of

Being as a logical principle. We here come upon a difficulty in Cohen's conception which must be analyzed and, if possible, removed. We have noted that divine transcendence is a logical and not a spatial distinction between Being and the world. How then can we believe in God's transcendence over the world and at the same time assume an immanent relationship between them? How can God, who is separate and apart from the world, be internally related to it? The answer is that the logical distinction between God and the world is self-subsistent, since it rests on the distinction between the logical qualities of Being and creation. This distinction is also the ground for the logical relation among the various elements, and it is precisely because Being is substance and distinct from the realm of relations—that is, creation—that these elements could be related. The distinction requires the two elements and is not abolished by the relationship between them. In other words, since the distinction and also the relationship are determined in logic and not in the temporal-empirical sphere, there is no contradiction between the two aspects of the relationship. The relationship has two aspects because of the logical structure of the sphere in which it is determined.

God, who is Being and the logical Ground of the world, is the *Beginning* of the world and not its *Creator*. We may say that creation in Cohen's system is an impersonal fact, unrelated to the act of creation or to the Creator who initiated it. Even in Cohen's second period God is not considered an active Personality (in this basic problem Cohen's conception underwent no change), and it is therefore impossible that the relation between God and the world should be personal—that is, that creation should partake of the personality of the Creator. Creation is a fact in the realm of logic and serves as an expression of a basic principle in Cohen's conception: namely, that the distinction between God as Being and substance, and God as Becoming in the realm of relations, is the same as that between a point and extension in space. Just as the transition from a point to an extended line is made possible by the continuity of thought, so the transition from God as Being to the world as Becoming is made possible by the logical-immanent principle inherent in the relation between the two. This positive transition is the meaning—although not explicitly stated—of the negative judgment: a point is the absence of extension.[126] We can thus say of God in a negative formulation that He is not the world, that He is the beginning of the positive transition to world. "Creation is not a concept foreign to God's reality and it can be derived from it."[127] Creation then means the logical and not the temporal transition from the concept Being to the concept Becoming. Creation is a conceptual category, not a temporal event; as such, it functions as a shuttle concept between the two irreconcilable poles, God and the world. The problem of creation is a conceptual-logical problem, not a physical one, and hence it finds its solution in Cohen's system in his elaboration of logical concepts.[128]

Another expression of this logical-immanent relationship between Being and creation is found in Cohen's view that creation is an original attribute of God.[129] Creation is not an event but one of the attributes that define the essential content of the concept God and the world; it is a corollary of the concept of uniqueness, which is the positive formulation of this distinction. God's uniqueness finds expression in Creation.[130]

It may be thought that Cohen's conception of creation is akin to the mystical, Neoplatonic doctrine of emanation—somewhat like that of Proclus, who taught that all things descend from the overflowing fullness of the Divine Intelligence, and that the farther they are removed from this primary Source the more gross, dense, and undigested they become. Although Cohen's doctrine of creation is not dependent upon a personal Creator or divine volition,[131] he argues against the mythological principle of emanation[132] which conceives of creation as an emanation of a divine Essence, and attempts, as it were, to describe the *history* of the world in *time*. Cohen, on the other hand, is not interested in describing the history of the world but in clarifying its logic. The transition from God into the world is a logical transition. God is the Founder of the world, but He did not pass into his own work in Creation. In emanation, reality proceeds from the potential to the actual. But for Cohen reality is not included in Being, put there surreptitiously in order that it may be able to be derived subsequently.[133] Cohen concedes a change with respect to Being, but this change is ef-

fected through a continuous, logical transition by means of creation. Since Cohen does not include creation within the realm of
temporal events, considering it an *attribute* rather than an *act*,
the world is for him an existent world, existing of necessity by the
very definition of the God-concept. Cohen's severe formulation of
the logical relation between creation and the concept of God emphasizes the absence in creation of volition and personality. "It
was necessary for God to create man."[134] Since creation is im-
pregnated with the God-concept and is an attribute of God, we may
say that creation is a *necessary* attribute—that is, that God creates
necessarily.

Creation as a quality or attribute is not a temporal act or event,
an accident in God's past. Time does not apply to creation, which
is eternal, so that its content may be described as renewal.[135] The
logical transition from Being to reality is a continuous, uninterrupted process of constant renewal. The concept of renewal, despite
the Biblical doctrine, has here no temporal significance, since the
transition from Being to reality is a logical process and does not
take place in time. This same concept also appears during Cohen's
first period in which God, who is the Guarantor for the everlast-
ing reality of nature, keeps renewing nature continually so that
it might serve as an enduring sphere for the embodiment of
ethical principles. In the first period the concept of renewal is
formulated within the framework of an ethical postulate; in the
second period it is a logical necessity that flows from the self-
determination of God as a unique Being.

Into this logical analysis of creation Cohen introduces a factor
that is not a part of the logical meaning of the concept Being:
Creation makes God himself responsible for man.[136] Since responsibility is not a logical concept, God's responsibility to man
is not derived from the sphere of logic, but from a special relationship between God and man, which is part of the larger relationship
of God to the world. God is related to the world through His attribute of creation and He is related to man by means of a supplementary relationship. The concept of creation serves as a bridge
between the concept of God as Being and the world as reality.
Creation is the relation of God to the world and has no special

place reserved for man. The specific problem of *human reason* arises from the manifoldness of Becoming,[137] a problem which finds its solution by means of the concept of Revelation.

The thought here pursued by Cohen, although not expressly acknowledged, is an essentially religious one. Revelation is a religious category that applies to the relation between God and man. God created the world and within it revealed himself to man alone. His revelation, furthermore, disclosed a definite content which imposed upon man a specific task. Cohen's concept of revelation combines it with reason: revelation is a bridge between God and man and it is addressed to reason.

From the outset Cohen made revelation a reciprocal relation between God and man. Revelation is not imposed on passive matter; it is directed to the only possible recipient of the mutual relationship—that is, to man.[138] Cohen, however, does not seem to be aware of the fact that by stressing man's active participation he is depriving revelation of its compelling heteronymic character with respect to man. Man is not merely a vessel that retains the divine Word; he is an active agent in his encounter with God. Cohen's tendency to emphasize man's activity is rooted in his idealistic philosophy, which induces him to relate revelation to human reason, an active, independent faculty that would not remain docile before the imperious claims of revelation. However, Cohen also saw human reason as a creation of revelation: Revelation is a continuation of creation insofar as it sets itself the problem of man's creation as a reasonable creature.[139] The correlation between revelation and reason, or between God and man, is to a certain extent dialectical: On the one hand, revelation is related to reason which is by its very nature an active force, and on the other hand, reason is a creation of revelation.[140]

The dual nature of divine revelation in relation to man, which is its essential relation, may be considered from still another point of view. Human reason, as a divine creation, conditions the relation of reason to God.[141] Since reason is created by God and serves as a bridge between Him and man, the relation between man and God is basically rational. Here we note a difficulty inherent in Cohen's conception of the principle of correlation with respect to revelation. Reason, being a divine creation, must be a principle for cognition of God's Being from the human point of view.[142] But reason, once created, is not passive; it stamps its own character upon the correlation. Reason constitutes the common ground of the correlation seen from above, from the standpoint of God, or from below, from the standpoint of man.

This relationship, which is conditioned by reason, is reciprocal. It seems as if God's Being becomes active through man's knowledge of Him. God's nature is communicated to man through knowledge acquired by reason, the faculty which serves as a methodological means to ascribe True Being to God's essence. Man is not only a creature of God; his reason makes him, by virtue of his knowledge and with respect to it, at least subjectively, the revealer of God.[143] God is conditioned by the correlation to man and man is conditioned by the correlation to God.[144]

The nature of the rational correlation between man and God is restricted with respect to both partners. Correlation does not signify union[145]; although man retains his independence before God,[146] his very creatureliness prevents him from becoming identical with the Creator. The members of the correlation do not forfeit their respective pretensions nor are they called upon to make unworthy concessions to each other. Man cannot abolish his independent status as a rational creature, which was freely vouchsafed him by God, nor can God obliterate the distinction between Himself as Creator and His creation. Union is impossible because each partner guards his original prerogatives against unlawful usurpation. The correlation reflects the tension between Infinite God and finite man.

Revelation rests on the rational relation between the correlatives. By making revelation a rational relation, Cohen deprived the concept of its historical essence. For him, revelation is not an accident that occurred at a given time in the past, but something given within the world, since it discloses the rationality of the world. Like creation, it is a constant renewal, and therefore cannot be restricted or limited. Revelation is the legacy of all men, for all men are rational creatures. Man, not the people and not Moses, man as a rational creature is related to the God of Revelation.[147] Cohen

strenuously opposed the mystery-religions because of their pantheistic element (the union of man with God), but his radical
idealism led him to accept their concept of revelation according to
which it ceases to be a historical fact and is made the possession of
the mystic who is deemed worthy to receive it. As an idealist,
Cohen makes reason, which is given to all men, the bearer of
revelation, thus rejecting revelation as a historical accident that
occurred at a definite time in the past and making it one of the
many concepts that define the nature of man.

Furthermore, revelation raises man from the vast world of experience and singles him out to enter into relationship with God.
Such a relationship must therefore be conditioned by the nature of
man. Since man is by nature ethical—that is, he strives for the
ought—revelation and the creation of human reason must of necessity be related to ethics. "The creation of ethics proceeded from the
circumstance that revelation can only apply to man, the bearer
of ethics."[148] Here we find the focal point of ethics within the
sphere of religion. Ethics is not ancillary or supplementary to religion, but makes up its essential content, since it finds its place
within the framework of the correlation between God and man.
Reason, in its fundamental relationship to man and ethics, presents
us with a concept derived from the sphere of this correlation between God and man, *viz.* the concept of the spirit of holiness.

The correlation between God and man finds its most pregnant
expression in the spirit of holiness. The spirit of holiness confines
that province of the spirit that connects God and man to holiness.[149]
The concept comprises two meanings: spirit and holiness. The essence of spirit and spiritual knowledge lies in the possibility of
continuous and uninterrupted renewal that gives it a primary position as a foundation or basis.[150] Spirit, as renewal, is the essence
of activity and spontaneity as it manifests itself in the concept
reason. Holiness imbues spirit with a dynamic, ethical impulse; it
is an expression of the excellence of divine ethics.[151] Holiness confines reason and spirit to the ethical sphere within which it determines the true correlation between God and man. In other words,
within the confines of reason, which serves as a bridge between
God and man, a place is set aside for ethical activity, the principal

means for bridging the absolute gap between God and man and the core of the problem of correlation. Ethics does not reside in the sphere of instinct and impulse, but moves in the realm of the spirit and has its moorings in the harbor of reason. From this point of view Cohen remained faithful to his first conception, which had introduced ethics into the system of reason and sought the connection between ethics and logic. Ethics was inserted in the sphere of reason in Cohen's second conception as well, with reason made a function of activity and spontaneity, although a created spontaneity.

The spirit of holiness, which means the spirit determined by the concept of holiness, raises the value of an act to a level where it can be reviewed by the spirit. At the root of the spirit of holiness we find *theoretical knowledge*. The theoretical knowledge that refers to nature is the knowledge of reason and of the spirit, but not a manifestation of that reason which is defined and determined by the concept of holiness. The force and authority of the spirit of holiness is confined to human conduct and ethical activity. Here again there is a deep-seated difference between Judaism and pantheism. Pantheism stakes out a common ground between man and God and makes the two co-extensive; all knowledge, of nature as well as of man, becomes part of the knowledge of God himself. Judaism limits the scope and force of the spirit of holiness to ethical knowledge, which is the source of ethical activity. Ethics is concerned with bridging the gap between human striving and the goal of perfection, or God.

Correlation in the sphere of ethics, or the concept of the spirit of holiness as the bridge to this correlation, is extended by Cohen to a point where he perceives an identity between man and God. We must bear in mind, however, that Cohen insists just as emphatically on the absolute distinction between the two. The spirit of holiness is a kind of faculty common to both man and God.[152] In describing the nature of the relation between God and man Cohen's formulation takes an extreme form. He assumes a substantial but not a complete identity between God and man, since the concept God is more comprehensive than the spirit of holiness. God is True Being and He is also unique, two qualities that preclude His identification with man. Such an identification is possible only by a consideration of the ethical aspect, wherein God is the Archetype of man's ethical activity and the Pattern for his conduct. From this point of view, there is no substantial difference between God and man. The ethical realm raises the correlation between God and man to a level where they are identical. In this respect it may be said that God exhibits His holiness over against man.[153] As the Archetype of ethical activity, God, so to speak, needs man. The concept of Archetype is basically correlative: It binds or obligates the opposite member of the correlation to which it looks as its guide and goal. Without ethical man as a correlative, God ceases to be the Archetype of moral endeavor.

The identity of God and man is also evident in the circumstance that God freely communicated the spirit of holiness to man and implanted it in his very nature. Since this spirit proceeds from the Divine Being, it is an indestructible and imperishable part of man, immune, because of its ontic character, to the ravages of the phenomenal order of the world. Cohen takes this ontic character of the spirit for granted and proceeds to build the ethical edifice on its foundation. Since the spirit of holiness is impervious to decay, it cannot be the source of sin and iniquity.[154] The indestructible spirit with its power of constant renewal is now identified with the indestructible nature of man and its ability to overcome sin. Sins shall be wiped out, but the sinner shall remain, for the sinner bears within him the spirit of holiness, which is not subject to destruction.

This brings to light another side of the nature of religion peculiar to Cohen's system. Religion has both an ontological and an ethical aspect. In the former, man is insured against the loss of the spirit, since the spirit is of divine origin; with the latter, man is enjoined to overcome sin through repentance, and through the moral dynamic of this redemptive process, which is a permanent condition of all spiritual achievement, to restore his filial relation to God. Repentance is possible because it is a permanent possession of the spirit, which is capable of constant regeneration. The God of religion, who in contradistinction to the God of ethics is the direct God of every individual and not just the God of mankind, has the unique function of acting as a Guarantor for the redemptive process of the individual, and serving as a divine pledge that the moral renewal of the individual shall not be a fruitless Sisyphean labor.[155] In Cohen's ethical theory God is the Guarantor for the continuity of *nature*; in his conception of religion God is the Guarantor for the continuity of *man*. In the former, the continuity of nature and mankind took place only within the framework of a postulate, whereas in the latter this continuity was *assured* at the very outset by a permanent, indestructible ontological element, the spirit of holiness.

This leads us to the connection between the concept of the spirit of holiness and the problem of the immortality of the soul. The soul is immortal because the spirit of holiness informs and animates it as it does the essence of man. Immortality refers to the immortality of the soul or, more exactly, to the spirit of holiness,[156] a vital regenerative principle that ensures the immortality of the ethical soul, which is identified with the spirit of holiness.[157]

In the concept of immortality as the indestructible spirit of holiness there is an additional factor, giving us another aspect of Cohen's conception of the spirit—the nonidentification of God and man which, in turn, depends upon an understanding of the concept of holiness.

The identification of man with God by means of the spirit of holiness does not remove from man the burden of his finitude. Man's redemption and reconciliation with God is not to be found, therefore, in the area between the finite and the Infinite.[158] Despite their common ground in the spirit of holiness and despite their correlative relationship, God and man remain distinct and separate. The difference between the finite and the Infinite is in proportion to the degree to which the quality of holiness is realized. God, as the Archetype of moral endeavor, is the perfect embodiment of ethical values and of virtue, and is seen as holiness in action.[159] Cohen here approaches the ideas set forth by Lazarus, despite his methodological criticism of the latter's position. Although holiness resides in man as a divine gift, it does not develop within him; the achievement of the holiness that is incorporated in God's Being has been imposed upon man as a task.[160] The difference between the finite and the Infinite, therefore, is the

difference between holiness in action and holiness that is the goal
of striving; in Cohen's words, "holiness for man is a task (*Aufgabe*)
to be achieved, but for God it determines His being."[161] God, then,
is the holiness that is in *Being* and man is holiness that is in
becoming.

This teleological aspect of man's holiness constitutes an important factor in ethical theory and exhibits an essential difference
between Jewish and Christian or pantheistic conceptions. Holiness
is not embodied in man's activities; it is a goal towards which man
strives[162] and he alone can achieve it. The goal is given since it
is embodied in God's activity, but the way to the goal must be trod
by man alone; no outside power, not even God, can help him.[163]
Man, however, having been given the task of embodying holiness,
has also been given the ability and the strength to perform it.[164]

A fundamental distinction between Judaism and Christianity is
related to this concept of holiness. Christianity enlists God in the
process of embodying holiness and thus vitiates man's independent
efforts. There is something tragic in the fate of pure monotheism
as exhibited in Judaism because it gives birth to a conception that
contradicts its very nature and tends to obliterate the distinction
between God and man.[165] This obliteration is inherent in the
Christian conception which enlists God or the Son of God in the
work of human redemption. Divine holiness, which in Judaism is
set apart from man, since it is holiness in action, is transferred in
Christianity to man himself; not only is God the goal of the
process, but He has become the process itself, the Light *and* the
Way. God descends from the level of Being to that of reality.

Man's distinctiveness at the other end of the correlation can also
suffer obliteration if we assume that the redemptive process is
finite and can be consummated in a given time. Another aspect of
the difference between holiness in action and holiness in existence
—that is, between the Infinite and the finite—appears in the
circumstance that divine holiness is realized, and hence Infinite,
and human holiness, because unrealized, is finite. Man's finitude
means that the process of realizing holiness is conducted under the
category of time. If, however, in the process God is accommodated
as a co-worker, then the process is consummated and is no longer

infinite.[166] The God of Judaism does not appear as a potent Agent involved in the human process of achieving holiness, but stands at the end of the process, where He whose nature it is to show mercy and forgiveness receives the penitent who return to Him.

The reconciliation of man with God—this is the entire problem of religion. Therefore, the first postulate of religion is: Man needs to be reconciled with God since man's aspiration and action are in contradiction with the task that God imposed upon him for his existence. This postulate, however, is accompanied by another: that man is capable of reconciliation with God in proportion to his need for it.[167] The reconciliation between God and man emerges from the difference between them—that is, between the process of human action towards holiness and the divine holiness that is an actuality. The two correlatives cannot be made to converge by having man overcome his finitude and placing him on the level of the actuality of holiness. Reconciliation bridges the gulf between man and God not by a series of continuous progressions (which is by definition infinite) but by divine grace bestowed on penitent man[168] by God alone. An Intermediary, by intervening in the human process and curtailing it,[169] would make man the bearer of infinite holiness and thus render divine grace superfluous. Man does not reach the end of the process by his own unaided efforts but by a special act of divine forgiveness.[170] The forgiveness of sin is the peculiar quality of God's goodness.[171] In this idea of forgiveness and atonement we find, more than anywhere else in Cohen's religious views, strong overtones of the concept of divine Personality. Cohen, who denies to God the attributes of life and personality, endows Him with these qualities indirectly by stressing the importance of forgiveness.

The logical status of forgiveness, reconciliation, and atonement is determined in Cohen's system by the spirit of holiness whereby the co-operation between man and God is effected; this co-operation, however, is incomplete since it takes place between unequal partners. This process, which approaches the Infinite, occurs in the sphere of the finite and is infinite in time. Man treads the road that lies before him, but he cannot know whether it will lead him to his destination. On the other hand, it is improbable that God

would deceive man and that the task He imposed on him should
be an ineffectual Sisyphean labor. The process of holiness must
reach an end if pursued long enough by man's persistent efforts.
God, whose nature it is to forgive, delivers man from the process. As
against the Christian view, in which God intervenes, Cohen puts
the process within the autonomous, practical sphere of man and
assigns God the function of forgiveness that draws man near Him.
Forgiveness is the assurance of God's activity within the process; it
puts an end to the process by means of grace, and thus breaks
through the conceptual relations between man and God.

Reconciliation exhibits three aspects: man's reconciliation with
God, with his fellow man, and with himself.[172] Man's reconciliation with God transports him to the end of the process of holiness;
his reconciliation with his fellow man establishes a relationship between equals based on both respect and love; and in his reconciliation with himself, which depends on his reconciliation with God,
man turns from the way of sin and voluntarily imposes on himself
an ethical imperative which constitutes the triumph of holiness.
A man whose sins are forgiven, therefore, becomes reconciled to
himself, and this transforms his soul into spirit, so that whatever
exists in his life becomes holy and all his acts are performed in the
service of holiness.[173]

Prayer is the psychological form of the religious factor of reconciliation.[174] In the objective sphere, reconciliation between man
and God relates human conduct to the process of holiness; in the
subjective sphere, this reconciliation is effected within the inner man
through prayer. A dialogue between man and God,[175] prayer is the
special form of man's reconcilement with God. In prayer man taps
the deep sources of his ethical strength, the spirit of holiness, which
is the divine part that dwells within him.[176] The veracity (*Wahr-
haftigkeit*) of man is revealed in prayer addressed to the God of
Truth. In short, we can say that Cohen considers prayer to be the
contemplative expression of man's reconcilement with God, as
forgiveness is the expression of reconcilement in the practical
sphere. But the circle of reconciliation remains incomplete as long
as no fixed place is found within it for the law and the imperative.

The ordinance, the law is only another expression of God's

essence as the Archetype and Pattern of human morality.[177] God with His virtues is the Paragon of ethical activity and is regarded by man as the One who commands him to practice these excellencies and virtues. As correlative concepts, Archetype and Pattern appear to man as obligations to be fulfilled. An obligation is an imperative carried out in conformity to God's teachings. God's attributes are virtues—that is, imperatives for the practical conduct of man in the world.[178]

What is the function of law within the context of reconciliation? Forgiveness is an aspect of reconciliation whereby God by a free act of grace delivers man from the endless process of ethical perfection: The complementary virtue of grace is righteousness, and if love is a religious attribute, then righteousness is an ethical one.[179] Reconciliation with God moves in two directions—the direction of God to man is that of grace and forgiveness, and the direction of man to God is that of righteousness and law. God prescribed for man the way that leads to Him.

The principal purpose of the law is not to make man a God, but to make him a more perfect *man* by raising him to an ethical level.[180] Law is always ethical law or an expedient for ethical law, that is, its task is to guide man by means of the discipline of education and the virtue of holiness.[181] The peculiar content of the law is expressed by the word *mitzvah*, commandment, in the two senses of that word, viz. as a law imposed on man and his obligation to obey it. The *mitzvah*, then, is an obvious example of the correlation between the divine and the human—the source of the law is in God and the obligation to obey it devolves upon man.[182]

To this idea, rooted in the concept of correlation and its various expressions Cohen added, even in his first period, the Kantian principle of the autonomy of the ethical law. The divine imperative is nothing but the religious expression of the ethical imperative, and is identified with it. The autonomous imperative is manifested in objective form beyond the ethical sphere. The ethical imperative is, strictly speaking, an imperative of pure reason, and not the product of man's instincts or emotions. That the pure will obeys the law is proof that the law does not spring from instinct but from the concept of duty or the ought. The divine origin of the law is the religious expression of the idea of obedience. Ethics in its pure form demands the objective ethical imperative and this objectivity is presented to it by religion as the law of God.[188] It is clear that the Kantian interpretation of ethical law deprives law of its religious character as the expression of the correlation between God and man. Ethical law, which is the product of the pure will, has two aspects which Cohen points out in the concept of *mitzvah* —the imperative itself, and the duty to obey it. These two aspects are found in the sphere of reason and the autonomous will, but they have not the dual aspect given them by Cohen—the imperative whose source is in God, and the duty to obey it whose source is in man.

The concept of correlation occupies a central position in Cohen's ethical system. By this means his understanding of the distinction between God and man was transformed from a metaphysical into a religious principle, which recognized that the true problem of religion is the problem of how an Infinite God is related to the perishable world and to finite man within it.

The correlation develops step by step. Its first expression is objective and appears in the creation of the world by God, a creation, however, that is without mutual relationships. Correlation then proceeds to establish a reciprocal relation between God and man—God reveals Himself to man and man is drawn into the orbit of God—and reason is made the bridge to unite these two disparate elements. But since man is a creature that desires the ought, the problem of the relation betwen man and God is transferred to the sphere of ethics and holiness. Man is now able to move towards God, just as in creation God moved towards the world, and in revelation towards man. Man's ascent to God is accomplished by the positive imperatives of ethical law. But the quality of righteousness inherent in ethical law is unable to lead man to the end of the process, and he is, therefore, in desperate need of the saving power of grace which is *the* religious virtue that can redeem him. The highest development of correlation is that of the sinner who looks for grace from the God of grace. The focal point of religion and correlation is transferred to the sphere where man and God meet under the auspices of grace. *Correlation begins with creation and ends with reconciliation.*

F. JUDAISM AND REASON

Cohen's conception of religion proposes to be a systematic treatment of its nature and a methodological exposition of essential features: The concept of reason is indispensable for the creation of the concept of religion.[184] Like all other manifestations of the spirit, religion falls within the scope and jurisdiction of reason.

Since religion has its roots in reason, it is *ab initio* rational and not a particular historical religion. The religion of reason is based on systematic concepts and derivations, not on historical facts or events. We must not forget, furthermore, that science knows but one discipline, mathematics, whereas religion includes many different religions, one of which is Judaism.[185] We shall now consider the special place that Judaism occupies in the comprehensive category of religion.

Since the religion of reason is derived from rational sources, its subject matter can be submitted to methodological and systematic analysis. The subject matter of Judaism—its historical and literary sources, which are the independent creation of reason—can be similarly investigated.[186] Cohen remains faithful to the transcendental method elaborated in his systematic works,[187] a method that seeks to extract from the various disciplines, such as science, law, and art, the fundamental principles on which they are based, and he applies this philosophical method to the sources of Judaism for the purpose of clarifying its basic notions.

Logic depends in its content and purpose on the one science of mathematics in order to clarify its own axioms. The philosophy of religion, however, has no one religion on which it can depend as a criterion. What then distinguishes Judaism, whose subject matter is amenable to philosophic methods of examination, from religion in general? Although Cohen believes that the essence of the religion of reason can be exhausted by the consciousness of no one people,[188] he places Judaism in a special category. The literary and historical sources of Judaism are distinguished by the fact that they are original sources of the essential features of the religion of reason, namely, the uniqueness of God and ethics, the two elements that raise Judaism above all other religions. The religion of Israel is not identical with the religion of reason, but is its principal manifestation in the history of religious consciousness. The sources of Judaism are not only original, but also pure, and purity constitutes for Cohen the very essence of reason.[189]

The people of Israel, the historical bearer of Judaism, is also placed in a special category. Here Cohen follows the ideas of the Reform Movement in Judaism although his methods differ from those of its advocates. The special status of Israel is related to its destiny as the chosen people, which Cohen interprets as meaning that Israel's election is its isolation and uniqueness. The historic fact of Israel's singularity is reinforced by the absence of a political basis for its collective life, such as other peoples enjoy. In fact, it was only after Israel had lost its political existence and national identity that it was able to realize its true mission[190]—an idea common to the early Reform Movement and espoused, for example, by David Einhorn (1809–1879), one of its ablest American exponents.

That Israel had no country not only isolated it from other nations but, according to Cohen, served as a symbol of destitution and impoverishment, calculated to awaken pity and love in men and endear it to God.[191] Israel's historic fate—to be scattered among the nations without a country of its own—has then a double significance; it emphasizes Israel's singularity in the world and at the same time serves as a symbol of man's lot.

Cohen also believed that historic Judaism and its literary products embody some of the concepts of the religion of reason and that Israel's historic destiny is intimately related to its internal structure. Israel's religion is an original source that can bear philosophical analysis, although it is only one of many historic and literary sources. (Cohen did not find it necessary to investigate the others.) Israel's suffering does not come from its breach with God but serves as a channel for His redeeming love. Cohen thus finds a justification for Israel's age-long vocation of suffering, and this explains his opposition to Zionism; as Franz Rosenzweig (1886–1929) observed, he saw it as a movement that would abolish Israel's isolation and suffering by restoring its national sovereignty.

G. FROM MENDELSSOHN TO COHEN

In his essay *Deutschtum und Judentum*, Cohen states that Mendelssohn analyzed the problem of the relation between ecclesiastical and natural law but failed to come to grips with the real problem, the relation between religion and ethics.[192] Furthermore, Mendelssohn restricted the problem to its formal, legalistic aspects instead of investigating its basic principles, an objection that we have already seen raised by Luzzatto. Cohen transferred the problem to the ethical sphere. In his first period he made religion the cornerstone of ethics; later, he attempted to discover special ethical concepts in the domain of religion. Religion is more than the formulation of moral principles and has an ontological ground not found in ethics.

This concludes our study of Judaism as an ethical system. The interest in Judaism now shifts from the ethical to the ontological; that is, it is apprehended as a reality with qualities and relations of its own, which develop in accordance with a unifying principle. In other words, Judaism is beginning to be looked upon as a metaphysical, and not primarily as an ethical system, and we now turn to the development of this view as it manifested itself in the last century.

5

The Religion of the Spirit

S. FORMSTECHER, S. HIRSCH AND N. KROCHMAL

A. TRENDS

Whereas the conception which made Judaism co-extensive with its ethical element rested on internal factors within traditional Judaism as well as on Kantian ethical principles, the later view, which regarded Judaism as a religion of the spirit, had its roots in metaphysical principles that arose after Kant, particularly those derived from the philosophical systems of Friedrich W. J. von Schelling and George W. F. Hegel.

The concept spirit, which dominated the philosophical thought of the nineteenth century, had more than one meaning. It was sometimes conceived as a realm of reality directly *opposed* to that of nature, and the content of Judaism was thus determined by its *opposition* to the religions of nature. It is instructive to follow this development in modern Jewish thought, in which the metaphysical element became the dominant factor for the *ethical* understanding of Judaism. In this view, which regards Judaism as a system of morality, we must consider a specific methodological factor. Although it proceeded basically from such concepts of morality as law and commandments, holiness and the ideal, the metaphysical concept was foremost among those that in themselves had no ethical significance and were nevertheless the vehicle for ethical meanings.

[106]

An ethical interpretation can be given to the metaphysical principle of spirit if spirit has become a part of a more inclusive reality, with the inevitable tension between its conquering impulse and recalcitrant nature. The two most prominent exponents of this metaphysical-ethical conception in Jewish thought of the last century are Solomon Formstecher (1808–1889) and S. Hirsch (1815–1889), whose views, despite some basic differences, we shall treat together.

The meaning of all-embracing spirit does not exhaust its content, which was broadened and deepened by the various philosophical movements of the nineteenth century, particularly by Hegel. Spirit is not regarded as a special, partial sphere, but as one that *embraces* all spheres, while ignoring the differences between them. It comprises reality as well as the knowledge of reality and thus tends to confirm a monistic rather than a dualistic conception.

An important consequence of the spirit becoming all-inclusive is that within the framework of such a unified conception no prominent place can be assigned to ethical problems. With the removal of diversity and the tension of opposites, which formed the background for the emergence of ethical imperatives, there is no place for the problem of ethics as the nucleus of a system. The harmony of reality deprives the ethical task of its urgency and its prominent position within Judaism. The best-known exponent of this view in Jewish thought of the nineteenth century was Nachman Krochmal (1785–1840), whose speculative gifts were not confined (like those of his successors, Formstecher and Hirsch) to method but also extended to content.

The different ways of interpreting spirit will help us considerably in classifying the various systems that regarded Judaism as a religion of the spirit.

B. SPIRIT AND NATURE

The religious content of Judaism was interpreted by Formstecher with the aid of the concept of the world-soul, derived from ancient cosmological speculations and revived in his day by Schelling. Some of the characteristics of this idea are enumerated by Formstecher:

a) the world owes its existence to the world-soul, but although it is upheld by the world-soul—and here Formstecher injects a purely subjective note—the world exists only in "the mind of whoever comprehends it."[1] Formstecher sees the world-soul as one reality and the world with its manifold phenomena as another, the former being the predicate or accident of the latter. The world-soul constitutes the essence of the world; the world itself is a manifestation of this essence[2] which is one and indivisible; it remains unimpaired by the world's manifold phenomena which have no independent existence of their own, being simply the appearances of the essence.

These two elements in the nature of the world-soul, which define its relation to the world, have actually no religious significance, being derived from the study of the philosophy of nature or from purely metaphysical principles. The concept of world-soul in Schelling's system performs an important although nonreligious function as a link between the organic and nonorganic spheres of nature.[3] The world-soul itself dwells beyond these two separate spheres and, because of its ubiquitous and indeterminate character, is ideally suited to serve as a common ground for the various natural spheres.[4] It is essentially material and not spiritual, as Edward von Hartmann (1842–1906) has pointed out, being a part of nature but not of nature divided into the spheres of organic and nonorganic. It is apparent that Schelling does not consider the world-soul as a being possessing consciousness but as a common creative faculty of the nonconscious spheres of nature.

Formstecher imparted a different meaning to this concept of the world-soul by pressing it into the service of religion. This was possible because of the very nature of the concept. Since the world-soul constitutes the essence of the world, it cannot be said to be dependent upon it. Because of its character as essence, it is not only independent of and superior to the world—as well as being its basic principle, as we have seen in Schelling—but constitutes an entity in and by itself, a circumstance that is related by Formstecher to the creation of the world.

Since the world cannot exist without the world-soul, which in turn has no need of the world, it is clear that the two have need of a common link. This common link is creation, a concept that takes the world-soul from the domain of the philosophy of nature and makes it the cornerstone of the philosophy of religion. It is not by accident that the identification of the world-soul with God is not explicitly stated or firmly established in Formstecher's system. If the world-soul is the essence of the world or its bearer, the question arises whether the separation between the two is a difference of degree or of real being. It is only by giving the world-soul an independent status that Formstecher could infer a real separation between God and the world: Without God there is no world, but without a world there is still God. God is God even though He does not reveal His attributes and even though the world were not renewed daily. It is not a matter of necessity but of freedom. Just as human freedom exists, even if it finds no concrete embodiment, so must we conceive God as existing even though He does not think Himself or permit creation to come into being.[5] Judaism does not look upon the world as independent because it is a product of creation;[6] this is the primary distinction between paganism and Judaism. Paganism conceives the world as the manifestation of God but conceives of God as dwelling only within the world (the pantheistic view), whereas Judaism, while believing that the world is God's creation and His dwelling place, insists on a strict separation of the two (the theistic view).[7] In other words, as long as the concept of the world-soul refers only to the bearer of the world and its essence, no advantage accrues to the theistic view or to Judaism. These systems come into their own only when essence (*i.e.*, the world-soul, God) is removed from the realm of the philosophy of nature and placed within that of religion—that is, when it is made independent of its manifestations, ceases to be a material principle, and becomes *God*.

Furthermore, the independence of essence from its manifestations and appearances expresses only a static relationship, forcing us to ascribe to essence an additional quality that is not shared by its appearances. Since essence is not dependent on its manifestations and can exist without them—but not vice versa—the creation of phenomena must be regarded as an act of freedom. Essence is free to create or to refrain from creating phenomena, since its decisions are voluntary. This quality of volition, deliberately initiated and acquiesced in, removes essence from the confines of the world-soul in the natural sense (as it appears in Schelling's conception) and makes it God; it converts the world-soul into spirit, because one of the essential qualities inherent in the nature of spirit is freedom.[8] In short, Formstecher transferred the concept of the world-soul from the realm of nature and the confines of matter to the domain of the spirit, a transference tantamount to one from the philosophy of nature to theology.

Formstecher ascribes to the world-soul not only the quality of freedom but also that of self-consciousness, which reveals itself in various manifestations, including man.[9] If there is a definite quality within the *manifestation* of the world-soul—that is, within self-conscious man—we should assume that it is also possessed by its essence, the world-soul, since the manifestation must necessarily be richer in content than the essence it reveals. It follows that the bearer of the manifestations is not only the physical world-soul, but also, by virtue of its self-consciousness and self-determination, a free, independent spirit—or God.[10] J. Schoeps has justly observed that the structure of this argument is reminiscent of the logical structure of the ontological proof of God's existence. Just as this proof derives the existence of God from the assumption that the sum total of qualities is incomplete if it does not include God's existence, so Formstecher derives the self-determination of God as the world-soul from the assumption that without this quality the world-soul would be poorer than man, who is but one of its manifestations. At any rate, it is clear that self-consciousness is the quality which, in addition to freedom, converts the world-soul into God and raises it from the material domain of nature to the spiritual realm of religion.

Formstecher departs from Schelling's conception of the world-soul in another respect. The world-soul is for Schelling the material basis of nature and as such is nonreflective and without self-consciousness; only man is self-conscious, a quality that defines his peculiar position in the world as the link between the organic and the inorganic, by virtue of which he possesses the additional gift of consciousness which is that of the world-soul. Formstecher, however, seeking to adapt the concept of the world-soul not to the needs of a philosophy of nature but to those of a philosophy of religion, went beyond Schelling and endowed the world-soul with the qualities of freedom and consciousness, thus making it possible for him to identify it with God.

We must not fail to note, however, the ambiguity that attends this transference of the concept of the world-soul to the speculative realm of religious essence. The world-soul is evidently a neutral element that existed prior to the division of nature and spirit and dwells in a region untouched by their separation. Formstecher, however, sees only the spiritual element in this union[11] and this emphasis is characteristic of all dualistic systems since Descartes, which regard the two substances, thought and extension (matter), as being equal, yet raise the thinking substance (at least from the religious and ethical standpoint) above that of the extended substance. This ambiguity is not absent, for example, from Spinoza's system which also considers thought and extension the two attributes of the infinite substance.

The consideration of the essence of the world-soul led to its identification with spirit, which in turn raised it to the level of God. This alone would make Judaism, which believes in the strict separation of God and the world, a religion of the spirit. It is also a religion of the spirit in the sense that it sets up an ideal for man, or imposes upon him the burden of a mission. Religion is the knowledge of this ideal shared by the entire community and the desire to realize it.[12] It is interesting to note that the definition of the essence of religion speaks of *knowledge* and not of faith; Formstecher, following either Mendelssohn or the speculative tradition, expressly rejects the concept that identifies the Jewish religion with faith.[13] Religion as the knowledge of the ideal and the desire to realize it falls into two types depending on the nature of the ideal; If the ideal is an individual one, we have a religion of the spirit; if it is universal, we have a religion of nature. Judaism is the religion of the spirit *par excellence* and paganism the religion of nature. This definition of the two types of religion is rooted in the nature of religion as knowledge of the ideal. The radical duality of religious phenomena is determined in accordance with the duality of the ideal.

The dual nature of the ideal is but an expression of the duality of the world or of the manifestations of the world-soul. The world can be conceived from the standpoint of nature as the manifestation of the world-soul, or the totality of the phenomena within it, or it can be conceived from the standpoint of spirit as consisting of individual phenomena. This division which depends on one's point of view, does not account, however, for the essential difference between the two spheres, viz. the absence of consciousness in nature and its presence in spirit; nature is governed by necessity, but the spirit is ruled by freedom and self-determination. Nature is complete and appears to us in panoply, immersed in the peremptory fulfillment of its own reiterated movements, whereas the spirit, summoned by beckoning goals, constantly deepens its insights and widens its horizons; nature is essentially object and spirit is essentially subject.

Having noted the inevitable duality of religious phenomena from the standpoint of the ideal, we can say that as long as the ideal is inexorably determined in nature as object, impervious to progress or change, we have the religion of nature or paganism; where the ideal is consciously struggling towards a larger freedom, we have the religion of the spirit or Judaism. Paganism and Judaism are not only historical phenomena but represent two categories of religious conception, differing not only historically but typologically.

We shall now examine more closely some of the basic principles of Judaism and paganism from a typological point of view.

Paganism has a god of nature and Judaism a God of the spirit.[14] Paganism deifies nature or the ruling powers within nature; its god dwells not above nature but within it, a blind force subject to the laws of nature and governed by fate.[15] Since the god of nature is not sovereign or all powerful, pantheism, which identifies God with the world, must be considered an inevitable philosophical offshoot of paganism. Furthermore, since pagan thought is directed towards nature, the principal type of human activity is the science of physics, which investigates nature and attempts to decipher its secrets. This is the esthetic ideal that summons man to the passive contemplation of the beauty and mysteries of nature, cultivating in the observer a certain detachment from human aims with a concomitant sense of satisfied desire;[16] all this is distressing to those engaged in the religious quest, whose ideals are beyond the pageantry of this world and the shadow of mortal things. In the religious conception of paganism knowledge has not yet reached the stage of self-consciousness—that is, the knowledge that constitutes the essence of its religion is not the knowledge of the spirit but of nature with which it is identical. In other words, in paganism knowledge has not yet emerged from the realm of the object to that of the self-conscious subject.[17] It may, therefore, be regarded from two points of view as a religion of nature: its god is the God of nature, and the knowledge of man, which is the specific characteristic of religion, is rooted in nature and co-extensive with its perfection.

Judaism, on the other hand, is a religion of the spirit from two points of view. First, the God of Judaism is the God of the spirit, who is sovereign and omnipotent in regard to nature, its free and conscious Creator. From the standpoint of knowledge within the religion, Judaism is also a religion of the spirit, in which the object of knowledge is not nature but spirit, and in which the spirit recognizes itself. The active manifestations of the spiritual human being (that is, the Jew) are logic on the one hand, and ethics on the other. When the spirit recognizes itself as the instrument of knowledge or as an activity of thought, it looks upon itself from the standpoint of logic; and when it recognizes itself as a striving towards the realization of the ideal that is not given in reality, it looks upon itself from the standpoint of ethics.

Formstecher thus derives the ethical nature of Judaism (as against the esthetic nature of paganism) from the very essence of spirit which, unlike nature, is a never-ceasing progression towards perfection. The essential characteristic of the spirit is its faculty of self-determination, which presses forward in the interminable struggle for the things of abiding value. This forward-moving human effort that reaches out to the unfathomable things of the spirit is an ethical ideal.[18] Judaism as a religion of the spirit is, by the same token, a religion of ethics.

We cannot fail to note the ambiguity inherent in Formstecher's view of the relation between spirit and nature. Every religion is, by its very nature, knowledge, the difference between them being determined by the nature of the object of knowledge. If the object is spirit, we have Judaism; if it is nature, we have paganism. All knowledge as such is a function of the spirit, and this led Formstecher to the belief that spirit has a double function, having at the same time a consciousness of self and a consciousness of nature. The two spheres are, of course, in no wise equal, that of the spirit being superior to that of nature. When the consciousness has recognized the object as object, it passes over to the concept subject, and the knowing subject and known object find in the concept itself the highest unity.[19] Formstecher here uses several principles derived from both Schelling and Hegel.[20] In Schelling's system man serves as a link between nonconscious nature and conscious spirit; in Hegel the dialectical process removes the differences between subject and object by uniting them at a higher level by means of the Idea. Formstecher needs both conceptions in order to lift spirit above nature or, more exactly, to make spirit the ultimate end of the conscious process. The tangible consequence of this view is the victory of Judaism which, as the religion of the spirit, is assured of ultimate triumph—a dialectical triumph—even as spirit is destined in the long run to overcome nature. The object, or nature, is not devoid of spirit; it is, on the contrary, constantly being subsumed under its conquering impulse. But Formstecher did not draw the logical consequences of this view and failed to show that the triumph of Judaism was the result of this conjunction within it of subject and object. On the contrary, in his historical conception of Christianity and Islam as apostles of Judaism to the pagan world, Formstecher attempts to prove that the absorption of pagan elements into the religion at that time was only a tactical expedient, adopted by Judaism in order to raise the pagan world to the level of a spiritual religion. The admixture of natural elements in Christianity and Islam seemed to Formstecher a temporary matter and not essential for the dialectical process of achieving a synthesis between nature and spirit; the possibility of such a synthesis, however, was implicit in the metaphysical assumptions upon which his conception rested.

The distinction between the religion of the spirit and the religion of nature helps us to understand the ethical nature of religion. Only the religion of the spirit can serve as the vehicle of ethical content. Ethics presupposes self-consciousness and freedom of decision on the part of man, two elements that constitute the peculiar essence of spirit and differentiate it from nature. It follows that only the activities of the spirit can be characterized as good or bad, while the manifestations of nature are beyond (or prior to) ethical decision. The realm of nature does not constitute a part of ethics; as long as man dwells within it without rising to the level of the spirit, he is not subject to ethical decisions and ethical criteria do not apply to him.

Within this ethical conception, however, Formstecher introduces another element related to his conception of God. We have seen how his idea of God wavered between the concept of God as world-soul or as spirit, that is, as a Power endowed with freedom and consciousness. This is the source of the ambiguous status of the two domains in Formstecher's conception. On the one hand, he regards nature and spirit as co-equal, since both are the manifestations of the essence of the world-soul; on the other hand, he regards spirit as superior since it is related to God who is Spirit. Traces of such wavering can also be found in Formstecher's ethical conceptions. An unethical deed, that is, a deed devoid of freedom or consciousness, thrusts man back to the realm of nature, but although it removes him from spirit, it does not remove him from God, who as world-soul includes both domains, spirit and nature. One who sins is hence extruded from the sphere of the spirit but not from the sphere of God. It is thus plain that if Formstecher had consistently adhered to his idea of God as spirit alone and not the totality of the two realms of nature and spirit, he would have acknowledged that the unethical act that removes us from the spirit also removes us from God. But since he conceived of God not only as spirit but also as a neutral being in relation to the two realms of nature and spirit, he was obliged to regard the unethical act as a mere passage from one realm to another without a consequent forfeiture of status within the total essence whose manifestation is spirit and nature together. The consequences of this view apply to the main principles of the religious conception. If the unethical act, which is tantamount to a sin, entails nothing more than a withdrawal from spirit and not from God, then there is no room for repentance and redemption in the sphere between man and God; these consolations are then relegated to the province of man himself, or to the relations between him and spirit. Just as the unethical act is a withdrawal from spirit and not from God, the good deed or the overcoming of evil is a return to spirit and not to God. This thought is elaborated by Hirsch and occupies a central place in his system.

The ethical problem, therefore, is a purely human problem, since man is a contradictory being perilously poised at the juncture of nature and spirit. As a child of nature, he is riveted to the life of the senses and bound by inexorable laws; as a child of the spirit, he is ethically free to modify and mold his character in the light of freely chosen goals. It is as if the wagon of life were harnessed to both winged Pegasus and the dull ox, and man condemned to fly with the one or creep with the other. The Christian doctrine of original sin seeks to dissolve this original collaboration between the two spheres by placing man within the realm of nature alone, from which he can be redeemed only by divine grace, since he is too exhausted to rise by his own efforts. By means of the ethical ideal, however, man can overcome his radical alienation from spirit and rise to the heights of perfection.[21]

This duality in the relationship between ethics and God has an additional aspect, demanding separate treatment because of its basic religious significance. It is plain that the essential element of the ethical act resides in its spiritual nature—that is, in its elective adoption and concomitant self-consciousness. But Formstecher places a severe limitation on this initial freedom by adopting the rabbinical dictum: "All is foreseen, but freedom is given," thus regarding the spirit as the common ground of man and God. Formstecher could thus assert that from the subjective, finite point of view man is free, but from the objective point of view man's will is displaced by God's freedom, resulting in an identity of divine Providence and human volition.[22] It is evident that if we take God as the world-soul that is neutral as regards the realms of spirit and nature, we cannot assume an identity between man's will and God as world-soul, since human volition is a manifestation of spirit and God is not only spirit. But if God himself is spirit and if the ethical essence of man consists in the rule of spirit over nature, the question necessarily arises concerning the identification of man with God in the common domain of the spirit. It appears that the duality inherent in Formstecher's conception of God as world-soul penetrated his entire system and left a marked imprint on his fundamental notions of ethics and on the ethical relationship between man and God.

Formstecher does not attempt to analyze the basic ethical principles of Judaism, but merely selects one which illustrates most impressively God's separation from the world—that is, his conception of God as spirit. In paganism man has his being in nature which is co-extensive with God; since man and God are on an equal plane, pagan ethics requires man to assimilate God. In Judaism, however, the chasm between God and man cannot be bridged; man is not required to be God, but to imitate Him and follow in His ways. Formstecher goes further and asserts that mysticism, which seeks the perfect union of man and God, is in fact but a legacy of paganism in a new guise. We are here confronted once more with a difficulty, since on the one hand, Formstecher assumes the identity of man and God in the spirit, with both in the possession of common ideals; on the other hand, a basic element in his system, the separation of God and man, prevents him from identifying man's ideals with those of God. It is this contradiction at the heart of his system that compels him to formulate man's ethical goal not as identification with God, but as striving to be like Him and to follow in His ways.

The gulf that separated the human from the divine is exhibited in still another theoretical aspect of Formstecher's system. God as the world-soul is essence, and the manifestation of this essence is the world with its two realms of nature and spirit in which alone essence can be recognized. For this reason the ethical ideal is placed in the sphere of the relationship between man and spirit, which is a *manifestation* of essence, and not between man and God, which is essence pure and simple. Man's task is to embody in his practical activities the manifestation of essence insofar as it is *ethical*, that is, insofar as it is spirit.[23] We can therefore say that the religious relationship, which depends upon knowledge, is by its very nature incapable of being a relationship between man and God, since God can in no way be the object of cognition. The religious relationship is one that exists between man and spirit and man is therefore required to identify himself with spirit (and not with God) and its progressive dominion over nature. Man's relation to God is in reality a relation to the manifestation or the phenomenon, that is, to spirit. Judaism insists on the increasing self-awareness of the spirit over against nature and attempts to overcome the duality between these two spheres in a higher synthesis.[24]

The problem of ethics leads us to a consideration of the methodological and metaphysical question of the relation of reason to revelation. Ethics is the product of spirit—that is, of freedom and self-consciousness—but the ethical act itself has a specific content. This gives rise to the question concerning the source and origin of this content, which is in turn related to the distinction between reason and revelation. Reason is the faculty that evaluates and compares a definite ethical act with the highest principle or the archetype of that act; it functions in a middle zone between seeming and actual facts, investigates their mutual accommodation and congruence and evaluates them in the light of a higher criterion. In the realm of esthetics, reason expresses itself as good taste and in the realm of ethics as conscience.[25] It cannot by itself determine what is good or beautiful, since it is nothing but an empty vessel that receives its content from without. Reason is to revelation as an instrument is to content, which is a manifestation of revelation. From the standpoint of finite man, revelation may be considered the knowledge of good and its essence bestowed by God upon the spirit of man.[26]

Content itself is granted to man and does not depend upon his self-consciousness, which is a basic quality of spirit. The spirit is in constant pursuit of the essence of revealed matter. A given content is elaborated into more perfect knowledge in the historical process of the developing consciousness. Content itself is impervious to change or development and is hence nonhistorical. In its efforts to comprehend content, reason is only a historical faculty and functions only within a process of development. In other words, the distinction between revelation and reason is rooted in the distinction between that which is given in its completeness and that which is subjected to the historical process. Revelation and reason are mutually related and complementary—the content (of revelation) is an objective fact, a gift that is presented to us from without and devoid of consciousness; and consciousness (of reason), an aggressive principle in search of docile matter, is devoid of content.[27]

Formstecher attempts to demonstrate the heteronomy of ethics by emphasizing the fact that its content is given to man and not created by him. Nevertheless, a complementary relation exists between the content and the evaluative faculty, or between revelation and reason, a relation that recalls Kant's well-known dictum concerning the relation between concepts and intuitions, viz. that concepts without intuitions are empty and intuitions without concepts are blind. Reason is constantly striving to discover the content of revelation.[28] Revelation that anticipates the historical process of knowledge is called prehistorical; reason that strives to disclose and decipher the content of revelation is historical revelation. We must not fail to note two basic distinctions between revelation and reason, that is, between prehistorical and historical revelation. Strictly speaking, revelation is one and indivisible and hence absolute. Historical revelation, which is reason's formative energy seeking to penetrate the content of prehistorical revelation, has by its very nature many facets and is hence relative. Every historical stage in the path of reason is a new and therefore relative manifestation. Formstecher here touches on a question which constitutes a basic problem in his system, namely, the relation between the spirit of man and the spirit of God. He finds it necessary to establish a complete separation between the two, and he is aided in this by his distinction between revelation and reason. The spirit of man, which is reason, is always historical and its manifestations are never absolute but always subject to temporal and spatial causality;[29] but the manifestations of the divine spirit constitute a revelation that presents the human spirit with content and therefore exists as an objective reality for man. It might have been possible for Formstecher to maintain this duality unimpaired, and to establish the transcendence of God and man's dependence on the content presented to him as a heteronomous gift. But the speculative element in his system, which stemmed from Schelling or Hegel (it is difficult to determine which), compelled him to overcome this duality by injecting the consciousness of human reason into revelation. The human spirit is impelled to lift revelation from the confines of its objective sphere to the level of consciousness and cognition, and this makes it possible for Formstecher to blur the distinction between the transcendent and the metaphysical content of revelation. The distinction between revelation and reason is made to rest on what occurred prior to history and what is history only. It is nevertheless plain that the emphasis on the prehistorical character of revelation is an expression of an ethical, religious conception and is designed to buttress the citadel of faith.

An unmistakable tension is apparent between the speculative and ethical aspects in Formstecher's system. This is the result of his attempt to inject an ethical element into a speculative background by emphasizing the sharp separation between nature and spirit, on the one hand, and between man and God, on the other. Sometimes the speculative factor gains the upper hand and this tends to vitiate the ethical ingredient; at other times the ethical constituent asserts undisputed sovereignty, and God's transcendence shines forth either as the world-soul or as revealed in objective contents. This casual interpenetration of the two elements, without a discernible principle of inner harmony or reconciliation, constitutes a disruptive force in Formstecher's conception of the religious consciousness. From this point of view, as we shall now see, Hirsch's system exhibits a more consistent and tenable approach to the problem.

C. FREEDOM AND SIN

The interpenetration of ethics and metaphysics is more prominent in the philosophy of Hirsch than in that of Formstecher. The metaphysical system, which sets off spirit against nature, serves to clarify the essence of ethics—the metaphysical concepts emphasize the antagonism among the contradictory ethical conceptions. The religious problem and the ethical problem are both in the same category.

The religious life, Hirsch says, is nothing else than this eternally actual and eternally creative freedom.[30] The *terminus a quo* of his philosophy is the cardinal problem of freedom. Although his criticism of Formstecher's book was uncommonly severe, he agreed with him in identifying spirit with freedom.[31] The transference of the concept spirit from the speculative to the ethical sphere, from the ontological realm without to the moral realm within, was more pronounced in Hirsch than in the idealistic philosophers of his day, including Formstecher. Spirit is conceived neither as a kind of substance of the world nor as the source of cognition, but as the faculty of man's free decision.

This pronounced shift to anthropology receives greater emphasis as a result of the identification of man's ego with the spirit. The word "I" exhibits that quality which makes man human. When a man designates himself as "I," he proclaims the essential quality of freedom within him; the assertion that he is an "I" reassures him that he is a free agent.[32] In other words, it is freedom that constitutes man's peculiar essence,[33] diverts his mind from instinctive fear, and lifts him above chaos.

The peculiar dialectic of the concept spirit, which distinguishes Hirsch's ethical and religious views, here becomes evident. If spirit is freedom and decision, it is never given completely in its finished form, a quality found only in nature where things lie outside of man. Spirit as decision is the promise and assurance of things to come; it does not enter directly into execution but requires training and preparation. Man is born for freedom[34] in the sense that it is incumbent upon him to acquire and cultivate it. Freedom is not a primary fact but an unceasing ethical task, achieved with the aid of freedom itself[35]—that is, man must lift himself up, as it were, by his own bootstraps.

The identification of spirit with freedom leads us to a consideration of Hegel's basic conception of history as a spiritual process whose goal is freedom. It may be instructive for the understanding of Hirsch's aims, however, to note some basic differences between him and Hegel in the treatment of this problem.

Hirsch, unlike Hegel, removed freedom completely from the objective-historical realm. Hegel viewed freedom as the goal of the historical process while Hirsch considered it the goal of the individual. We might say that this removal of freedom from the objective sphere indicates a determined opposition to one of the deepest philosophical urges of Hegel, namely, to free history and ethics from their dependence on subjectivity and place them in an objective context beyond finite man. This desire to establish human behavior on solid foundations of objectivity led Hegel to prefer the State to a subjective morality. Hirsch, on the other hand, regarded freedom as residing in the subject and hence he identified it with the subject's faculty of self-determination; that is, he made ethics dependent on the power of decision and not on a consolidated social structure such as the State.

The concept of freedom expounded by Hegel has many meanings, but it is enough here to note one of them—freedom as identified with intellectual maturity, whose opposite is intellectual obtuseness. The exercise of freedom implies a knowledge of its basic elements and motives. Freedom does not remove man from reality; it raises reality to the level of consciousness, seeks to divest it of its sensuous wrappings and to make it more amenable to cognition. From this point of view, we can say that freedom has no ethical significance but only a theoretical, speculative meaning. Hirsch's conception, however, identifies freedom with spirit and places it in opposition to existence, ignoring the mutual complementary relationship between freedom and reality, wherein reality is the given content and freedom the conscious knowledge thereof. Hirsch emphasizes the sharp differences between freedom and reality whereas Hegel identifies freedom with reality.[36]

These differences between Hegel and Hirsch are not fortuitous. Since the problem of ethics does not occupy the central place in Hegel's system, it is not surprising that his concept of freedom should not have an exclusively ethical significance. Whatever ethical meaning it has is derived from the presence of the concrete individual within the general Whole, not from the subjective decisions that man is required to make. Hirsch's approach, however, is from the very outset closely bound to the ethical problem and to the antagonism between spirit and nature, in which ethics seeks to assert itself and acquire and independent status. In other words, Hegel's concept of freedom is part and parcel of his monistic system and Hirsch's concept is, like that of Formstecher, based on a meta-physical dualism of spirit and nature.

The proper task of religion is the actualization and the inward acquisition of freedom as the result of man's self-determination in the face of nature. The entire life of religion is imbued with ethical meaning because it is based on the relation between man as he is and the acquisition of freedom, the object of his striving, and emerges from the dualism in man's existence between nature and spirit or freedom.

Hirsch's radical treatment of the ethical problem was the result of his efforts to introduce ethical content into religion and to place it in a dualistic context at a point where nature and spirit intersect. From a negative point of view, an even more significant factor was his failure to grant religion an element of paramount importance, namely, man's relation to God. The explanation for this has many aspects but fundamentally it is rooted in a basic principle of Hirsch's system, which considers ethics to be part of anthropology, a principle that requires additional comment.

We cannot speak at all of a relation to God; only finite things are related to one another.[37] In order to exclude God from a religious *relation* Hirsch made use of a logical, metaphysical reason. Since the category of relation can exist only in the finite world, it was necessary at the very outset to exclude the relation between finite man and Infinite God, since it can hardly be confined to the limits of the relational concept in general. As expounded by Hirsch, this concept, moreover, is necessarily a reciprocal one—that is, if man is related to God, it follows that God is related to man,[38] and this in turn detracts from God's uniqueness and singularity as conceived by religion. Hirsch believed that the chief error in modern religious thought (he undoubtedly had in mind Friedrich Schleiermacher [1768–1834], who was sharply criticized by the Hegelian school) was to base religion on the relationship between man and God. Schleiermacher, who defined the religious consciousness as the sense of man's absolute dependence on God, thus making feeling the ultimate test of religious truth, was in fact obliged to stress the other aspect of the relation, namely, God's dependence on man.

From this it may be inferred that the sphere of practical ethics, which is co-extensive with that of religion, is confined solely to human activity. The emancipation of spirit from its entanglements with objective reality and its removal to the subjective realm of feeling is here expressed in an extreme form. Religion can now dispense with one pole of the theological axis, God, since religious activity takes place in the human sphere alone,[39] between man as nature and man as spirit, and derives its content from the struggle of the spirit to overcome and eventually to subsume nature.[40]

Besides a logical-metaphysical reason, which is designed to investigate the meaning of the relational concept in general, there is also a religious reason for excluding God from the religious relation—namely, that an Infinite God is too exalted to be related to man. The introduction of this religious motive gives rise to an astonishing paradox in the religious consciousness—a religious reason is advanced for transferring the central core of religion from God to man. This humanizing theology, which Hirsch believed to be the essence of religion, is in fact nothing but anthropology, and was used by Feuerbach to deny existence to God, except as an idealized object of human consciousness, the outward projection of man's inward nature.

The conception of religion as anthropology raises the question of the nature of the religious relationship, which is clearly not between man and God, but an immanent activity within man himself towards the realization of greater freedom, an inner struggle between the natural and spiritual elements in man that strives to convert potential into actual freedom. This view tends to approach Feuerbach's conception of religion as the deification of man but, properly speaking, Hirsch's religious ideal or his principle of freedom has no personal image. Man is not related to himself as a personality with definite qualities (as in Feuerbach's view), but to an impersonal inner ideal, characterized by the metaphysical element of spirit or by the ethical element of freedom, elements not endowed with a personal image. We can therefore say that for Hirsch the religious relation is that between man as he is and the endless task of perfecting his innate capacity for freedom.

The principal problem of this anthropological conception of religion is to determine God's place in it. Since God has been displaced by man in the religious relation, Hirsch is constrained to restore him surreptitiously by introducing the principle of *imitatio Dei*. "God and not nature is sovereign, and man, like God, must be the ruler and not the servant of nature."[41] God is not the object of the relationship and even the imitation of God does not take place within the religious relation, but merely serves man as a pattern of behavior. The ideal of the spirit's dominion over nature, which man strives to realize, finds its perfect consummation in God, imposing on man the obligation to follow in His ways. That which in man is an incomplete striving and volition is in God brought to perfection.

Spirit is the element that man and God have in common, according to Hirsch, and it is therefore incumbent upon man to develop his latent capacity for freedom and within the limits of the human sphere to support the spirit in its struggle against nature. It is this activity, not prayer, or adoration, or even attachment to God, that brings man closer to the divine Being. When man lives in conformity to his own nature, he lives in conformity with the Creator.[42] But even this life of the Creator is not lived beyond the confines of the human sphere. Hirsch does not speak of living in conformity with the *will* of the Creator, but with the Creator, since the Being of God as spirit, not the imperative which has its source in being, is here the predominant factor. This element that man and God have in common is expressed by Hirsch in extreme form: The human and the divine will is essentially the same.[43] Man's desire for freedom, which is itself a product of freedom, has a metaphysical aspect in that freedom or spirit rooted in God's being. In this conception God, and even man, to the extent that he is identical with God, is nothing but spirit in the metaphysical sense. In other words, man identifies himself with God in the sphere of the spirit, which includes being or active spirit as well as the aspiration to sustain and promote the spirit.

Hirsch maintains, nevertheless, that the life of God is not of this world and differs from that of the human spirit.[44] After he stresses the identification of God and man in the common sphere of the spirit, he proceeds to point out the differences between them. Since

God is an active spirit, he transcends God and the world. An appreciation of the distinction between the *desire* for spirit and freedom and the actual *existence* of these qualities is necessary in order to understand the transcendent nature of God. What is the source of this human aspiration for spirit and freedom? Why is man only potentially free, and why is he bound to the endless task of converting potential into actual freedom? The answer is to be found in the circumstance that man is a curious mixture of two metaphysical elements, nature and spirit, a combination that has an ethical character derived from the metaphysical nature of the combination itself. The more man seeks to overcome nature, in order to ensure the triumph of the spirit, the greater the danger of embracing the life of the senses. Freedom is a quality of the spirit that makes man a spiritual being—that is, it gives him the freedom to choose one of two alternatives: to transform potential into actual freedom, or to refrain from doing so and remain in the sphere of nature. A decision in favor of spirit is an ethical act that constitutes the very core of ethics and the decision to forgo this prerogative is, in the religious sense, sin. It follows that man, who has the power to decide between nature and spirit, is by the same token a being who can sin—that is, embrace nature and remain within its confines. God, on the other hand, is pure spirit, and his spiritual nature does not oblige him to make choices in favor of either spirit or nature. In contrast to man's spirituality, which consists in the struggle to reach a goal, God's spirituality is a given fact that flows from His unique nature and gives Him a singular status in relation to man and the world. The religious ideal, which we have formulated as the supremacy of freedom, is for Hirsch the identity of man and God, which every individual should strive to establish.[45] Hirsch rejects a relationship between man and God that is not logically justified as a relationship of the finite to the Infinite, insisting that man and God are united only in spirit; consequently, man's duty is to free himself from nature and become pure spirit. Man does not aspire to be one with God; his goal is an autonomous human activity directed towards higher human ends. *Man identifies himself with God by becoming himself.* It is interesting to note how the mystical idea of the union of man with God found its way into this idealistic-ethical conception, although this union here is not consummated at the intersection between immanence and transcendence where the finite and the Infinite interlock, but within the sphere of immanence itself where the luminous spirit confronts opaque nature and where the potential yearns to become actual.

Considering the general consistency of Hirsch's religious argument, it is surprising that he should make God transcendent and proceed to draw from this consequences of considerable religious import. We can sum up his position in brief by saying that religion is the relation of man to himself by virtue of his innate capacity for freedom. This would incline us to believe that man's liberation from the state of nature and his ascent to the level of spirit would also be the result of his own unaided efforts, and his deliberate decision to avail himself of his unique prerogative of freedom. But at this point Hirsch finds a nail on which to hang the relationship between man and God; he finds it necessary to introduce God as the source of this relationship of man to himself, a relationship which is the essence of religion.[46] Religion is not the relationship to God but the relationship of man to himself whose source is in God.

This thought requires further comment, since it contains a view of the nature of man's dependence on God from which we can draw certain consequences concerning the idea of Creation. We have already observed that man is a combination of two disparate elements, nature and spirit, and that his ideal task is to aid the spirit in its progressive illumination of nature, a task in which man asserts his true essence and at the same time emulates God. The problem that faced Hirsch was to determine the source of man's ability to choose between these two metaphysical elements. The static metaphysical point of view gives priority to neither and provides no criterion to determine preferences. From a dynamic ethical point of view, however, spirit is clearly the superior element and asserts its unmistakable sovereignty. How is this transition from the metaphysical equality of the two components to the ethical superiority of one of them achieved? In answer to this question Hirsch found it necessary to posit man's dependence on God. Man is unable to make the decision without reliance on his dependence on God, who induces man to effect the transition from the static existence of the two elements to the dynamic ideal of the one. *God does not appear within the religious relation but at its beginning.*

A unique idea of Creation emerges from this exposition by Hirsch (whose incomplete elaboration drew sharp criticism from Steinheim), since it is not related to the two metaphysical elements on which the static ontological nature of man rests. The two elements are given, one active (nature) and the other potential (spirit), so that it is not the *combination* of the elements of which man and the world are composed whose existence is dependent on God, but the *relation* between them. As the predominant factor that favors the spirit, God is not the Creator of the elements but the Architect, as it were, of the ethical edifice erected on the given elements—not a cosmological edifice, such as we find in various Gnostic systems which conceive God as a demiurge. In other words, as the source of man's relation to himself, God does not fulfill a metaphysical-cosmological but an ethical function, and this restriction of God's function to the ethical sphere detracts from the idea of God as Creator. Creation, according to Hirsch, is not the relation of God to a world composed of nature and spirit, but the determination of relation between nature and spirit.

In Hirsch's religious system God's function may be regarded from two points of view:

(a) God is the Lord of nature and His being pervades it through the active superiority of spirit over nature. From this point of view God is conceived as man's ideal, summoning him not to emulate God's ethical nature (as advocated by those systems that make God the Paragon of morality and man's practical conduct) but His metaphysical nature. If, then, man's ethical striving, which is the essence of religion, consists in the emulation of a metaphysical Being, we can better understand how these two lines of thought, the ethical and the metaphysical, converge in Hirsch's system—namely, by raising metaphysical being to the level of an ethical ideal.

(b) God as pure spiritual Being dwells beyond nature and has no need to overcome it, but He makes it possible for man to do so within the human sphere and thus ascend to true essence. In Hirsch's system God is assigned a double function. From the standpoint of man, God serves as the Pattern for human conduct; from the standpoint of God himself, He is the Source which inclines man to decide in favor of spirit. We can sum up Hirsch's position as follows: Just as we observed previously that the relation of man to God through imitation is in fact an immanent relationship of man to himself, of potential to actual man, we now see that this is a transcendent relationship. Man is not related to himself as an active spiritual being except through his relation to God, who initiates and fosters man's relation to himself and who dwells beyond the confines of anthropology in the realm of metaphysics or theology.

The aspect of man's dependence on God gives Hirsch's conception a religious complexion. Man does not acquire dominion over nature by his own unaided efforts. This power comes to him as a boon from without and by virtue of it he becomes the recipient of freedom or God's mercy.[47] Here we feel the full force of the religious paradox: Dependence on God is the source of man's freedom and his power over nature. This paradox can be reconciled, however, when we consider that it is not dependence that is the source of freedom but God's mercy that comes as a result of it. This divine mercy or grace does not forgive sins, as in Protestant theology, but comes to man as a gift of freedom to make a decision in favor of spirit and to refrain from sin. This grace is to be found at the beginning and not at the end of man's career and for this reason Hirsch rejects the Christian doctrine of original sin: The goal of divine government is nothing more than the eternal self-liberation of man and of mankind, the life of mankind in freedom.[48]

The problem of man's dependence on God requires further clarification from the standpoint of revelation. Steinheim distinguished between the two meanings of this concept that are generally confused: (a) the manifestation of the nonsensual by the sensual; (b) the oracular words, statutes, and laws explaining the source of Creation and the origin of the world and its formation.[49] From the first point of view, the nature of revelation is seen as the penetration of the spiritual being into natural existence; from the second, which Steinheim accepts as the biblical idea of revelation, it is the communication of truths from God to man for the purpose of instructing him. What has previously been said concerning Hirsch's philosophy and religious views does not coincide with what Steinheim considers the biblical concept of revelation. God does not communicate to man the content of His teachings; Hirsch emphasizes, rather, that general truths are not foreign to man's spirit—that is, they are not conveyed to him through revelation. "The spirit of man immediately attests that these truths are truths of the spirit."[50] Hirsch is thus led to differentiate between common consciousness and the philosophical concept: The former perceives these truths without being able to find a firm basis for them; the latter renders them positive since they are rooted in spirit. The spirit subdues the content to which it has always had an affinity[51]—that is, from the standpoint of the content of the ethical and metaphysical conception, spirit is not dependent on God and need not be communicated by means of revelation. For Hirsch, God's revelation is His guarantee for the metaphysical order of the world; this is not Creation *ex nihilo*, however, but simply the guarantee for the fixed order of the world. This guarantee also serves to urge the world to follow ethical ideals. Revelation, according to Hirsch, has no instructive or edifying meaning; its significance is ontological.

The consideration of Hirsch's religious and philosophical principles leads us to the concept of sin which occupies a central place in his system. Religion is defined as the relation between the active "I" in nature and the potential "I" in spirit. Sin repudiates the spirit and resists the efforts of the authentic "I" to liberate itself from nature. "Sensibility and nature, although known to man as something relatively external, seek to assert themselves at the expense of freedom. They seek to enhance their customary activities and to offer man greater sensual pleasures. If man succumbs to these allurements, then pleasure becomes for him the surrogate value for his "I" and for his freedom—and this is sin."[52] Sin constitutes a shift of values in the autonomous human sphere—nature and the senses instead of the spirit and freedom are taken to be the highest value.

Neither nature nor the senses in and of themselves constitute sin. These are but given metaphysical factors, and as such they are indispensable to the constitution of the world and of man. The transition from the metaphysical-ontological facts to their ethical evaluation is bound up with man's decision, either in favor of nature and the life of the senses (in which case he enters the realm of sin), or to invest the metaphysical entity with value (in which case the ontological-factual view is transformed to an ethical-axiological view).

In other words, the possibility of sinning is a necessary quality of man's nature, since he is a mixture of both nature and spirit. This possibility cannot be removed, since it inheres in the ontologically given entities themselves. Man sins when he transforms this latent possibility into an active reality. Man must of necessity sin—this inclination is rooted in the very nature of existence as it is—but it is also incumbent upon him to forgo this possibility and to resist the temptation. This imperative is the essence of ethics which is, in the final analysis, nothing but religion. This possibility of sinning must remain within the confines of possibility only and should never be realized.[53]

Additional light is here cast on the quality of freedom, whereby man is enabled to emerge from the sphere of nature to that of spirit. The same quality of freedom, however, also enables man to decide to adhere to nature and not to venture into the realm of the spirit. It can thus be said that freedom is an instrumentality of the spirit that operates in two directions: If man casts in his lot with nature and identifies himself with its essence, he *sins*; if he decides in favor of the spirit and the realization of its potential powers within him, he has embraced the life of religion.[54]

In this conception the order of the two metaphysical elements that constitute man's essence has been reversed. Hirsch first affirms that nature is the active element in man and spirit the potential element, but in discussing the essence of sin he holds that, as part and parcel of nature, it is a potential element. This change is the result of the altered perspective from which we now look at the problem. From the metaphysical point of view with its exclusively ontological interest, nature is active existence and spirit ideal or potential existence. But in ethics, which introduces the element of the moral imperative and the ought, the order is reversed—active nature becomes potential, and potential spirit becomes active. This new order brings with it a change in the level of existence. The possibility of sin, as we have observed, is derived from man's nature. But sin as a reality is accidental; as a creature endowed with the power of making decisions, man can decide not to realize the potential.[55]

It has been made clear that for Hirsch religion is the relation of man to himself; and sin, which is the opposite of religion, is also the relation of man to himself. Religion is the relation of the natural to the spiritual man, which comes into being by virtue of an ethical decision. Sin is the relation of natural man to natural man, and it, too, comes into being as the result of decision. The relation between man and God is absent in both. Sin is not directed against God or His imperatives; it is a violation of man's essence, an autonomous category of man. Formstecher observed that, from the standpoint of God, an unethical act is a sin, and an ethical act a good deed. In Hirsch's conception there is no room for such a double point of view. An unethical deed is a sin from the standpoint of man himself; there is no criterion that can be applied external to man. Typically, Hirsch here, introduces into the autonomous sphere of ethics a religious category derived from a heteronomous conception.

The problem of sin sheds light on Hirsch's idea of God and the distinction between Him and man. Sin adheres only to man, for he is a creature of nature, composed of two elements; it cannot apply to God whose essence is only one element, active spirit.

This metaphysical distinction between God and man lends additional emphasis to the principle of the imitation of God, which is an important aspect of Hirsch's religious ideal. The decision not to sin is a human obligation. Sin is not to be regarded as necessary and innate, since man is free to imitate God, who is the Lord of nature; it is part of the human sphere and does not apply to God's imperatives but signifies a *metaphysical* withdrawal from the divine Being. The distinction between man and God is best exhibited in the phenomenon of sin, which is the failure to rise above nature, a realm of existence not found in God at all. Since sin is an autonomous fact confined to the human sphere, from God's point of view, it must be understood not in its ethical aspect as the abrogation of an imperative, but in its metaphysical aspect as a withdrawal from God's being. The peculiar mixture of meta-physics and ethics in Hirsch's conception is again evident. In God's sphere there is no room for ethics or for the imperative to overcome nature, since God must be viewed ontologically and is devoid of nature; nature is present, however, in the human sphere and it is man's specific task to rise above it, a task which is the inevitable result of his double nature. If we now apply the relation between ethics and metaphysics to the problem of man's imitation of God, we can say that ethics is the instrument by virtue of which man, who is a combination of nature and spirit, is able within his sphere to insure the victory of the latter over the former. According to Hirsch, ethics is identified with religion as a necessary category of human reality; the purpose of ethics and religion, however, is not to arrest and immobilize human nature as it is, even to express it, but to overcome actual existence by infusing it with spirit.

It is somewhat surprising that Hirsch, who starts from rational-istic presuppositions derived from the speculative philosophy of the nineteenth century, should advocate the reality of miracles. A miracle is an infraction of the physical process by God's direct in-tervention in the natural order. It expresses God's sovereignty and the subordination of nature to spirit and clearly reveals that God and not nature is the Lord of the world.[56] Through miracle, God, who is devoid of nature, is able to establish contact with it and display His power by abrogating and annulling its laws. Just as God overcomes nature through miracle, man in his own sphere performs a miracle by refraining from sin.

To this view of miracles Hirsch added another aspect, not from the sphere of the relation of God to nature, but from the sphere of the relation of God to man. Since man is always prone to sin and desires to remain in its toils, God created in miracle the means to oppose sin and its dire consequences without detracting from hu-man freedom.[57] Even if man does not decide in favor of spirit but clings to nature, he does not remain entirely without hope and when his autonomous acts have lost all merit, God's grace reveals itself. Miracle is here directed to man, not to nature, and is iden-tified with a grace that is designed not to pardon sin, but to rescue man from the toils of nature when he can no longer save himself. Hirsch's view of sin occupies an intermediate place between the Christian doctrine of original sin and the position set forth by Hermann Cohen; the latter considers grace a divine gift to reconcile the penitent with God, who does not desire the death of the sinner but that he repent and live. According to Hirsch, man is able to liberate himself from nature and sin by his own unaided efforts (which is not the Christian conception), but if he fails, God appears and rescues him by means of a miracle.

The antagonism between religion, which assures the spirit of its victory over nature, and sin, which adheres to nature, became a standard principle in the typological description of the historical religions. Hirsch, like Formstecher, made a typological distinction between Judaism as a religion of the spirit and idolatry as a religion of nature, but he laid greater emphasis on the ethical aspect and found no need for the cosmological aspect of Creation. Idolatry clings to nature or, to put it negatively, in idolatry the spirit is loath to be spirit.[58] Idolatry is basically not devoid of spirit, since the decision to cleave to nature and not follow spirit is itself a decision of the spirit. Krochmal, who insisted on the spiritual element in all religions, emphasized the existence of an objective element that appears in the various religions in the form of God, whereas Hirsch emphasized the existence of a subjective element that resides in man's power of decision. The contradiction at the heart of the idolatrous religions, however, springs from the fact that in them spirit succumbs to itself. Idolatry aids and abets nature in its antagonism to the spirit.[59] Thus it negates the reality of human freedom, which basically means liberating man from the chain of causality in the natural order and placing him within another chain of causality, that of the spirit. The antagonism of idolatry to the causality of the spirit is pure deception[60] since opposition to spirit and subjugation to nature are also decisions of the spirit.

Seen from this point of view, idolatry appears to be the religion of sin—that is, a religion that adheres to nature and seeks to invest it with value. The contradiction within idolatry cannot be grasped from its nature, but is best seen when placed in opposition to the religion of the spirit: Idolatry is the religion of sin and Judaism is the religion of ethics. Idolatry widens the breach between man and God, for in sin man sinks deeper and deeper into nature, the realm that is completely absent in God. There is no room in idolatry for the positive religious ideal, since it does not believe that man can liberate himself by his own efforts and is also ignorant of the *imitatio Dei*. Judaism bases human life on spirit and draws man nearer to God's metaphysical essence; the primary task of a Jew is to establish the unity of man and God.[61] Here again we note the mystical element that appears within the metaphysical conception. The religious ideal is that of the unity of man and God; it means giving allegiance to the ethical imperative in order to sustain the spirit in its struggle against nature, the ultimate goal being the union of man and God, a goal which is both metaphysical and mystical.

Whereas idolatry is the religion of nature and sin, Judaism is the religion of spirit and freedom which regards the *possibility* of sin as a necessary quality in man, but enjoins him to forgo its realization. Here also lies the difference between Judaism and Christianity, although Hirsch is careful to distinguish between early Christianity and that of St. Paul. Judaism looks upon early Christianity as a daughter religion,[62] but realizes at the same time that this added nothing new to the fundamental principles of Judaism. The breach between Judaism and Christianity became irreparable with the Pauline doctrine of original sin, with the doctrine of the inevitable participation of all men in Adam's transgression and the assumption that man is unable to free himself from sin.[63] Paul teaches not only the possibility of sin latent in all men but its necessity, thus basing religious experience on the fact of sin—that is, on man's irremediable need to adhere to nature, abrogating his relation to the spirit. Pauline Christianity shows us how an idolatrous element entered the original conception of Judaism and succeeded in changing it completely. Each in his own way, Hirsch, Formstecher, and Steinheim, consider Christianity a religious syncretism composed of Judaism and idolatry. It does not put the union of man and God at the center of its religious thinking; on the contrary, it removes man from God; we might even say it leaves him destitute and abandoned by his Maker.[64]

An additional factor that distinguishes Judaism from Christianity, one that had already appeared in apostolic times, concerns the central place occupied by the personality of Jesus. From the Jewish point of view, Jesus accomplished what he did because he was born a Jew, studied the Law and the Prophets, and strove to be what a Jew should be,[65] in order that every Jew might attain the level of Jesus.[66] (We must bear in mind that the birth of Jesus as a Jew was emphasized by the Reform Movement in Judaism in which Hirsch had a prominent part.) Christianity believes that Jesus alone was able to free himself from sin—that is, to transcend the natural realm and rise to the sphere of spirit; Judaism, however, believes that every Jew has the strength to undergo Jesus' spiritual development and rise to his high level. Hirsch himself mentions Abraham as a perfect type of God-fearing man who succeeded in realizing the religious ideal. Clearly, Hirsch is here opposing the Christian view by introducing the basic principle that the religious life is the autonomous life of man, that man *qua* man is obliged to strive to realize the religious ideal and is in a position to do so by virtue of his autonomous efforts and innate powers. Hirsch has here restricted the scope but not the significance of autonomy; he no longer speaks of man as man but of Judaism and of the man within Judaism, injecting the objective factor of birth in order to emphasize this restriction.

This analysis of Hirsch's philosophical and religious conception[67] reveals its framework as metaphysical but its content as ethical. Ethics, however, is a manifestation of man's finitude and his desire to participate in the Divine; the realization of ethics lifts man above himself and draws him closer to the metaphysical Being, that is, to the Spirit that is God. In the reaffirmation and consummation of the ethical ideal the metaphysical framework itself is transformed into content. Moreover, the elevation of ethics to the level of content is possible in Hirsch's religious conception only when the metaphysical framework is nourished by the two ontological elements of nature and spirit. Ethics itself constitutes religion, since religion is here closely bound to the principles of dualistic metaphysics.

D. THE ABSOLUTE SPIRITUAL

The intellectual world of Nachman Krochmal (1785–1840) was characterized by idealistic concepts common to the nineteenth century, derived from philosophical tendencies that stemmed either from Schelling[68] or from Hegel. From this point of view there is a striking similarity between Krochmal and the exponents of Jewish philosophical idealism in the nineteenth century (Formstecher and Hirsch), although we know little of the literary and personal relations of these thinkers. The idealistic strain in Krochmal's thinking was, however, not as prominent as the influence of traditional Jewish thought, particularly that of Maimonides. Krochmal's systematic problem appears to be a dual one. On the one hand, he defined the essence of Judaism by emphasizing its uniqueness and isolating it from other religious conceptions, although the typological problem did not concern him as much as it did the other Jewish idealists; on the other hand, he sought to find a basis for the absolute value of Judaism, and in this respect continued the traditions of medieval Jewish philosophy.

Krochmal's method of dealing with the essence of Judaism differs from that of his contemporaries. The central theme which had engaged idealism up to that time was the antagonism between nature and spirit and the position of Judaism as a religion of the spirit. This antagonism is not to be found in Krochmal's philosophy, which falls entirely within the realm of the spirit. All religious faiths are spiritual, he states; even in the awe felt by the lowest savages who inhabit the wilderness, there is an immaterial aspect, something that is not particular, limited, and evanescent but contains a spiritual core which abides through the infinite number of external and material changes to which it gives rise.[69] Since no religion is utterly devoid of a spiritual core, there is no point in making a distinction between a religion that is attached to nature and one that is attached to spirit. The differences between the various religions must be regarded as differences of *degree* within the realm of the spirit, depending on the scope, depth, and quality of their spiritual insights. Interestingly, Krochmal, who came from Galicia and was steeped in Hebrew literature, had a more tolerant attitude to religion than his enlightened contemporaries of the West, the exponents of the Reform Movement who were attached to German philosophical idealism.

Two basic consequences flow from the religious conception set forth by Krochmal as against the positions of his Western contemporaries. Krochmal sees no antagonism between spirit and nature, and hence no need for religion to decide in favor of spirit in its struggle against nature. Since the central problem of religion is not ethics, or the place of practical conduct within the religious sphere, as stressed by Formstecher and Hirsch, they receive no systematic treatment in Krochmal's philosophy. He confines the content of religion to the speculative realm, so that the religious ideal is converted into a speculative ideal: The Enlightenment is the perfection of man's inner capacity—that is, his spiritual self-consciousness. There is no need to establish a relationship between the spiritual basis of religion and the practical deed, since the latter is part of a cognitive content that is comprehended through speculation.

The second of the two consequences concerns Krochmal's interpretation of spirit, the primary concept of religious idealism. For Formstecher and Hirsch, spirit was endowed with two fundamental qualities, freedom and self-consciousness. Formstecher emphasized both qualities equally, whereas Hirsch placed the greater emphasis upon freedom, the quality that confers ethical meaning on spirit. For Krochmal, however, the meaning of the concept spirit is completely speculative and possesses two related qualities: On the one hand, it is the content of cognition (the objective pole, as it were, of theoretical speculation); on the other hand, cognitive insight or conception (the subjective pole of theoretical speculation). In Krochmal's system, spirit is also endowed with self-consciousness, which is called "spiritual consciousness in itself."[70] But this quality is not a cognitive faculty or the power of decision accompanying consciousness. Since self-consciousness is the highest degree of conception, its content completes itself and has no need of external insights. The shift to the speculative realm in Krochmal's system is clearly seen in the neutralization of ethical conduct in the human sphere, and in the activity of the spirit becoming a content that conceives and comprehends itself.

A distinction also emerges between Krochmal and his contemporaries with respect to the ideal of religious perfection. With Formstecher and Hirsch, this ideal was the decision of the spirit to triumph over nature, an ethical decision in favor of one sphere of being and only one; the ideal implicit in Krochmal's religious and philosophical conception is the ideal of totality. The highest level of religious development, Judaism, is bound to the most total spiritual content. This level, however, does not include spirit and nature as one, since nature as purely material existence is, as we have seen, only a transitional step to the sphere of religious speculation. Totality is richer and more comprehensive than the isolated and fragmentary spiritual elements. Needless to say, this change in idealism also linked the speculative aim to the ideal of totality.

The conclusion we are bound to draw, although somewhat extremely formulated, is that whatever pantheistic elements are to be found in Jewish idealistic philosophy of the nineteenth century are contained in Krochmal's system. Formstecher and Hirsch completely dismissed pantheism as an expression of idolatry that identified God with nature, whereas the ideal of totality set forth by Krochmal served to support a pantheistic interpretation. At any rate, just as we speak of panlogism in Hegel we can speak of a panspiritualism in Krochmal.

Krochmal's central problem in propounding the essential concepts of Judaism, finding a basis for its absolute value as against the prevailing philosophical systems, was not new. Indeed, his solution is not essentially different from that put forward by the Jewish philosophers of the Middle Ages. Since there are certain given facts that constitute the essence of absolute value, Jewish philosophy was chiefly concerned with identifying them with Judaism, or, to put it differently, with demonstrating that those absolute facts which are not specifically related to Judaism nevertheless appear fully developed within it. This approach does not depend on changes occurring in the course of time that might affect the content of these facts. The principal element in this approach endures throughout all attempts made to find a basis for the absolute value of Judaism in terms of the cognitive element embodied within it. This was the method adopted by Krochmal when he sought a solution for his problem. He accepted the known concepts as fixed and unalterable and then proceeded to demonstrate that they were compatible with Judaism. The critical question that immediately arises concerns the meaning of these concepts and their religious content. For the sake of brevity, we can describe this method as the identification of religion with philosophy.

Raising the content of Judaism to the level of an absolute value is made possible by identifying it with the "absolute spiritual." This removes the partition dividing religion from philosophy and permits us to describe the philosophical data as absolute.

The "absolute spiritual" has more than one meaning. It is defined as the source of all spiritual being and containing all things.[71] Here the "absolute spiritual" is defined by Krochmal from the standpoint of its relation to individualized spirits—that is, to specific fragmentary spiritual existences which he mentions in connection with the character of various peoples. In contradistinction to these individualized spiritual beings, the "absolute spiritual" is an all-inclusive spirit which is at the same time the source of these beings. The individualized beings have existence only insofar as they are dependent upon the "absolute spiritual," which is thus both the source and the content of the totality. This is one way of defining its essence. The "absolute spiritual" is also defined as the highest content of cognition, rising step by step from sensible images to universal concepts;[72] this is not from the viewpoint of its position in the world of spiritual beings which are dependent on it as their source and included within it, but in terms of its position among the graduated steps of cognition which are related to concepts. If any religious significance is attached to these distinctions within the absolute spiritual (Krochmal himself does not make them)—that is, if we make them dependent on the concept of God—then the first distinction serves to emphasize the nature of God as the source of existence and the origin of intellect,[73] and the last to emphasize the nature of religious consciousness whose object is the "absolute spiritual."

How did Krochmal proceed to identify the content of Judaism with the "absolute spiritual"? He saw the peculiar character of religious consciousness in its similarity to the philosophical concept. The content, he says, found in faith in the form of thought or feeling is also found in the intellectual analysis of faith carried over from sentiment and imagination to the form of universal intellectual concepts.[74] It is necessary, in other words, to discover and formulate the inner meaning of the religious imagination. The infinite and absolute spiritual is "the rationalized form of the speech of the Lord God" and of the words: ". . . that I may dwell among them: I am the Lord their God" (Ex. 29:46) which, in logical language, means, that all spirituality is rooted in Him and emanates from His spirit.[75] In other words, from the outset Krochmal sets up a scale of cognitive steps for faith wherein he finds room for the corresponding cognitive ideal. The task of cognition is to take the sensible forms given to it from outside the soul or from the soul itself and convert them into concepts—that is, into universal forms joined and united to one another.[76] Faith, whose cognitive instruments are the forms of original thought, is a step towards perfect cognition in which instrument and content coincide. We thus find that faith has no peculiar characteristic of its own; its ideal is simply the speculative ideal. The speculation, moveover, is not realized in its purest form, since it is still attached to the instruments of cognition which must be overcome in order to arrive at the completely purified thoughts of reason.[77]

By this identification of religion with philosophy religion is deprived of its special value and independent basis—which was given it by medieval philosophy—as well as its revelatory character. Regarded as an instrument of cognition, religion is a purely psychological concept, unsupported by the analysis of the nature of religious consciousness or by prophecy (as in Maimonides). Religious consciousness has no criterion of its own that is independent of an external cognitive criterion and religion has no alternative but to submit to it. Krochmal sees Judaism as the typical bearer of religious content and feels no need to offer proof in support of this hypothesis. But among the questions that he designates as debatable we find the question concerning the possibility of knowing God. It is clear, however, that his general tendency (since he relegates religion to the speculative realm) is decidedly in favor of religious content, even though religion is thereby deprived of its proper sphere and peculiar character.[78]

The failure to grant religion a sphere of its own is related to the concept of the beginning of things. Krochmal advances a number of methodological arguments in opposition to the tendency that seeks to go back to the primal source and beginning of things, that would automatically clarify questions and invalidate opposing derivations.[79] This aims at a middle course among the conflicting views; it regards religion not as a sphere existing side by side with philosophy, but as a transitional step to a more perfect sphere of pure speculative cognition. This compromise is based on the existence of given spheres, and attempts to find a definite content between religion and philosophy that would serve to mediate between them. Going back to sources defines the place occupied by the spheres, but without accepting them as given. From the speculative point of view, we can reverse the order of the spheres and assign the highest place to religion. Krochmal, however, avoids this possibility by restricting the essence of religion to the speculative *process* and by relating the special nature of this process to "the early conceptions at the beginning of thought," which inevitably are superseded by the more perfect cognitive instruments—that is, by the concepts of reason. Faith in God and in His Law is beyond doubt the beginning of knowledge, learning, and man's education, and is prior to them in time and nature; the knowledge of faith, however, is last in time but first in rank, being higher than reason; that is, general, divine understanding implanted in man is higher than conceptions at the beginning of thought and, needless to say, higher than sentiments of the heart.[80] The priority of faith in time is due to a psychological reason—that is, at the very beginning it was bound to the image, and not to the intellect or the concept. But this priority in time has no metaphysical-religious ground; what was given it by medieval philosophy and by philosophy at the time of Krochmal, the certainty of religious perception, was merely a widespread assumption. Krochmal rejected every possibility to establish religion as a special province and merely assigned to it a place in the scale of cognition; as such it cannot be regarded as a necessary expression of the absolute spiritual. There is no place in Krochmal's system for the principle found in Hegel, that even the finite, subjective spirit (not just the absolute spirit) is a necessary vesture of the idea,[81] and that all individual forms of the spirit develop within it as in a seed. We are generally obliged to assume a psychological and not a metaphysical necessity for the religious form of perception. The "absolute spiritual" is the content of faith, but from the essence of faith we cannot derive the necessity for binding it to this particular content and to no other. Krochmal was able to find a basis for the absolute value of Judaism by making it a speculative, cognitive realm of faith, the conceptual forms at the beginning of thought simply being instrumental in making the transition to a more perfect conception.

The idea of establishing the independence of religion by adopting the view that it is the imaginative expression of rational truth was also dealt with by Hegel, and variously interpreted by his followers. The question that arose in the Hegelian school of thought was: How is it possible to take the content which has acquired a conceptual form and transform it into a content of religious consciousness; or how is it possible to retain the immanent content within its transcendent shell? Since they regarded transcendence as attached to the imaginative form, they tried to preserve it even after they had raised consciousness to the level of reason.[82] Such reservations, which result from the attempt to make religion an independent sphere by giving it a fixed place in a developing system, are not to be found in Krochmal, who in this matter uncompromisingly decided to do away with characteristically religious form in favor of more perfect rational knowledge.

The same question appeared in Jewish idealism, of which Krochmal was a foremost exponent. Hirsch had also advocated the view that identified religious content with philosophy; however, he defined the task of philosophy as against religion not as that of changing the imaginative to the conceptual form, but of finding a basis for the *necessity* of the content. In other words, philosophy does not abolish the religious form in order to put a higher form in its place. In everyday consciousness the content is known, Hirsch maintained, but its necessity is only felt and not based on conceptual reasons. The task of philosophy, changing neither the content nor the form of religious knowledge,[83] is to find the ground for the necessity of the spirit to posit the content that is only felt by general consciousness. The difference between religious and philosophic knowledge may be formulated as a difference in mode, not in form; that is, philosophic knowledge *knows* the ground for the necessity of the content whereas religious knowledge *receives* the content as *given*. To be sure, this conception assigns a superior place to philosophic knowledge rather than religious knowledge, but at the same time it preserves both the content and form of the latter. Krochmal does not attempt to distinguish these two forms of knowledge; the distinction he makes is between the form and the content of the religious consciousness.

We have thus far considered the relation between the two spheres of religion and philosophy. An analysis of the elements in the content of religion reveals that in Krochmal's system religion is completely subsumed under philosophy; the reason for the absolute character of Judaism is the fact that it can be assimilated by philosophy. The concept of God, which Krochmal identifies with the "absolute spiritual," is devoid of all the characteristics that adhere to a personal God.

The content of this religious conception can be summed up in the one phrase: God is the "absolute spiritual." It seems that Krochmal was of the opinion that the "root" element in the "absolute spiritual" is the one that brings this concept close to the God-concept and he defined this root as the nascent intellect,[84] the cause that contains within itself all the different kinds of causes.[85] Evidently, the "absolute spiritual" as root or source is distinct from all that is dependent upon it and serves as a concept having a different status and value than those of the effects. But in reality it is not possible for the "absolute spiritual" to maintain this separate status since it, too, is a whole that contains everything[86]—that is, every spiritual content is contained within it. From the standpoint of the concept of source it could be inferred that the "absolute spiritual" is separate from the various contents dependent upon it, just as effects are separate from the causes on which they depend; but from another point of view we must identify the "absolute spiritual" with these definite contents. Krochmal's words contain no suggestion of a dialectical reconciliation of this difficulty; by assuming the "absolute spiritual," the source of the spiritual development is limited in its actual content through the individual spirits alone. But we can, perhaps, interpret Krochmal's thought by saying that the "absolute spiritual" is the source of the process whose aim it is to provide the contents which unite into a complete entity.

It seems, however, that Krochmal was not of the opinion that the content of the process is the result of a development; he thus identified the source of the spiritual from the very outset with the content of these spiritual elements. The absolute spiritual is *ab initio* a general content to which nothing is attached for the purpose of development. Krochmal saw the content of the "absolute spiritual" sometimes as definite, individual embodiments, fragmentary spiritual elements distributed among the nations, and sometimes as a complete, inclusive embodiment which is the portion of Israel. There is no metaphysical reason for this reduplication and it seems that the two embodiments represent an ultimate fact. But since the source of its content is nothing more than the totality of the partial spiritual elements, we can understand the dependence of the individual spirits on the "absolute spiritual" as a dependence of the individual on the whole. The individual is included in the whole from the very outset. If there is any transition from one to another, it is a transition within the sphere of contents and not an ontological transition—that is, the whole does not create the individual by means of a definite act in time. It is evident that Krochmal placed the "absolute spiritual" in the sphere of contents and not in the sphere of beings; hence it is difficult to combine his system with the concept of causality, that is, to regard the "absolute spiritual" as an *active* cause. The dependence between the "absolute spiritual" and the individual spiritual elements is in reality the dependence of the "absolute spiritual" on itself. To designate the "absolute spiritual" as infinite does not remove the concept from the category of content, nor does it impart a shade of transcendence to the concept, since even an infinite concept means the totality of contents over against their fragmentation: the existence of a principle of spirit lies in its absolute truth.[87] It is clear that Krochmal sought to establish the special nature of the "absolute spiritual" by granting it the status of a source of spiritual reality. But as a source it performs no real function, since the source is identified with individual contents which are necessarily dependent upon it. *The "absolute spiritual" is a substance consisting of content, and does not of itself create reality.*

In this sphere of the relation between the "absolute spiritual" as the total content and the individual spirits included within it, there is obviously no place for the volitional impulse. The source, in the sense of the "absolute spiritual," has no volitional meaning. If Krochmal ascribes to the source a volitional aspect, he does so to preserve some distinction in the "absolute spiritual" and save it from being swallowed up in the sphere of contents. The will as a special function that is not theoretical and is also without content is able to assert the independence and the primacy of the absolute spiritual. It is paradoxical that the individual contents included from the very outset in the "absolute spiritual" should appear as the product of its volitional impulse. The will can break through the closed circle of contents and displace them. But no such volition, nor indeed any dynamic urge, is to be found in Krochmal's conception, at least not in the metaphysical sphere—as against the historical sphere which was his main concern. The spiritual contents are given both in the complete embodiments of the "absolute spiritual" and its fragmentary embodiment in individual spiritual elements which are the gods of the various peoples. Even though Hegel's dialectical method deprived spirit of its volitional character, it was still left with a certain vitality. The dialectical movement, which is the development of the latent contents, preserved an element of activity, albeit an activity that is theoretical and immanent and not volitional and transcendent. Here, too, we find a distinction between Krochmal and his contemporaries, Formstecher and Hirsch, who emphasized the element of freedom in the essence of the spirit and identified it with self-determination. They thus introduced the volitional factor at the beginning of their systems and assumed the active intervention of God in the order of the world through the agency of either Creation or of miracle. In Krochmal's conception the active aspect of spirit is not considered— spirit is content and the absolute spirit, the God of Israel, is the total content. Krochmal's spiritual monism here borders, as has already been suggested, on pantheism. Spirit is all and includes all within it, and the more it includes the higher it rises. The spirit that includes all is the God of Israel.

Needless to say, the "absolute spiritual" is devoid of personality. The immanent content of spiritual existence is not an active personality. It should be pointed out that Krochmal himself saw the crystallization of the spiritual content in the form of personality as a hypostasis and his thought here is surprisingly similar to that of Feuerbach. Take the sum of all the spirits that prevail within a people, Krochmal says, and make it a particular entity simply in name, along with the attributes that adhere to it, and you will note that just as the king displays within his person the representative qualities of his people externally for all to behold, a people's God represents its inner life in time and space from generation to generation; and this is the *rational form* assumed by the conceptual content.[88] This clearly explains how a definite spiritual quality becomes a distinct, divine power endowed with attributes and a personal image. Furthermore, the manifestations of the divine Essence as a power seemed to Krochmal to be an interpretation of the rational content within the intellectual conception. In other words, the inner meaning of the concept of Divine Being as personality is the immanent spiritual content raised to the level of the divine. A personal God is an intellectual concept, but a divine Being as immanent content is a concept of the understanding or else an idea. It seems that Krochmal took this general description of the nature of the understanding and of the rational essence from Hegel. The speculative task of the understanding is to separate the elements and the function of reason is to combine them. The activity of the spiritual content in separating the elements is the product of the understanding, but the activity that gives rise to the immanent modes in which this content manifests itself is the product of reason.

Krochmal's words are directed against the individual, spiritual elements, such as the "gods of the earth" and the "strange gods of the people," not against the "absolute spiritual" or the God of Israel. Even with respect to the latter, Krochmal attempts to give a rational interpretation of the intellectual form and concludes that the "absolute spiritual" and the infinite are rational forms of the words: "the Lord God is God."[89] Thus, in Judaism also the personal aspect of the "absolute spiritual" is conceived by Krochmal as an outer vesture or covering and nothing more. But even in this sphere he deprives the God-concept of this outer covering and seeks to understand its true, impersonal nature. The absolute value of Judaism is here given a basis by removing the God-concept from the sphere of the conceptual form that still clings to the personal covering, and transferring it to the rational sphere which discards the personal aspect and makes God a *neutral*, spiritual content.

This is not the place to analyze Krochmal's historical conception[90] in his attempt to find a basis for the absolute value of Judaism. But in metaphysics, where the problem properly belongs, it is clear that Krochmal identifies Judaism with philosophy, or rather with a definite philosophical system, whose fundamental principles, however, he fails to explain adequately. This identification of religion with philosophy applies to their respective spheres as well as to their content. The religious sphere is a transitional stage on the road to complete, philosophical knowledge, just as the religious concept of God is a transitional stage to the perfect concept of God, that is, the "absolute spiritual."

Steinheim was not acquainted with Krochmal's philosophical system, since his principal writings appeared before Zunz published Krochmal's *Guide to the Perplexed of Our Time*,[91] but it probably would have remained unknown to him in any case because of his ignorance of Hebrew literature. It is certain, however, that had he known it, he would have criticized it more severely than he did Formstecher and Hirsch.

6

The Road Back

S. L. STEINHEIM AND FRANZ ROSENZWEIG

A. THE TOTTERING FOUNDATIONS OF IDEALISM

The two currents of thought discussed thus far have in common the tendency to explain and justify the concept of Judaism in the light of rationalism, whether it be a rationalism rooted in ethical principles or in speculative theory. In Luzzatto's theory it is not faith but ethics that is placed in opposition to knowledge.

Contemporary with the idealistic movement in Jewish philosophy in the nineteenth century we find in discussions of the nature of Judaism a gradual shift from rationalism to irrationalism. From the negative point of view, this tendency sprang from the philosophical criticism of idealism prevalent in European philosophy in general and in Jewish philosophy in particular. During the 1830's idealism came under attack not only from Feuerbach and Marx, who impugned the religious strain in Hegel's philosophy, but also from religious thinkers who had adopted a theistic position. It was chiefly criticized for its insistence on deriving existence from logical principles which are incapable of comprehending the fullness and subtle texture of the phenomenal world. At the same time these thinkers sought to wean philosophy from its attachment to pantheism and restore its original allegiance to theism. This conception brought to the fore once more the importance of the volitional element in religious thought.

[149]

It seems that Steinheim's philosophical theory depended on this criticism of idealism. In his effort to make Judaism a pure faith he repudiated the conceptualism that characteristizes idealism, as Rosenzweig would do almost a century later. But whereas Steinheim based faith on the empirical world outside man, Rosenzweig identified it with the experience of man himself. Steinheim's strictures against idealism applied principally to the physical sphere and Rosenzweig's to the anthropological, a distinction that reflects the development of philosophical thought in the century that separated these two thinkers but does not detract from the essential affinity between them. (Rosenzweig mentions Steinheim only once in passing, and it is doubtful whether he was acquainted with him while writing his *Star of Redemption*.) Negatively expressed, the affinity consists in their common distastes for idealism; positively expressed, in their effort to restore to faith its nonrational basis.

B. REVELATION

The various currents of Jewish philosophical speculation in modern times to a large extent adhered to traditional Jewish thought. They attempted to justify the religious or theoretical content of Judaism by comparing it with certain philosophical systems or schools of thought and identifying it, in one way or another, with concepts or conceptual systems derived from philosophical currents outside of Judaism. This philosophical tendency of the generation was aptly described by Steinheim when he observed that Moses had become a follower of Hegel or Schelling. The attempt to attach philosophical significance to the Torah or to Moses is rooted in the fundamental notion that faith must be provided with a philosophical apparatus and imbued with speculative content, and the task of Jewish philosophy is seen as removing faith from traditional attachments and making it amenable to philosophic elaboration.[1]

This was not the course adopted by Moses Mendelssohn, for he made no attempt to justify the inner content of Judaism in the light of prevailing philosophical conceptions or to identify it with some accepted philosophical system. He circumscribed the religious sphere at the very outset and saw no need to submit it to philosophical scrutiny, since these two systems are totally diverse: Judaism moves in the sphere of practical deeds and commandments, and philosophy in the sphere of reason and speculative truths. Mendelssohn refrained from combining the two spheres not because of the autonomous nature of faith or Judaism, but because he confined Judaism to the realm of ethics. Against this view of Mendelssohn two basic arguments were advanced by Steinheim, one dealing with the social implications of this view and the other with the relationship between it and the body of principles laid down in the Torah. The Mendelssohnian conception of Judaism that confines it to practical deeds and an ethical way of life is described by Steinheim as one that leaves Judaism nothing but a wig and a beard, deprived of all contact with the basic things of life, both in the realm of speculation and of ethics, so that it was not strange that the wig and the beard were quickly transformed under the impact of secular Judaism into curls and braids in the latest style.[2] Mendelssohn further restricted the content of Judaism by holding that the purpose of divine Revelation was to acquaint man with the Law and not with the existence of the living God, thus removing God from the sphere of Judaism and changing its character from a faith to a system of laws, unaware that the Law is inferior to the assertion of the object of religion, God.[3]

The philosophical speculations of the generation were doomed to failure because of their tendency to introduce a foreign element into the inner content of Judaism, depriving its essence of religious character by denying that faith constitutes a special form of knowledge. This failure did not stem from the desire to preserve the autonomous character of Judaism, but from philosophy, principally that of German idealism, which had such a marked influence on Formstecher and Hirsch as well as on Krochmal. Steinheim described the God-concept of P. K. Marheineke (1780–1846), who was professor of theology at Heidelberg, as typical of the speculative philosophy of the right-wing Hegelianism; The God of Marheineke is not One who reveals something to *us* but One to whom we reveal something.[4] Hegel's philosophy, according to Steinheim, emphasizes the conscious, cognitive process and looks upon historical development as divine manifestations and the ways in which God knows himself. Pantheistic tendencies are foreign to this view, which stresses the distinction between God and the world. Steinheim felt that in this conception the world and man become the incarnation of God. Since the world and man are indispensable to God, human consciousness becomes an inseparable part of God's essence. From this point of view man is not a mere creature but a being that acknowledges and reveals a hidden content, one who is no longer dependent on God but, on the contrary, one on whom God is dependent. In this reversal of religious values man, who is endowed with consciousness and the faculty of making decisions, occupies the center of the world: The true *knowledge* concerning the Absolute is nothing more than this *Absolute* itself. This view of God's essence makes Revelation an independent creation of man, and denies that it is heteronomous and a gift from without; in other words, it rejects what for Steinheim is the most prominent aspect of Revelation and the one that he stressed most.

The antagonism to the speculative method of religious philosophy in general, and especially in Judaism, as well as the unsuccessful attempts to reconcile the Jewish religion with philosophy, bring to mind the approach of Judah Halevi (1085–1141). Surprisingly, Steinheim does not mention Halevi but Maimonides, in connection with several points on which he finds himself in agreement. Steinheim's knowledge of Hebrew literature was very limited and, besides, a fundamental difference separated him from Halevi: the latter isolated the faith of Israel from philosophy in order to preserve it as a nonspeculative sphere for the relations between man and his Maker, the two foci of the religious ellipse, and to this end cleansed it of all speculative and cognitive accretions. He opposed philosophy not because of its rationalism but because of the wide gap that separates faith rooted in experience and philosophy rooted in discursive thought.

Steinheim's purpose, however, was not to transform faith into a relational sphere between God and man; he opposed philosophy not because of its cognitive but because of its *rationalistic* element. He left faith its speculative and cognitive contents, but only on condition that they discard all rationalistic influences.[5] His purpose was not to find a basis for knowledge in the sphere of faith but to make faith an independent sphere of knowledge not identified with rationalistic knowledge. To this end he relied on his analysis of the concept of Revelation and on empirical, *a posteriori* cognition.

Revelation is defined as information of an instructive nature conveyed to man from without,[6] information that can be transmitted to man in no other way. Revelation is characterized by two fundamental qualities:

a) It transmits instructions to man, teaching him the way of faith and its principles (*e.g.*, Creation, et cetera). God appears in Revelation by means of instructive principles, and not in the world or in existence as it is. Steinheim presents two interpretations of Revelation which are sometimes confused: It is possible to regard Revelation as the embodiment of nonsensible being in sensible existence. Revelation thus understood as the incarnation of the spirit implies the ontological identity of the two main elements of existence, the supersensible or spiritual element and the sensible phenomena in the empirical world of man. Revelation in this sense does not speak of a God who exists outside of man and of man who receives the content transmitted to him by God, since, strictly speaking, Revelation is not a relationship of incarnation between the two elements of existence. As set forth in the Bible, Revelation is Torah in the radical sense of this concept, designed to teach man to comprehend Creation and the world. In the religious sense of the word Revelation is a theory concerning God and His work,[7] that is, a theory that is confined to the sphere of speculative and cognitive assertions and not to the sphere of reality and its various dimensions.

b) Although Revelation is a special theory that comes to teach man concerning God and His work and although it is a system of theoretical assertions, it is not the creation of reason. Revelation provides reason with information from without, but reason contributes nothing to the content of Revelation. From the historical point of view reason does not elaborate the content of Revelation; it receives content, but it cannot create content out of itself. This fundamental aspect of the nature of Revelation as knowledge transmitted to man from without can be summed up as follows:

Reason knows, after a rigorous self-examination (cognitively conducted), that the content of Revelation is basically different from that which reason can produce out of itself; that is, reason by itself cannot produce the instructive principles given to it by Revelation. Reason acknowledges its shortcoming over against Revelation and dependence on the content received from it.[8] In the inevitable tension between them, the spontaneity of reason succumbs to the heteronomy of Revelation.

The problem of faith, then, goes back to the question of the fundamental distinction between reason as a cognitive method that leads from man to God and Revelation as a cognitive method that leads from God to man, a basic distinction that Steinheim makes the criterion of Revelation. It may be said that the instructive content that is a product of Revelation differs formally from that of reason, and is even opposed to it. The formal characteristic of the content of Revelation is its nonconformity to our consciousness and even conflict with it.[9] In this tension between reason and its content on the one hand, and Revelation and its content on the other the emphasis is in favor of Revelation—despite this distinction, as Steinheim sometimes puts it, or even because of it.

This, of course, means an abandonment of the traditional ways of Jewish philosophy. The faith of Israel cannot be reconciled with philosophy, since faith is based on Revelation that comes to man from without and philosophy is based on reason which produces its own content by its own effort. The content of faith also differs from that of philosophy and owes its allegiance to a different source. It is therefore necessary to examine the special content of Revelation, which breaks through the closed, rationalistic world of philosophy and creative reason and introduces active elements that are foreign to it. The first principle of Revelation concerns the nature of the relation between God and the world, expressed by reason as the ontological affinity between God and the world. The world is a garment, as it were, in which God clothes himself, or it is the product of His emanation; from this point of view, both God and the world appear within a common system. This thought is also closely related to that of prime matter. In the rationalistic view God is not the Creator of matter, a position which Steinheim, as we shall see later, identifies with idolatry. In the act of Creation, God fashions matter that is given Him and endows it with form.[10] In any case, the existence of God as conceived by rationalism is not an existence outside the created world but one dependent upon it, two mutually interdependent elements existing on the same plane.

Revelation presupposes a breach in the closed rationalistic system that unites God and the world; that is, it assigns to God a place outside of the world and it makes the world dependent upon God and God alone. Instead of the immanent causal chain within the world which embodies the unified system, God appears as the absolute beginning of the world, as a Creator endowed with will, the One who created the causal chain itself. The breach in the unified system signifies that among the elements of the world an external, nonrational factor was introduced—namely, the element of freedom. In the rationalistic conception which seeks to impose form on a closed, circular system everything is determined and proceeds by inexorable necessity; to make a breach in this fixed system of causal necessity means the introduction of a free factor which induces activity in and of itself.[11]

Furthermore, the closed, circular system of the world as understood by the rational mind arises of itself; its necessity signifies its eternality. Since this system is fixed and determined, it has no beginning in time and there could never have been a time when this system was nonexistent. The assumption of a temporal beginning cancels the *inner* reason of the system and its contingent character.

It follows that the difference in the rational approach and that of Revelation with respect to content is rooted in a number of conceptual alternatives—creation and infinite past time, necessity and will, determination and contingency. The difference between the two approaches may be interpreted as a difference between the instructive principles themselves. Just as it is impossible to reconcile the inner with the outer source, so it is impossible to reconcile the substantive outlooks that are based on diverse sources.

This opposition between the system that is enclosed in itself and the system that has been breached to include the Creator is formulated by Steinheim with the help of traditional theological concepts—creation from an undifferentiated *materia prima* and creation *ex nihilo*. The rational system has no absolute beginning; every event occurs within it and constitutes a causal transition from existence to existence. The beginning of Revelation, however, lies outside of the system itself which, having been created from without by an external being, is a system created *ex nihilo*. The difference between rationalism and Revelation with respect to content may be formulated as follows:

a) Nothing comes of nothing—*ex nihilo nihil fit*—is the rational principle; *all is created out of nothing* is the principle of Revelation.

b) Rationalism holds that there is no effect without an adequate cause; Revelation holds that the will of God alone is the cause of matter which He created *ab initio temporis*.[12]

The principal distinction between rationalism and Revelation revolves around the notion of freedom, the principle that breaks through the closed rationalistic system. Steinheim made Kant's antinomy of causality and freedom analogous to the fundamental antinomy of reason and Revelation; that is, what Kant took to be an antinomy within the sphere of reason itself was understood by Steinheim as an antinomy between two separate spheres. The principle of reason is causality and the principle of Revelation is freedom. Since Steinheim stresses the antirationalistic element as the one that breaks through the closed circle, he requires the anti-rationalistic elements of will and freedom to account for the formation of the system, instead of explaining the congruence and harmony of elements within the rational system itself. Just as Steinheim mentions freedom as the basic principle with respect to God's relation to the world, he also stresses it with respect to man's position in the world. In the rational view man is part of a closed system and there is no ontological difference in existence between man and the world. Naturalism is the inevitable corollary of a rational conception with its rigorous, all-pervasive laws. Even God is not exempt from these laws; *a fortiori*, man. Steinheim stresses the affinity between two ideas: active man and immanent God. Revelation needs reason to break through the closed circle, both from God's standpoint and man's. Man creates his own circle, since he is a creature of freedom, which has been bestowed upon him by the will of God; by virtue of this freedom, man can move freely within the circle he has created for himself. Steinheim here draws our attention to the inner affinity between the physical and the ethical conception.[13] From the physical point of view, the world is not a closed system bound by a logical nexus of inexorable laws; also from the ethical point of view, the world is not an exclusive, self-contained system, but one that welcomes man's intervention and the free exercise of his active powers. The ethical principle must at the very outset posit a nature that is not dependent on the laws of cause and effect.[14] The difference between the rational and the revelatory principle, therefore, is analogous to that between the naturalistic conception which regards man as an integral part of nature and the ethical conception which places him in a realm of free, ethical activity. The closed, rationalistic circle is pierced both from the side of God's being, and that of man's ethical nature. The religious conception that separates God from the world, and the idea that man is responsible for his deeds, would be groundless without Revelation.

Freedom expresses itself in man's relation to sin. The fact that I can sin constitutes my glory, Steinheim argues, since it signifies that I can also refrain from sinning, that I can act properly whenever I so desire.[15] Freedom then expresses itself in man's ability to choose to sin or to refrain from doing so and in his obligation to decide in favor of the latter. Man's awareness of the alternatives and his power of decision prove that the world is not a closed circle but subject to human influences and decisions. The things of the world do not appear ready-made, nor do they endure in their original form; they are constantly being changed by man's free decisions and refashioned by his intervention. The things that remain untouched continue to be part of the rational world and the iron chain of cause and effect. Man's freedom breaks through this causal chain.

The nonrational character of freedom is apparent not only in this matter of freedom that pierces the rational system but also in the inexplicable nature of the ultimate fact of freedom, which cannot be derived from other facts or presuppositions. Every ex-

planation proceeds by way of derivation—that is, the obscurity of
a phenomenon is clarified in the light of one that is already known.
Explanation, then, is based on a logical sequence; if this is disrupted by freedom, the latter can in no sense be said to constitute
an explanation. Freedom is an ultimate fact, and as such is
described by Steinheim as an inexplicable contingency.[16] Freedom
as an unillumined phenomenon cannot be reconciled with a
translucent system, so that an ethical conception is possible for
Steinheim only in the sphere of Revelation; no place can be found
for ethical activity within a rationalistic system. In this matter there
is a marked resemblance between Steinheim and his contemporaries,
Formstecher and Hirsch, who regarded Judaism as an ethical conception, since it was a religion of the spirit rather than of nature;
whereas Steinheim regarded Judaism as an ethical conception,
since it was a religion of Revelation. Both Steinheim and his contemporaries made a distinction between Judaism and the religion
of nature. In Steinheim's conception, Revelation is confronted by
its opposite, reason, which expresses itself in naturalism and
mechanism. According to Formstecher and Hirsch, however, the
ethical character of Judaism has its source in a spiritual principle
innate in man; according to Steinheim, in Revelation as knowledge
conveyed to man from without. The former based ethics on spirit,
for they regarded spirit as a dynamic factor, like freedom; Steinheim based ethics on Revelation, understanding it as a disruptive
element which breaks through the rationalistic framework, and
without which freedom would find no place. But these differences
in method cannot obscure the similarity in the three conceptions of
the philosophy of Judaism that we have considered, viz. they all
raised the ethical content of Judaism to the level of essence. Here
we can say that the metaphysical conceptions concerning the nature
of Judaism rest on notions derived from the sphere of ethics.

Freedom is also the reason and the cause of the belief in the
immortality of the soul which, after Creation and freedom, is the
third principle of Revelation. We must not fail to note the difference, however, between the place occupied by this principle and
that taken by the others. It has already been made clear that the
opposition between Revelation and reason depends on the tension

between Creation and infinite past time, or between freedom and necessity. The content of Revelation is that of Revelation alone and its opposite is the content of reason. The third principle, however, the immortality of the soul, is not only one of the elements of the religion of Revelation, but also constitutes the main content of reason, or of idolatry, regarded by Steinheim as the religious embodiment of *reason*.[17] The difference between Revelation and reason in this connection is a difference of basis and not of content. Reason—or idolatry, which is the religion of reason—finds the basis for the immortality of the soul only in physical reasons —that is, since the world has no beginning in time, it is eternal, and has no end in time. The natural, immanent laws of the world account for the eternality of the soul as a natural fact. In other words, the soul as part of the world is also subject to its general laws, and like the world exempt from destruction. This is not true of Revelation which rests on the principle of creation *ab initio temporis*, that is, the creation of the world by God at a given moment in time. The physical world cannot, therefore, serve to demonstrate the eternality of the soul, since the world itself is not eternal. Furthermore, Revelation does not include man in the physical world as does naturalism. God as the Creator of the world has imparted to man, whom He created, a spark of His freedom. The naturalistic argument to explain the immortality of the soul is therefore unconvincing. Steinheim regards even the immortality of the soul as a contingent fact which cannot be derived from any other principles; it is not the product of natural causes but a free gift of God's grace to man who was created in His image.[18] The world as it is cannot serve as a basis for the immortality of the soul, since this immortality was created by God and its explanation lies outside of man and the world.

This principle of immortality breaks through the circle of the world which is constructed of rational elements. Since this principle is not grounded in the inner system as a physical fact, it is the result of external intervention. After a system is broken through by intervention, it is no longer closed, since it is not self-explanatory and is dependent on a transcendent cause. The difference between Revelation and reason, as we have already noticed, is not a

difference within the content itself, but a difference in the basis of
the content, which results from the distinction between immanent
facts and transcendent cause.

The opposition between Revelation and reason also appears in
another area—namely, in understanding the meaning of the unity
of God. It is not clear from Steinheim's words, however, whether
he regards the unity of God as a principle of Revelation, but this
can be safely assumed. At any rate, a fundamental opposition between a closed system and one that has been broken through is
here evident.

Steinheim realized, as did Hermann Cohen two generations
later, that unity is one of the basic concepts of reason. The difference between reason and Revelation cannot be made to depend
on the assumption of the concept of unity but on the essence of
its true content. The difference or opposition between reason and
Revelation is that between abstract, impersonal unity and real,
personal unity. The unity that is a principle of reason is a concept
and not a reality. It arises in the sphere of concepts and is hence
not an active, thinking unity, since such attributes are derived from
real being and are not qualities of isolated concepts. Rational unity,
then, is only a fiction created by our thought processes and is therefore an unreal unity.[19] Rational unity is not given to the understanding from without, but is created by the understanding out
of its own resources. Such unity is characterized by the fact that it
is a concept and not a reality; indigenous to reason, it contains no
knowledge that comes from without. The concept of the unity of
God based on this rational, conceptual element is called "bad
monotheism."[20] True monotheism means *faith* in the unity of God,
who appears as an active personality. True monotheism is personal or real[21] and is not based on the rational *concept* of unity but
on a definite reality. The rational framework is here pierced at its
core and we no longer have a closed circle with a conceptual content. An element of reality has penetrated the rational sphere and
as such can find no place in a rational system replete with concepts.
In understanding the concept of the unity of God a peculiar distinction arises between reason and Revelation which may be stated
in Hegelian terms as follows: In Revelation we deal with real,

ontological facts, but reason creates out of itself a pale world of shadows.

Unity, the main principle of reason, cannot give rise to One within the system. The number One stands at the beginning of a numerical series, but is not separate from it with a distinct content of its own; it is on the same plane with the numbers that succeed it, *primus inter pares*.[22] Conceptual unity does not break through the system which is internally one continuous unity of unbroken, transitional steps. The real One of faith, however, is One and Only One[23] with no internally articulated steps. If we assume continuous transitions, Creation must be viewed as necessary and the immutable laws of nature would also apply to God. But if Creation, the first principle of the religion of Revelation, is understood as informed by will and freedom, we cannot assume an unbroken transition that flows from the One who is the Creator of the entire world system. True monotheistic unity is real and personal, not a numerical One followed by the number two. This unity is separate and unique; it knows itself, thinks, has a will, and contemplates.[24] The opposition between unity that is included within the system and unity that is separate and apart from it is reduced by Steinheim to the opposition between the One and the unique One,[25] a dinstinction which is similar in content and terminology to that made by Hermann Cohen, which we have already touched upon, between unity and uniqueness. Cohen also emphasizes God's transcendence and real being implied in His uniqueness, but he is careful to make a distinction between God's being and its ontological-volitional content. Steinheim, however, stresses God's transcendence by making a distinction between the Only One and the One and interprets unity as a unity of Being, at the same time insisting that this Being has attributes of conception that is conscious of itself and a self-created free will that is not within the bounds of comprehension.[26] In giving prominence to God's uniqueness, Cohen remains within the confines of rationalism, albeit a metaphysical and not formal-logical rationalism; Steinheim posits the concept of uniqueness in order to remove God from the rationalistic system.

At any rate, it is clear that with this concept of God's unity

Steinheim desired to draw attention to an instructive principle of the religion of Revelation, which breaks through the rational system even though it expresses itself in the opposition between concept and reality, and between transcendent God and a system that contains everything within itself. A closed system cannot endure transcendence.

We thus have four instructive principles of the religion of Revelation—Creation, freedom, the immortality of the soul, and the uniqueness of God—which have in common the fact that they all break through the rational, causal chain and introduce an element from without that is foreign to it and that disrupts the system because of its unexpected appearance. The ways of Revelation are inexplicable to reason, for the content of Revelation is strange and baffling to the rational mind.

It may be helpful at this point to indicate the historical place occupied by Steinheim's conception of the cardinal doctrines of Judaism in the development of Jewish thought. Our purpose is not to trace historical sources, it seems that Steinheim had but scant acquaintance with traditional Jewish philosophy, and even Maimonides' system was not sufficiently clear to him. If we compare Steinheim with several Jewish philosophers, it is only to shed light on some of the religious and philosophical ideas that underlie his system.

Revelation in its traditional formulation as *the divine origin of the Bible* is one of the thirteen principles of Maimonides and one of Joseph Albo's (c1380–c1435) three principles. Maimonides derives the principle from the verse: "And Moses said, Hereby ye shall know that the Lord hath sent me to do all these works; for I have not done them of mine own mind" (Num. 16:28)—to indicate that the Torah comes from an external, transcendent source. The belief in Revelation is one of the substantive principles of Judaism. Steinheim does not make Revelation itself the cardinal principle of Judaism, but he makes the instructive content of Judaism (Creation, et cetera) provide the principles of Revelation. The logical relationship between Revelation and the other principles is totally different for Steinheim than for Maimonides and Albo. For him, Revelation is the basis for positing the principles of Judaism, but it is not on an equal plane with the other principles. Just as it cannot be said, for example, that reason and the law of continuity are on the same plane, since reason is the source and the instrument of its manifestations, so also is it impossible to say that Revelation and its specific, substantive principles occupy the same plane. Steinheim removes Revelation from the general content and basic principles of Judaism and raises it to the level of a root (or a supposition) of Judaism. Revelation is at bottom synonymous with faith, and you cannot make faith a substantive principle and at the same time speak of the principles of faith. It seems that Steinheim was here confronted with the problem of finding a basis for the principles of Revelation and this obliged him to make a distinction between Revelation as a presupposition and a point of departure, and the principles themselves, or the instructive content of Revelation.

We have thus far treated the methodological aspect which must be regarded as more than merely formal, since it touches the religious and philosophical tendencies in Steinheim's system. There is one point with respect to the content of the principles themselves that should not be overlooked—namely, that *creatio ex nihilo* is not to be found among Maimonides' thirteen or among Albo's three principles. In Albo it is relegated to a minor subdivision that includes those instructive contents which can be denied without incurring the stigma of heresy. It is plain that creation *ex nihilo* is not given a significant place among the principles set down by either Maimonides or Albo. Steinheim, however, makes this a cardinal principle, for he sees it as corroborating the conception of Revelation in its attempt to break through the rational frame. On the other hand, reward and punishment is absent from Steinheim's list of principles, which includes only those that tend to emphasize the antirational character of the world. The principle of reward and punishment is based on human conduct, and Steinheim showed little interest in the problems that attend human action or in the consequences that flow from it. He included freedom as one of the principles, because he understood it as the *root* of ethical activity and because it best illustrates the rupture within the sphere of natural laws. It could also be said, moreover, that the principle of reward and punishment is an expression of the results of ethical activity in terms of law and one of Steinheim's main interests was to ascertain the nature of the ethical act.

The existence of God is also not included among Steinheim's principles of Revelation; he seems to have considered this principle as a logical presupposition in discussing the nature of Revelation and its content. Since Revelation means knowledge transmitted from without, an agent who conveys this knowledge must necessarily be assumed. It seems that Steinheim took God's existence as a self-evident assumption (and here we get a glimpse of the speculative manner of treating Jewish doctrines, especially that of Hasdai Crescas, ca. 1340–1420). Revelation itself is not a doctrine of Judaism, since it depends for its reality on God's existence as a *conditio sine qua non*. We have already observed that Revelation is a presupposition for doctrines; by the same token, we can now say that principle of God's existence is a presupposition of a presupposition.

One of the doctrines included by Steinheim is that of God's unity, which he understands in the same way as Maimonides. He is not like one of a pair or one of a species, or the first in a numerical series; He is the exalted One in a unity which is beyond compare. God's uniqueness is accepted as a doctrine because it adds an antirationalistic attribute to God's existence, indicating the distinction between this divine existence and the world, and the absence of an unbroken line of transitional steps between them. God's uniqueness does not refer to His existence but to the transcendence of that existence; for this reason it was included by Steinheim among the doctrines he formulated.

In short, Steinheim did not intend to include Jewish beliefs and doctrines in his list of principles or to extract their literary values. It was the antirationalism of the doctrines that served as the criterion of his selection and as the guiding principle of his doctrinal system.

Since Revelation has a basis of its own, Steinheim does not make Revelation a content of faith, but its presupposition. As a conception, Revelation is a definite cognitive phenomenon, and therefore occupies a conspicuous place in the theory of knowledge;

although it provides a ground for antirationalistic doctrines, it also serves as a scientific, although nonrational, basis for antirationalistic assertions. To secure a basis in religion, Revelation must acquire a scientific basis. Revelation is the final authority in the highest *cognitive* sphere.[27] Moreover, the assumption that Revelation has an exact cognitive-scientific basis assures theology, which is rooted in Revelation, of the certainty of its truths. Religion finds in Revelation a firm ground on which it can build its structure with assurance. To deny religion this cognitive ground is to confine its deep insights to the sphere of theosophy and the vague, unscientific religious feelings of the individual. Steinheim seeks to understand Revelation from the cognitive point of view in order to make theology a science like astronomy or chemistry.[28] Revelation thus becomes a basis for antirational content and antirational doctrines of faith, but is not removed from the cognitive sphere; it is itself one of the manifestations of cognition. The tendency of religious philosophy was to recognize Revelation as a mode of cognition and to assign it a place in the comprehensive system of a general theory of knowledge.

There is still another aspect that contributes to our understanding of the nature of Revelation. Religious thinking that relies on individual experience and subjective feeling (represented chiefly by Jacobi and to a certain extent by Schleiermacher) provides no valid criteria to test the certainty of its assumptions. Our chief concern is the religious content and our allegiance to this content absolves us, as it were, from seeking its cognitive basis. For traditional theology the true content is supplied by intuition, and it therefore has no need of a basis. Metaphysics, on the other hand, has a basis in the form of proofs and demonstrations, but is bereft of content. The abundant content of theology is thus without a cognitive basis and the solid basis of metaphysics is from the cognitive point of view destitute of content.[29] Steinheim seeks to provide religious content with a solid, cognitive base whose content is antirationalistic but whose solidity is nonrationalistic, that is, not derived from feeling or dependent on the noncognitive aspects of the soul. Steinheim distinguishes between an intellectual-formal and a cognitive-substantive basis, between one that rests on *a priori* and one that rests on *a posteriori* presuppositions. But the cognitive certainty of Revelation, although not less convincing, differs from the formal certainty of metaphysics.[30]

The place occupied by Revelation in the cognitive system is closely related to two modes of cognition which differ from each other. Steinheim accepts Kant's distinction between thought and cognition proper in defining the cognitive nature of Revelation. Thought, considered by Kant a function of the understanding rooted in spontaneity, detects and combines resemblances in the consciousness with the aid of concepts; it takes place in the sphere of the understanding and is a product of that faculty. The understanding is not dependent on thought and remains unaffected by an external object. Cognition is the *relation* to the object and does not fall within the province of the understanding and the concepts; it bursts the bonds of the understanding, since it really belongs to the realm of the contemplative where its activity revolves around the synthesis of the concept, which is a manifestation of the understanding and the sensible perception of the external world of things. One important aspect of Steinheim's conception of the nature of cognition should be noted. Cognition does not lie outside of the concept; without the concept, in conjunction with intuitive perception, it would be unable to function at all. In the Introduction to the *Critique of Pure Reason*, Kant states that all cognition begins in experience, but is not derived from it. Deep within the recesses of cognition we find this element, rooted in the understanding—that is, the concept as well as that element not derived from the understanding but coming to it from without.

Although not expressly acknowledged, Steinheim's view of cognition in general and of Revelation in particular depends on Kantian dualism. He carefully distinguishes between an object that is given to thought alone and an object that is given to cognition.[31] This Kantian distinction, however, takes a different turn in Steinheim's system. An object that is given to thought can be proved *a priori*; an object given to cognition is one that is subject to *a posteriori* experience. The distinction between thought and cognition is for Steinheim a distinction between the construction of an object and the object as given in experience. According to Kant, even the empirical object—the object that is the product of the synthesis of the concept and the intuition—is a constructed object; in other words, construction applies to the sphere of experience and not only to the formal-logical or mathematical sphere. It seems that Steinheim based his distinction between thought and cognition not on the relation to intuition, viz. that thought is not to be found in intuition but in cognition, but rather on the place occupied by the concept that constructs all the different modes of perception. Steinheim seeks to remove from cognition the *a priori* conceptual element that Kant assumes to be inherent within it. Kant's distinction between thought and cognition is used by Steinheim for his own distinction between a conceptual structure and knowledge received from without by way of experience. Thought as construction is called by Steinheim the faculty of synthetic judgment,[32] which departs from Kant's terminology and meaning. According to Kant, synthesis does not apply to the sphere of formal thought but to the intersection where the concept meets the intuition and is a synonym for that fruitful meeting. Steinheim employed this misleading terminology to emphasize the free structure in synthesis and the independent creative activity of the understanding. Instead of synthesis, he considers the inductive faculty of judgment an empirical, cognitive method, which begins not with reason but with the given object.[33]

The distinction between thought and cognition receives additional emphasis from still another aspect of Steinheim's system. Thought in itself is the product of the spontaneous activity of reason or the product of innate ideas, and as such is empty from the very outset, since it contains no objects. (Steinheim here confuses the element of spontaneity derived from Kant with that of innate ideas derived from Descartes and Leibnitz.) Thought can acquire content only from external reality. The difference between thought and cognition thus amounts to the difference between what is indigenous to reason and what accrues to it from without, a later addition or adventitious efflorescence.[34] The difference between these two modes of comprehension is formulated not only from the standpoint of their relation to objects, but also from the standpoint of their relation to time. Here the temporal factor penetrates the cognitive structure. Empty cognition, thought, dwells outside of time, since it is not susceptible to accretions from without. Full cognition, which is cognition in the exact sense of the term, functions within time: There was a definite moment in time when cognition was not full and then at a definite moment later it was filled with content.

The difference between what is innate and what is absorbed from without is also formulated from the standpoint of cognition. Thought that springs from reason alone, the source of innate ideas, is impervious to matter that comes to it from without; it finds its own matter by reaching down within itself. Thought comes into being by means of Platonic recollection. Content lies hidden in the depths of reason and needs only to be lifted to the surface and recollected. Speculative idealism, against which Steinheim directed his criticism, adopted the Platonic view, which regarded the inner structure of the world as rational. In contrast with this thoroughgoing rationalism of Platonism and speculative idealism, we have the Aristotelian method with its adherence to a mode of cognition that is necessarily dependent on the external world. Realism, of which Aristotle is the most prominent exponent, disputes the power of reason to create the world out of its own resources; the world is given to reason and is absorbed by it in the process of experience.

The fact that thought is not related to intuition and to external objects is not its only characteristic. Steinheim finds some inner characteristics which he takes to support his theory of Revelation. The principal weapon wielded by thought is the Law of Contradiction. In the realm of thought a decision must be made in favor of A or non-A for both possibilities cannot exist at the same time.[35] The whole edifice of thought rests on this antithesis[36] between two mutually exclusive logical possibilities, and it is this restricted choice of alternatives that gives thought the character of necessity.[37] Thought is thus a mode of comprehension ruled by the Law of Contradiction and the Law of Necessity and its method is that of conceptual derivation, which is nothing but the drawing of inferences from given presuppositions.

Empirical cognition that is related to the object is altogether different from thought, not only because it relies on knowledge transmitted to it from without, but because it takes the facts as it finds them without submitting them to the Law of Contradiction. Thought acknowledges only two possibilities, of which it can choose only one, whereas cognition knows of no such possibilities. Thought is ruled by the alternative "either-or" and cognition by "thus and not thus." Reality and not antecedent possibilities is the starting point of empirical cognition, which recognizes and accepts an incommensurate, unaccountable element at the heart of reality that cannot be dissipated in the clear air of thought or digested by its voracious instruments.[38] The object it confronts is not a concept produced of necessity by reason, but a given fact and hence contingent.[39] Man is therefore faced with the choice of living in a world of mathematics, a world of shadows and fictive realities, or resigning himself to the real world of brute, thick facts and contingency.[40] Thought moves in the sphere of empty space and not extension, in a sphere of development that disregards time. Emptiness is identified with the concept and with necessity; and fullness is identified with contingency and reality.[41]

In his theory of antinomies Kant points out the contradictions that reason must necessarily fall into the moment it seeks to transcend experience. Steinheim attempts to demonstrate that the antinomy is not an attribute of reason in itself but of reason in its relation to experience; its source lies in the distinction or opposition between thought and cognition or between necessity and contingency. The empirical world of accidents and eruptions is not docile to the rational mind and yields up only some typical, anemic specimens. The physical atom, Steinheim argues, is an extended point and the mathematical point is a nonextended point. It is an apparent contradiction to speak of an extended point, a contradiction that stems from the fact that we have no way of capturing the elusive phenomena of the world in a gossamer web of logic. The substantiality of the world cannot be deduced from formal or rational suppositions. The fact that substance is given makes it distinct from a formal or rational system, for substance is by its very nature antirational.

The ontological proof of God's existence, which consists in

enumerating the qualities that constitute His essence, is an attempt made by quasi religion to bridge the deep gap between formal thought that is devoid of content and cognition that is filled with content. Existence is not to be found in the sphere of thought, for existence is a contingent element superimposed on the concept and not derived from it. God, whose existence the ontological argument seeks to prove by means of rational demonstration, has become a *necessary* God, but necessity is not real, since it is a quality that adheres to the formal-logical sphere, not to the sphere of reality. Reality and proof are contradictory.[42] The attempt to derive the contingency of reality from the necessary nature of concepts is doomed to failure from the very outset, since it seeks to relate two wholly disparate elements. Here again we can see Steinheim's dependence on Kant (who pointed out in his criticism of the ontological argument that existence is not a conceptual quality), except that Steinheim makes the various Kantian distinctions the subject of a special problem—that is, he uses them to prove the antirational nature of faith.

Against the ontological proof of God's existence Steinheim brought not only the cognitive argument connected with the content of the concept existence but a religious argument as well. He held that at the basis of the ontological proof was the assumption that existence represented the height of perfection and it is impossible that what is perfect should be absent from God who is the highest Being. The ontological proof reverses the order of values by placing existence above God, and then attributing it to God, since without it He would be less than perfect. Existence and not God is made the highest criterion, but the basic assumption of all religious thought is that existence is *created*—that is, it is necessarily lower than God and subject to Him. Without God no existence is given to cognition. How, then, can the ontological argument attempt to explain divine essence by demonstrating its necessary existence without involving God in a glaring contradiction?[43] It would seem that the ontological argument undermines the very basis of religious faith by making existence and not God the highest Entity.

Implicit within the religious claim, however, there is a cognitive argument concerning the relation between the concept and existence. Necessary, uncreated existence that is above God, and is also placed in the sphere of the concept and hence of necessity, results in a contradiction, since existence and concept are mutually exclusive. The fact that existence is by its very nature contingent means in religious language that it is *created*. Contingent is that which cannot exist by virtue of itself; given is that which could not exist without an anterior cause. Existence or the created world do not exist by virtue of themselves but because they were created. The world which lacks necessity has its source in the Divine Will.

These arguments on the nature of cognition are not set forth as part of the theory of knowledge but rather to indicate that Revelation is an independent mode of cognition not subject to the postulates of formal and rational cognition. Actually, Steinheim identifies Revelation as a mode of religious perception with *a posteriori* cognition. There is no fundamental methodological difference between them; both break through the rational system and introduce into the cognitive sphere an accidental and unexpected element and both compel reason to submit to the given facts. The only difference between the two is simply one of content: Revelation is concerned with God and the totality of the world, and empirical cognition is concerned only with such physical entities as the atom, the atmosphere, et cetera. But these differences in content do not detract from the basic similarity between the two modes of cognition. Revelation, which has a cognitive base, can thus serve as a root for instructive principles and not merely as one principle among many.

The difference between formal thought as an original mode of comprehension, based on recollection and material cognition as a mode of comprehension that depends on additions absorbed from without, also appears in Steinheim's system in connection with Revelation. The distinctive feature of Revelation is the fact that it has a definite beginning in time; there was a moment in time prior to Revelation and a moment in time subsequent to it.[44] Here also lies the difference between Revelation and natural religion. The former is a novel event that takes place in time, whereas the latter is rooted in reason from time immemorial and presents nothing novel. We can therefore say that the religion of Revelation is a religion based on additional knowledge that comes to it from without and natural religion is nourished by its own private resources. Revelation depends on external matter which cannot keep pace with the changes in man and thus stands still while man develops,[45] whereas the intrinsic content of natural religion keeps changing as man develops.

Steinheim regards Judaism as a religion of Revelation and paganism as a religion of reason or as a natural religion; Christianity is a mixture of the two and may be regarded as paganism that has absorbed Jewish elements or Judaism that has absorbed pagan elements. The third volume of Steinheim's principal work is devoted entirely to an analysis of Christianity and its historical development in the light of this distinction. Steinheim treats Christianity as a historical phenomenon; paganism, which is more than a historical phenomenon, is treated typologically. He tries to discover the basic elements in paganism as a timeless phenomenon that is independent of special circumstances or a particular environment. Paganism is based on reason and is, indeed, but another name for rational laws and postulates.[46] Steinheim defines the essence of natural religion or paganism as all that the human soul expresses by means of its aptitudes and capacities concerning the nature of God, spirits, the world of matter and its creation.[47] The emphasis in this definition is on "the human soul," and its innate powers. Natural religion is the expression of the knowledge latent in man and pressing toward rational formulation, to be embodied in a closed system of clear principles such as prime matter, natural causality, the principle that nothing comes of nothing—all opposed to the basic notion implicit in Revelation.

Steinheim considered paganism as a way of looking at the world and not as a particular-historical phenomenon. He went further, however, and identified it with philosophy, especially since the philosophical idealism of his generation rested on the unhampered activity of immanent reason. This does not mean that post-Kantian idealism was based on formal reason devoid of content. On the contrary, its primary concern was to provide content as well as intellectual illumination; the content, however, must be purified by reason and subject to its laws within a closed system, so that no necessary antinomy arises between reason and experience. Revelation itself becomes an expression of reason, which here discloses its content unto itself and puts on an outward garment, as it were, that it may not pass unseen among men. Idealistic reason does not absorb knowledge from without; it is, to use a modern figure of speech, a broadcasting rather than a receiving station. Steinheim thus identifies paganism with philosophy and holds, furthermore, that both are part and parcel of reason and subject to its eternal laws. Revelation sees the world as for the first time, "old yet ever new"; paganism sees it as an ancient, recurrent phenomenon. In both paganism and Revelation, however the rational framework is disrupted—in one by the penetration of external knowledge, and in the other by creation; in one by a new beginning and independent development, and in the other by a closed chain of causality initiated by God at the beginning. The God of natural religion is a slave of necessity and His power; goodness and love are not real.[48]

Steinheim's appraisal of philosophy in general and of idealism in particular led him to an interesting conclusion. Religious thinkers generally place philosophical idealism above materialism, since idealism finds room in its system for the God-concept and seems to have a close affinity for the spiritual aspect of religion. But it is precisely idealism, according to Steinheim, that imperils religion in that it negates God by confining Him within the limits of a closed, rational system. It needs the word "God," but must reject the true content of the word which is antirational, since it refers to transcendent existence. Steinheim therefore prefers materialism to idealism, since it must necessarily assume a spirit outside of matter that directs it. This is the view that Steinheim attributes to the ancient Greek philosopher, Anaxagoras.

Steinheim considered Judaism a religion of Revelation in the sense in which he understood the concept of Revelation. In a letter to Derenbourg, Abraham Geiger relates that when he questioned Steinheim as to where his cardinal doctrine of Revelation could be found, the answer was, "in the Synagogue." Steinheim even went on to say that even if it had been invented by him, it was destined to be the typical doctrine of the Synagogue.[49] Steinheim's system was more intimately connected with the development of nineteenth-century German idealism than with the development of Jewish thought, and it contained more elements derived from general philosophy than from traditional Jewish philosophy. While his contemporaries, Formstecher and Hirsch, sought a basis for Judaism within the framework of idealistic philosophy (for, like Steinheim, they regarded Judaism as a typical religion and paganism as its opposite), Steinheim tried to understand and to justify the essence of Judaism against the background of the crumbling edifice of German idealism. Steinheim was the most formidable Jewish opponent of idealistic philosophy in the nineteenth century and the most notable exponent of the new direction in religious thought. The anti-idealistic arguments in Steinheim's system are known to us through the works of Christian Hermann Weisse (1801–1866) and the works of Immanuel Hermann Fichte (1797–1879).[50] Steinheim's basic religious conception, namely, that reason must look upon itself as created, is also to be found in the works of the historian Johann Gustav Droysen (1833–1913). Speculation is confounded the moment the slightest bit of content penetrates its closed circle. Here we also find stress laid on the volitional factor.

Steinheim's system expresses the same religious sentiment that pervades the "negative theology" of our own day, the sentiment that impugns and discredits idealism for having obliterated the distinction between God and the world. But whereas this negative theology emphasizes the deep gulf that separated God from *man*, Steinheim stresses the deep gulf between God and the *world*. Steinheim's problem is thus not anthropological and historical but ontic and physical.

It could perhaps be said that Steinheim's point of departure is the existential world, if by existential we understand the recalcitrant facts that slip through the rational net. Existentialism is an attribute of the external world, and here it is co-extensive with the objective sphere; it is in this sense that we shall see that Rosenzweig's religious philosophy was rooted in existential man.

C. CREATION—REVELATION—REDEMPTION

Steinheim found a place for faith within the sphere of empirical cognition which acknowledges the existence of a real world and is not the product of the free play of discursive thought. Faith lays claim to a sphere of its own, the sphere of empirical cognition, which is identical with that of Revelation. Rosenzweig[51] also assigns to faith a place in empirical cognition, but he has a different understanding of the nature and aim of this sphere. He calls his philosophical method "absolute empiricism"[52] and defines its aim as the pure and complete description of experience,[53] experience as it is without any superfluous mental constructions or intellectual accretions. The method that Rosenzweig adopted was a description of simple, human experience which he at times calls the philosophy of sound, human understanding,[54] but it would be unwarranted to consider him a disciple of the philosophical school of common sense. He insists that his system is not constructed *in vacuo*, the lucubrations of an isolated mind, but is rooted in the living man of flesh and blood, a being nailed down by his finitude and eager to overcome himself.[55] Rosenzweig acknowledged his indebtedness to Feuerbach, who attacked idealism and Christianity in the name of sound, human understanding, the real understanding of real man.[56] A closer examination of the nature and purpose of this philosophical trend called "empirical philosophy,"[57] will aid us in studying Rosenzweig's religious conceptions. The two elements in his philosophy that deserve particular attention are "the healthy understanding" and "experience."

These two elements are meant to indicate that the new philosophy looks at things in their positive and absolute facticity,[58] that is, without conceptual constructions that would fit given facts into preconceived systems. This gives rise to the question as to where these facts are to be found, and what is the source of their facticity. In the systems of Kant and of Hermann Cohen this is to be found in the "consciousness of culture," in the basic forms created by man, such as science, politics, art, et cetera, objective realms whose logical structure is made the subject of philosophical investigation. But Rosenzweig's facticity is not primarily directed to these crystallized forms of human culture in their historical development, but confines itself to the individual consciousness and attempts to shed some light on the elements imbedded within it.

This insistence on taking things as they are, in their *Gegebenheit*, is also revealed in Rosenzweig's conception of the religious consciousness: Religiosity is always positive religion; it begins with the fact and not with its source or its essence.[59] These words are by no means unambiguous. It is not clear whether Rosenzweig is referring to the individual religious consciousness or to the historic embodiments of this consciousness, the historic religions. This ambiguity is not accidental but inheres in the very nature of the concept of facticity and reflects Rosenzweig's ambiguous conception of the problem.

The second characteristic of common consciousness, the consciousness of plain understanding, is found in the fact that it comprehends things in their relations and interconnections. The given things of the world do not appear separate and isolated but as part of the flowing circle of reality.[60] Common consciousness is by its very nature one of *plurality*, which grasps the multifarious aspects of the world as they are without the superimposition of an artificial construction that would reduce multiplicity to unity. It seems that the two characteristics of common consciousness are related to each other—to see things as they really are is here interpreted as seeing them in their diversity and bewildering variety without mental restrictions or preconceived systems of unification. Facticity and multiplicity, like constructive creation and unity, are related to each other.

Common consciousness is closely bound to time, the element in which it moves and has its being. It is not given to man's plain understanding to see all things at once; he must wait patiently for future events to unroll before his field of vision. We can thus say that the world of simple understanding is by its very nature open and incomplete, its expectant gaze turned to the future.

This characteristic of the simple, healthy understanding is also apparent in Rosenzweig's interpretation of the nature of experience as the interrelationship between things. In Kant's critical philosophy interrelatedness is made a criterion of experience in its exact sense—that is, of scientific experience which is identified with scientific cognition. Whereas perception sees phenomena as separate and discrete, experience sees them in their relations and interconnections. These are also stressed by Rosenzweig, but his conception of experience is not the Kantian product of conceptual construction, since he takes experience in its unscientific sense as the bridging of gaps between things. The pagan or scientific point of view sees all things in their isolated state; religion sees them in their relation to one another. In this sense the cognition that characterizes religious faith is identical with experience.[61]

The quality of multiplicity also appears in Rosenzweig's view of experience which preserves each element in its independent state. The relatedness that constitutes the nature of experience consists of a multitude of relations. Every element within experience has an independent status and value of its own, and is on an equal plane with all others. This also applies to the concept of God, which is a concept of experience or of common human consciousness; like man and the world, it enjoys no favored status. Not one of these elements is given to cognition by itself, in its isolated state; each comes to cognition enmeshed in a web of interrelationships.[62]

No one element, then, occupies a privileged place in experience, which, like the consciousness of the simple understanding, takes place in time; and it is this temporal element in which experience occurs that is given a special status. But here again all moments are on an equal plane and each moment is important in its own right. This is expressed by Rosenzweig when he says that a momentary experience does not occur *in* nature but *above* nature, a distinction whereby he indicates the transition that takes place from blind indifference to expressive significance within experience. Each moment has its own individual character and its own nuance. Multiplicity, which characterizes the objective aspect of experience (God, man, world—entities that exist independently), is also a quality of the subjective aspect of experience, since every event experienced is incomparable.

The foregoing analysis of the nature of experience revealed some religiously significant concepts, including that of God. What was said about the function of time within experience also applies to the relation between experience and faith. Faith abhors the isolated object and its constant attempt is to bridge the gap between the elements. It has been well said by G. Scholem that in this basic function faith expresses its heteronomy—that is, its dependence on matter from without. The spontaneous element in consciousness itself is unable to perform this task; although it has the elements, the connection between them is the product of the free gift of Revelation. The heteronomous nature of faith does not express itself in the substantive existence of its elements, but in the net of relationships among them as they appear in experience. This gives us a significant insight into the religious world of Rosenzweig. He ignores the question of God's essence—the concern, he declares, of the intellect and not of faith, which deals with the activity of the elements, including the activity of God. It is not substance, but function that constitutes the content of faith or the content of the religious consciousness. The paradoxical aspect of this concept is worth noting: Rosenzweig is not concerned with the substantive *source* of things but with their mutual interrelations. The system, then, is the sphere in which faith lives and moves, not one that sacrifices distinctions in the interest of intellectual coherence and unity, but of manifold relations.

An additional characteristic of experience is its affinity or even identity with faith. Rosenzweig distinguishes between the assertive aspect of experience, that states a fact or relates an event, and the imperative aspect, that tells man what he is to do. This distinction illumines the nature of faith, since the imperative element in experience implies an obedient and receptive attitude. This is further clarified by Rosenzweig's statement that the experiences of God are assertions and imperatives for the world and that philosophy and mysticism are acquainted only with assertive experiences.[63] With these words Rosenzweig touches a special phase within experience, its suitability as a sphere of intersection and as a meeting place of contending forces.

The experience involved in meeting is called by Rosenzweig "theological experience." Man does not merely absorb dumb objects; he meets the life he finds before him and experiences it.[64] The background of this meeting is the authentic background of religious faith, the relation between living man and the living God. "Theological experience" makes no general assertions about the nature of God, but asserts only what God is at a given moment when He meets man, not a meeting of dumb substances but a real encounter between struggling man and the living God.[65] The general nature of experience here receives an additional dimension derived from faith. The Bible was, for Rosenzweig, such an area of experience between man and God and not a speculative study of fragmentary episodes. This view led him to a profound interpretation of anthropomorphisms in the Bible which he regarded as "plain assertions of encounters between man and God,"[66] not fixed, unalterable assertions but momentary confrontations of the Creator with creation.[67] Since every moment of true experience is unique, every meeting bears the imprint of a special nature and specific relationship. We might say that in the general sphere of experience there is a special sphere of religious experience where man and God meet. An affinity should be pointed out between this conception and Hermann Cohen's theory of correlation, as well as Martin Buber's dialogic form. In other words, faith is nothing more than the experience of the meeting between man and God, the encounter between the Creator of life and His creature.

To this description of experience Rosenzweig adds an aspect derived from Kantian or, at any rate, neo-Kantian philosophy. It has already been stated that critical philosophy was chiefly concerned with the objective facts of cultural creation, science, law, art, et cetera; we might also say that it revolved around experience that is cognitive, ethical, esthetic, et cetera. Rosenzweig attempted to base religious faith on "theological experience" that had an independent character of its own and he opposed those who sought to solve the problem of faith by ignoring the poignant experiences of frail man. He tried to find a basis for his view in the sphere of human activity, where the assertive and imperative aspects meet, and in theological experience untouched by mental constructions, examples of which are to be found in the Bible where wretched man encounters his Maker and enters into a dialogue with Him.

In short, from the standpoint of system, Rosenzweig attempted to proceed in two parallel paths: What he called "absolute empiricism" is nothing more than an interpretation of the facts of consciousness and experience in order to find in them the seeds of religious faith. Rosenzweig's purpose, as against religious or antireligious constructionism, was to keep faith within definite limits by insisting on the given fact of religious experience as an ultimate fact from which there is no recourse. He considers the basis of faith as valid as any other creative sphere of human activity. The relationship of faith helps us understand that experience as bridging the gaps between things, and to the nature of religious experience as a living encounter; experience enables him to impart to the religious relationship an assurance derived from the given, hard fact that cannot be ignored.

The notion of "common consciousness" and of "experience" is formulated in a negative and critical manner in opposition to philosophic idealism. Rosenzweig's strictures give us a comprehensive view of idealism and its characteristic features which may be classified as follows:

a) In the interest of unity and generality, idealism prefers the pale world of quantitative truth to the warmth and color of particular things in the visible world. Disregarding qualitative multiplicity and the quiddity of individual things, it constructs a philosophical edifice of barren propositions that conform to the contours of the human mind.

b) Since idealism stresses rational articulation performed by the mind and reason (*mente ac ratione*) in subduing the stubborn facts of existence, it shifts the emphasis from the external object to the form and the subject that comprehends it, viz. to the philosopher and to his philosophical fabric or system.[68]

c) Idealism can thus shift the object to the subjective sphere, since it does not believe that reality is given but that it is created, derived from the sources of the Ego.[69] There is a continuous transition from the "I" to reality, the "I" being a constant, durable point that serves as the source of the world. We no longer find here the two antithetical entities of the Ego and the world confronting each other, but both are comprehended by the unifying activity of the mind and confined to one system wherein the Ego gives rise to the world. The religious view, however, cannot acknowledge this sovereign position accorded to the Ego, since it believes that the world is dependent on a transcendent Source. Rosenzweig no doubt had this in mind when he said that idolatry was brought into existence by idealism[70] (words that remind us of Steinheim's attitude to paganism).

d) Reality as conceived by idealism ignores multiplicity and attains unity at the expense of content.[71] Reason and the Ego clasp the empty air and end in a self-embrace. Rational thought beats its wings in a void; it is nourished by its own substance, like a serpent that bites its own tail.[72] It is condemned to continue its own reiterated, circular movement and can find no outlet to transcendence.

e) Reason thus goes its own way, self-sufficient and self-contained, cut off from living consciousness and human experience. Idealism is the exact opposite of empiricism which is based on general consciousness. Empiricism, as understood by Rosenzweig, analyzes the data of experience *a posteriori*, whereas idealism seeks to create the data of experience by *a priori* means; the one is a cosmological view that attempts to explain how existence is derived from reason and is thus inimical to faith; the other is a religious view that seeks to understand human existence in terms of faith.

f) The difference between the empirical and the idealistic view is also apparent in the problem of the relation of truth to existence. Idealism is committed to the search for truth, the highest principle on which every assertion depends, and it makes truth the basic principle and law of existence. On the other hand, Rosenzweig's fundamental allegiance is to existence and his empiricism takes the data of experience as they are. Existence cannot be said to be dependent on truth because truth is an integral part of existence, constituting its content and not its principle. Existence does not depend on truth; the *generality* of truth is inherent within existence itself.[73]

The distinction between general consciousness and experience on the one hand, and idealistic speculation and system-building on the other, properly belongs to the theory of knowledge. It serves to support the claims of faith to occupy an independent sphere; claims that have, however, a cognitive basis. To the cognitive distinction, therefore, Rosenzweig adds an existential distinction by relying not only on human cognition but also on man's position and conduct in the existential world. What is the nature of this real man, the bearer of general consciousness, who is irremediably caught in the toils of existence? The cognitive and existential aspects of reality have in common their interest in facticity, their respect for the stubborn facts that resist rational schemes.[74] The qualitative multiplicity of the world cannot be rationally articulated or classified; similarly, the unpleasant fact of man's wretched existence cannot be ignored or brushed aside. Man's realization that he is a creature of dust and ashes is the beginning of religious speculation. Man must come to terms with the dread fact that he stands alone as a sentient being amid the multifarious things of the world. Idealism with its attachment to abstract forms and values has no room for empirical, struggling man; Rosenzweig's empiricism, on the other hand, celebrates the sin, guilt, and agony of man in his existential state.

Existential man stands alone in a world of things, but he cannot be classified among them and stands out as an eternal, irreducible fact.[75] Man as man is but dust and ashes, but as an individual he glories in his privileged position. Rosenzweig sometimes speaks of the "effrontery" of those philosophers who refuse to be swallowed up in a sea of abstractions and who dare to look at life as it is, philosophers such as Schopenhauer and Nietzsche. At any rate, this existentialist philosophy has two sides: It sees man as a miserable creature of dust and ashes, and at the same time as an individual of power and influence within the empirical sphere. Rosenzweig devotes the first part of *Star of Redemption* to describing the nature of this existential man, whose most enduring quality is obstinacy.

Rosenzweig finds in his existentialism corroborating evidence for his theory of faith. Man is ideally suited to serve as one of the poles of the theological axis over against God: the living God reveals Himself to living man.[76] This correlative, dialogic relation between man and God expresses the religious aspect of Rosenzweig's existentialist conception, which attempts to bridge the gap between man who is confined to the empirical world and transcendent God. This is the element that existentialism has in common with empirical philosophy. Both stress relationship—one, the relationship between God and man; the other, the relationship among the elements in human experience.

A prominent trait of idealism is its aversion for the disagreeable facts of man's earthly existence. It conquers its fears by denying reality and by making light of man's plight, by spreading a blanket of abstractions, as it were, over life's ugly features. Its highest wisdom is to deny the reality of death.[77] Its futility lies in trying to uproot man from experience and remove him from reality.

Rosenzweig's philosophy can best be understood in the light of the philosophical currents of thought which exerted a profound influence upon him. He himself mentioned on one occasion his appreciation of the views of Martin Heidegger, the chief exponent of existentialism in his day. A closer look at some of these modern movements may prove valuable is casting light on the problems of religion and Judaism with which Rosenzweig was primarily concerned.

The characteristics of existentialism have been enumerated by Eduard Spranger: a) a sharp distinction between theory and life; b) the significance of the element of time in existence and the difference between the past and the present; c) opposition to all closed systems with their artificial classification of facts; d) the qualitative distinction between the finite and the infinite; e) creaturehood, or the feeling that man is a created being that owes its existence to forces outside himself.[78]

These five characteristics apply to the philosophical conceptions of both Rosenzweig and Heidegger. However, we must be careful to distinguish between existentialism that rests on faith and atheistic existentialism, a distinction emphasized by Karl Löwith in his valuable study of these two thinkers.[79] Rosenzweig's philosophy seems to be closer to that of Karl Jaspers than to that of Heidegger, since Jaspers also stresses the transcendent aspect of man's existential nature.

Jaspers sees man's existence as the arena of human activity dependent on transcendence, an area of tension between an existence whose gaze is turned in upon itself and one that looks beyond its narrow confines.

At this steep juncture to which man is confined he is impelled to take the leap across the narrow isthmus from immanence to transcendence, from temporal existence into pure being.[80] Here Jaspers comes close to Kierkegaard's conception of finite man's *saltus mortale* to the divine source of his being. He sees man at-tempting to escape from his finitude and to rise above himself, which is the essence of his religious impulse. But whereas Jaspers speaks of the *leap* to transcendence, Rosenzweig speaks only of the dialogue between God who reveals Himself and man whose soul is born in the process of Revelation.

We should not overlook Rosenzweig's relation to dialectical theology, a basically religious tendency in existentialist philosophy that was prevalent in Protestant circles. Rosenzweig mentions this current of thought in Protestant theology and in this passage speaks of *Deus absconditus*, one of its cardinal notions. Rosenzweig's observation is meant to be critical, but it reflects a fairly wider ac-quaintance with this school of thought.

Heinrich Barth defined the nature of existentialism as a relation to something beyond itself.[81] Against the background of tran-scendence in human existence, he emphasizes the dialogic or dialectical character of this concept, which he interprets as a matter of question and answer.[82] This line of thought is close to that of Rosenzweig when we think of his conception of bridging the gaps in existence or of the correlation between real man and the living God.

From these presuppositions dialectical theology drew two conclu-sions that are close to Rosenzweig's thinking: Existence is funda-mentally *decision*, a decision in favor of something transcendent beyond itself and the will to realize it. Existence is therefore inter-preted as a realm of possibilities not yet realized.[83] The inevitable consequence of this is to raise the *deed* to the level of a religious value. If we recall Rosenzweig's thoughts concerning human conduct as the mature product of wisdom, we can note the resemblance to the conclusions drawn by dialectical theology except for differences in terminology. In any case, the question that was of deep interest to Rosenzweig was a basic, existentialist one: If existence means decision and if every decision takes place at a definite moment in time, does the decision occur for the sake of the moment—that is, immersed within the element of time—or through the moment—that is, for the sake of something beyond time.[84] Dialectical theology disagrees with existentialism at this point (its argument being directed chiefly against Jaspers) and argues that this philosophy is condemned to eternal subjectivism. From this point of view, Rosenzweig's philosophy cannot be regarded as subjective, for it takes man's existential nature as the starting point for bridging the gap between man and God.

Despite Rosenzweig's philosophical affinity to dialectical theology, however, there are some basic differences that call for more detailed notice. Dialectical theology stresses the distinction between the finite and the infinite and asserts, furthermore, that man is the finite that contains within itself an element of the infinite, the grace of God, without which man would be cast adrift on a dark ocean of matter without faith or deliverance. In seeking to bridge the chasm between man and God, Rosenzweig recognizes not only the act of God's grace but also the fact that it is the product of Revelation rooted in God's nature. In dialectical theology, grace is a free gift of a distant God; for Rosenzweig it has its source in Revelation that links man with God, who is both transcendent and immanent.

Dialectical theology rejects the notion that the finite is capable of containing the infinite.[85] This thought is also found in Rosenzweig; in the religious sphere, however, man and God meet in a moment in time when the infinite enters the finite and endues it with transcendence. Dialectical theology insists on the unfathomable distance that separates God from man; Rosenzweig seeks a way of bringing them into a closer relationship. In this respect Rosenzweig is closer to Paul Tillich and his conception of time that is filled with content (*Kairos*) than he is to dialectical theology. We are dealing here with two different approaches—the world of dialectical theology, disrupted and cleft in two, with no harmonious principle of reconciliation, and the world of Rosenzweig which, despite its starting point in the confused, empirical world of multifarious phenomena, strives towards an ultimate harmony through his concept of Redemption. It is clear that at the end his circle closes (in spite of his opposition to Hegel) with a God who constantly returns to Himself in a process of self-redemption.

In the sphere of theology itself we find a difference between Rosenzweig and dialectical theology with respect to Revelation, the latter understanding the biblical Revelation of a transcendent God as a unique event, and the former considering it both an objective fact and an inner experience, a harmonious combination of an external event and an internal sentiment.

Rosenzweig treats the subject of Revelation against the background of his existential philosophy, a subject that is central to his basic philosophical conceptions.

There are two aspects to experience, the elements within it and the relations between them. The first is described by Rosenzweig as containing three contents—God, man, and the world, each provided with its own qualities. God has both nature and is an active Power; man is a private individual with a character of his own, and also a being related to others; the world is the meeting place of the universal and the particular, the species and the individual. All three possess a content of their own as elements given in experience, but experience conceived as *faith* finds its content not in these elements themselves but in the interrelations. From the standpoint of the elements themselves, the experience of faith is no different from any other experience, and the pagan conception no different from the monotheistic. The operations of the healthy understanding was, for Rosenzweig, intimately connected with these three elements—God, man, and the world—and he therefore examined the general concept of experience to find the specific characteristic of faith.

The essence of faith, therefore, lies in the dynamism of the elements and in their active, mutual relations. In short, when we speak of faith, we speak of the function of every element of one experience in its relation to another. The emphasis placed on the function and the dynamism of the elements is clearly not meant to deprive faith of its constant, constitutive ingredients, since even the content of the elements changes in accordance with the varying relations and interconnections among the elements themselves.

The main point that deserves notice in this discussion of the rational structure among the substantive elements of experience is the tendency of the structure to convert experience into *faith*. The connection among the elements is a formative one, the result of a real event which moves forward on different levels in time and is not confined to a closed, circular movement. Three levels are discernible in this progressive movement: Creation, Revelation, and Redemption. From the standpoint of method, Rosenzweig relies on the traditional concepts of the religious consciousness, and attempts to weave them into a net to capture the experience of faith. While making this attempt he succeeds in imbuing each of them with special significance.

a) Paganism, in contradistinction to monotheism, is characterized by the absence of relations among its elements. God and man are both confined to their respective spheres without an active principle of communication or co-operation. Monotheism, which is the true experience of faith, is primarily concerned with establishing relations between man and God and also in determining the *fons et origo* of this relationship, which the religious experience conceives as the living God, the Creator of life.[86]

The question that now arises concerning the act of Creation is whether it is a unique occurrence on the part of God or a manifestation of His nature, whether it is an event that happened once for all at some point in the past or whether it is an ever-recurrent, continuous process without end. Rosenzweig was much concerned with this time factor in Creation and in his attempted solutions seems to have followed Cohen in confining the time relation to the finite realm of man and the world, contesting its validity when applied to God.

Rosenzweig repeatedly insists on regarding Creation as an objective fact based on the relations among the elements. He argues against the theology of the nineteenth century, which shuts its eyes to the fact of Creation and concerns itself mainly with the problem of Revelation.[87] Rosenzweig attaches great importance to this objectivity of Creation, since it serves him as an absolute, initial point in the chain of relations among the elements. This objectivity is also expressed by the circumstance that the act of Creation took place in the past and is hence far removed from us and beyond our control. From the standpoint of the world the act of Creation was not completed in the past and is not a temporal act confined to a closed system; from the standpoint of God, however, Creation constitutes a past event. The fact that God created the world tells us nothing about the manner of the transition from God to the world—that is, whether it took place in time and whether time existed before and after Creation. To say that the transition occurred in time is to introduce a time factor into God's province and to widen the sphere of relations between God and the world from the standpoint of the world. Rosenzweig here becomes involved in the complex problems of traditional speculation concerning freedom and will in Creation. Time is real only when it refers to man and the world, and has no validity when applied to God.[88] The difference between the finite and the infinite finds expression only within the temporal sphere.

For Rosenzweig as for Cohen, creation is not a volitional act of God occurring in time, but a logical-immanent relationship between God and the world, so that Creation is an *attribute* of God, a quality that defines His being. In other words, when we say "God exists," we mean "God is Creator," since Creation is but a quality of the existing God. Furthermore, since Creation is the nodal point in the net of relations among the elements, and since faith is concerned with the relations that exist among the elements and the elements as they are, the existence of God means God in His capacity as Creator, since it is this quality that determines God's character within the net of relations. Existence that is devoid of relationship is not the concern of faith; the existence of God endowed with relationship is God the Creator.

Cohen supports his conception of Creation as an attribute of God and not as an act of divine will with the logical assumption that God as Being does not exist in and of Himself or for the sake of Himself, since all being exists for the sake of becoming. This is the logical-cognitive argument that takes the basis of substance as being and as the support for relationships and becoming. Cohen transfers the problem of the concept of substance and its accidents from the cognitive to the divine sphere, and by identifying substance with God he finds the way to initiate the logical-immanent transition from God, conceived as substance, to the world, conceived as accidents that are dependent on this substance. Rosenzweig does not employ the logical-cognitive method, but relies entirely upon the argument based on faith. He makes a distinction between the distant God who is unknown to man, and the God who is nigh to those who call on Him, and he makes this distinction basic to the question of Creation. If we say that Creation was an act of the will that took place in time, then it is possible for such an act never to have occurred; in such an event the world would not have been created and God would have been isolated from the world and from man. God could then not be the object of faith, for there would be no paths that lead to Him and He would remain the object of pagan worship, a pococurante God of independent, detached elements.[89] If we look at Creation from the standpoint of a God who is hidden from men and dwells in a realm where relations do not apply, it must be regarded as an arbitrary act. But if we see it from the standpoint of a God who has made Himself known to man, then creation is a real quality of a revealed God.[90] The fact of Creation as a conception of the relations among the elements is derived by Rosenzweig from the content of faith. Since the existence of the elements is beyond doubt, being a given fact of common understanding, Rosenzweig arrives at the basic principle: The relation of God to the world is that of a Creator to the created.

This view of Creation raises a number of religious questions that are touched upon in Rosenzweig's system. The central question, however, upon which the others depend is: What is the nature of the faith relationship against the background of Creation, or what is the element of faith in this sphere? The problem of cosmogony is here interpreted with the aid of the religious concept of the revealed God, but we are not told of the religious nature of the transition from the world to the revealed God. On the basis of the concept of Creation, Rosenzweig defined the place assigned to each of the elements of the relationship. God is the active factor and the world is the passive factor.[91] Creation reveals God as a powerful entity;[92] the world, by virtue of the fact that it is created, is accompanied by the consciousness of having been created,[93] reflected in a feeling of dependence and inadequacy. If we would formulate the new relationship of the primacy of faith that emerges from this conception of Creation, we might say that the fact of Creation introduces no change whatever in the nature of God, for the essential nature of God is to be a Creator. The world, however, does undergo a change, like every content of experience that is touched by faith, by becoming conscious that it is created and no longer an independent, self-contained entity. The change that takes place in the sphere of the world is both one of consciousness and reality; Rosenzweig makes no distinction between the two.

From the standpoint of God, Creation is a fact and not an event, an impersonal fact that is not dependent on a decision of the active will. From the point of view of the world, but not of God, Creation is an occurrence. The notion of Divine Providence is related by Rosenzweig to the idea of Creation. Providence means the active intervention of God in the affairs of the world and their supervision; a divine act whereby God comes close to the world. By depriving the concept of Creation of this active aspect, Rosenzweig is unable to relate Providence as an act with Creation as conceived from the standpoint of God. The act of Providence, then, is related to Creation not from the viewpoint of the Creator but from the viewpoint of the created world: The consciousness of being created is realized in the notion of Divine Providence.[94] We are here confronted with the paradox that is inherent in the concept of Creation as it appears in Rosenzweig's system. In Creation, God's active power reveals itself over against the passivity of the world, and this is the principle that applies from the standpoint of cosmogony to the natural, factual transitions from God to the world. From the standpoint of faith, however, the order changes: The active factor now is not God the Creator but the created world, a world transformed by faith and conscious of its dependence on the Creator and on Divine Providence. Rosenzweig attempted to make the concept of Creation the objective root of faith, but it could not function as such because of the subjective factor of consciousness that accompanies it.

That Rosenzweig was aware of these problems related to the concept of Creation can be seen in his view of Creation and science. Rosenzweig regarded Creation as the content of *knowledge*; in one of his letters he states that science belongs to the world of *Creation*, and is pagan."[95] These two characteristics of

knowledge—its connection with Creation and its pagan nature—
deserve to be examined more closely.

In what way can science be said to belong to the world of Creation? Science revolves around constant facts and not around
incomplete occurrences in time. It is concerned with impersonal,
nondialogic facts, but what it gains in its much-vaunted objectivity
it loses in religious value. Two correlative entities—God and man—
are at work in the sphere of faith. This basic thought, which Rosenzweig received from Cohen and Buber, finds no place here, for
as long as God is active from the standpoint of cosmogony, the
world remains passive; and as long as the world is active from the
standpoint of faith, God remains passive. The absence of mutual
co-operation in Creation is evident from the fact that Creation, as
in Cohen's conception, is a relation between God and the *world*
and not between God and *man*. The absence of the personal factor
deprives the relationship of its efficacy. This helps us understand
why Rosenzweig relegates knowledge to past time.[96] From God's
point of view Creation is a fact that belongs to the past. All knowledge, insofar as it is knowledge, originates in something that is far
removed from us and that has its cause in the distant past.

The other characteristic, the pagan nature of knowledge, stems
from the circumstance that the pagan gods, although alive, are not
related to the world and are not the creators of life. The purpose of
Creation is to bridge this chasm and bring God closer to the world
and the world closer to God. Rosenzweig criticizes the religious
notion that Creation serves as a ground for faith. As long as the
bridge between man and God is a fact and not an occurrence in
time, we have not touched the secret springs of faith. Creation
alone and of itself provides us with the reason for the existence of
things, but does not explain the dynamic character of their relations. Knowledge that arises from creation is pagan because it is
based on being and not on an occurrence, to which access can be
obtained only through the gateway of Revelation. The knowledge
of the mere creation of things tells us nothing at all; there has
never been a form of paganism, from the Babylonian priests to
Hegel, that has not had its own creation-myths. It is only when
"created" things have been created for the sake of an end, and
the first is also the last (as in Isaiah) or the Alpha and Omega

(as in John), that we have knowledge.[97] The principal defect in knowledge resides in the fact that it regards things as complete and ignores the empirical occurrence as an event that takes place in time. The experienced event is conceived by Revelation, Redemption, and the Knowledge of Truth, which is real faith, as nourished by three sources at once and not alone by Creation.

b) Creation determines the relation between God and the world. But if we were to remain simply in this relationship, the world would be blind and dumb; it emerges from this state only when God illumines it with His light and man finds the strength to speak the redeeming word.[98] This observation concerning the transition from the inarticulate stage to the spoken word leads to the second step on the road that defines the immanent essence of existence. This step takes us to the place where God and man meet, not as the impersonal poles of the theological ellipse, but in a personal relationship which is defined as Revelation.

Hermann Cohen, as we have seen, also took Revelation to be a correlation between God and man, not simply one between God and the world. This view is in keeping with the essential character of Revelation which, as an adjunct of Creation, speaks to man and man alone. In Cohen's idealistic conception, Revelation is understood in its relation to *reason*, not to man; more precisely, it is the procreator of reason. If man is a being endowed with reason, then rationality has its source in Revelation. We can thus say that Cohen stresses the *instructive* aspect of Revelation, since its purpose is to teach man; and reason, by virtue of its theoretical function, promotes this purpose. Cohen was thus able to preserve man's independent activity within Revelation by insisting on the spontaneity of reason. In Revelation there is a correlation between man and God, a mutual relationship in which man plays an *active* part.

A similar conception of Revelation is to be found in Rosenzweig except, of course, that he removes it from the sphere of reason as this term was understood by idealism. Revelation gave birth to *man*, to the human soul, not to reason; if reason finds its crowning expression in scientific achievement, we can say that it is related to the *fact of Creation* and not to the *event of Revelation*.

In Revelation, God reveals Himself to man himself—the accusative and the dative together, Rosenzweig says, constitute the unique content of Revelation.[99] Revelation is meaningful only in such a mutual relationship between the One who deigns to reveal Himself and the recipient to whom Revelation is directed, a relationship wherein the distant, inarticulate God of Creation is transformed into the God who is close to man.[100] In contrast to the pagan God who dwells beyond the life of this world, Creation represents a kind of bridge, an opportunity for God to make Himself felt in the world and approach closer to man. From this point of view, Creation is regarded by Rosenzweig as a kind of inchoate Revelation, wherein the face of Divinity is turned towards the world. But as long as Creation is considered only an attribute, not an act or event, it cannot be taken as Revelation in the full sense of the word.

Creation emphasizes the inner transition from a God who is remote from man to a God who is near him. Revelation emphasizes the relationship between man and this nearby God. This God has now acquired an inviolable unity, not subject to an inner duality. This is true for two reasons:

a) This inarticulate, remote God of Creation is now the indwelling God, the Redeemer who was found the liberating Word.[101] Revelation, in other words, adds nothing to God's essence, but is merely another aspect of a new relationship of God to man brought into existence by the depth, power, and reality of faith. Revelation does not define God's *nature* but rather, His *relation* to man.

b) Even though Revelation is another aspect of God, it does not draw us any closer to a knowledge of His inscrutable essence; it merely acquaints us with His existence in its relation to man. His essence remains hidden from us:[102] "What God is and what He was before Creation . . . these are questions that are beyond any comprehension."[103] The remote God may even be subject to demonstrative proof,[104] but the indwelling God is the object of faith and concepts do not apply to Him. Revelation, then, may be regarded as the mediating latch or bolt of faith.[105]

The distinction between Creation and Revelation may be formu-

lated from still another point of view. We have seen that within
the sphere of experience Rosenzweig distinguished between the
assertive phase of given facts and the imperative phase addressed to
empirical man. We can now relate these two experiential phases
with the two aspects of God's relation to the world and to man:
The imperative belongs to Revelation and the assertion to Creation.[106] Since knowledge revolves around Creation, the inarticulate
facts in this sphere simply remain given in their original state. The
fact of the world's existence, that is, its having been created, constitutes the content of assertion. It is otherwise in the sphere of
Revelation, in which God meets man, to whom He deigns to
reveal Himself and with whom He enters into a dialogic relation.
The ground is here prepared for the growth of the *imperative*.

Religious factors, both historical and theological, can be discerned in this conception of Rosenzweig. The relation of Revelation
to the imperative points to the central function that Rosenzweig
assigns to language and speech in this sphere. He is here able
to stress the instructive element and to identify it with the imperative, as in the biblical conception of Revelation. In Rosenzweig's
interpretation, Revelation is related to man and to the birth of the
soul, the first step toward the traditional concept of Revelation as
obedience to the imperative. In order that the imperative be meaningful and obeyed, it is necessary to posit One who issues the
commands and one who obeys them, and to determine the essential
relationship between them.

From the historical point of view some notice should be given
to the relation between Rosenzweig's conception and Maimonides'
doctrine of attributes of action and negative attributes by which
alone God's relation to the world can be recognized. It is in this
sphere that Rosenzweig places his concept of Revelation, and his
revealed God is the active God of Maimonides. Here Rosenzweig,
intentionally or not, expounds the doctrine of Maimonides by em-
ploying concepts derived from Cohen's interpretation of this
doctrine. There is, however, a fundamental distinction between
Maimonides' rationalism and Rosenzweig's fideism, a distinction
best illustrated in their attitude to the question of anthropomorphisms in the Bible. Maimonides, as is well known, would purify

the God concept of all its anthropomorphic elements, including the human attributes of activity. Rosenzweig, however, considers anthropomorphism a proper category of faith in man's relations with the indwelling God. He does not understand on what basis of comparison our language, our thought and our experience can be blamed as deficient.[107] In order that God's counterpart in the dialogic relationship could be man and not reason (as in Cohen's philosophy), there are no other means of expression man could employ; to replace these by clear, rationalistic concepts would vitiate the intimate relation between the revealed God and man who is commanded to hearken to Him.

Revelation is basically a dialogue between two active participants: As he stands before God, man is conscious of his inadequacy, and looks to God to take the first step; at the same time he hears a compelling voice which urges *him* to take the first step—and thus an endless dialogue is initiated.[108] This passage gives us the outline of Rosenzweig's conception of Revelation as consisting in a simple dialogue *conducted in words*, between God who opens it and man who brings his own contribution. Each of the participants has his say, although God sets the tone, since He has the first and the last word, and is thus able to exercise a controlling influence in the conduct of the dialogue.[109]

The dialogue opens with a question that God addresses to man, "Where art thou?"[110] It is not asked to ascertain man's nature or essence, but to discover the "thou" in order to communicate with him.[111] Rosenzweig here raises Revelation to the level of a mediating bolt or latch in the religious experience. The existence of God and man as they are belongs to the sphere of given facts that Rosenzweig accepts without question and whose separate and unrelated natures he explains in the first part of his system. The basic question of faith, therefore, is: How are these two existences, each with its own well-defined essence, related to each other, and how are their isolated states bridged? In the question, "Where art thou?"—that seeks out man and requires him to answer— Rosenzweig sees the initial step of the relationship between the human and the divine within the framework of an interminable dialogue that is to reverberate down the ages.

In this first step of the relationship man is addressed in the vocative voice by a God who has emerged from his remoteness to engage directly in a dialogue with man, not as an Abstraction but as the living God who bears a Name which is synonymous with the content of Revelation. Since this content is based on a relationship of faith, it is manifest to man and comprehensible in terms of human language.

Into this dialogic framework Rosenzweig injects something of the content of Revelation. Man beyond the theoretical-practical system, man in his quality as "I" demands that God return his love, even that God love him first; for his "I" is speechless and waits for God's redeeming word: "Man, where art thou?"[112] It is God's concern for man that makes Him ask. In Rosenzweig's view man takes the initiative; it is he who first asks for God's love and insists on an answer. Man's love is transferred to God and the love of God is returned in recompense. Rosenzweig here seeks to find support for the sentiment of love experienced by the individual in daily life and to transfer this dominant emotion to the religious consciousness and make it part of Revelation. Man seeks God in vain unless his path is illumined by God's love. Rosenzweig here follows Feuerbach, for whom love was a primary relation, except that he uses it not to deprive man of his transcendence but to draw God and man closer together. In any case, it is clear that the central position assigned to love in the sphere of faith necessarily determines the nature of faith and the object of its allegiance.

Love is the content of Revelation from two points of view. God loves man—this is the novel factor in Revelation that draws God closer to man; and God commands man to love God—which is a quality of Revelation from the standpoint of man. In other words, two elements meet in Revelation: a divine act directed to man and the imperative that flows from this act originating with man in his relation to God. Rosenzweig here makes a distinction between Creation and Revelation from the standpoint of content and status. The assertive aspect in Revelation applies, therefore, to the divine act and there is no place here for the imperative, since we are moving in the sphere of a beneficent and all-powerful God. The assertive aspect affirms the love of God for man. The imperative is by its very nature a category in the human sphere and its function is to requite God's love. *Thou shalt love the Lord thy God* because the Lord thy God loves thee. This distinction between the divine act directed to man and the imperative that proceeds from man to God is also expressed by Rosenzweig's saying that the love of him who loves is directly opposed to the love of him who is loved, and is without basis.[113] God's love of man is a manifestation of His being and an expression of His power, but man's love of God is based on God's love of man. The mutual relation between man and God has its origin in God, who initiates the process to which man reacts.

Man reacts by requiting God's love and thus promotes the mutual relationship, which from the human side rests on trust in God.[114] Rosenzweig here distinguishes between trust and faith. Trust is not an intellectual category but one derived from the sentiment of love and piety and therefore makes no assertions concerning God's nature or essence; it is merely man's attachment and loyalty to Him whose desire is in man.

Some explanatory words should be devoted to the reasons behind this religious conception that makes love the content of Revelation and the imperative to love its chief ingredient. It is apparent that Rosenzweig here departs from the traditional conception of Revelation, which rests on the assumption that the relation between God and man already existed, being rooted in Creation which was traditionally conceived as an act of will whereby God manifests His existence. Rosenzweig obviously departs from this traditional view by making Revelation the sole foundation and not a superstructure erected on the prior foundation of Creation. He thus seeks to make Revelation conform to the covenant between God and man. He who had often inveighed against mysticism now unknowingly adopts its views and considers Revelation to be a covenant and the aspiration to be one with God and not a dogmatic content. In this Rosenzweig's conception differs from that of Steinheim who emphasizes the instructive content of Revelation as its principal ingredient.

The concept of Providence is also part of the consciousness of being a creature; the relation of the world to God and its dependence on Him is understood from the standpoint of the world in relation to Providence. This concept also appears in connection with Revelation and this helps us in understanding a significant point in Rosenzweig's conception—namely, that just as Creation was the origin of Revelation, the idea of Providence implicit in Creation was the origin of Providence in Revelation. It is the Providence within Creation, however, that expresses the essential connection between the world and God and does not express God's actual intervention in the progress of the world and in the affairs of men. It is the fact of an unlimited Providence, that not a hair of man's head falls to the ground without God's will, which constitutes the new concept of God introduced by Revelation.[115] It should not be overlooked that in this explanation of the nature of the new concept of Providence the volitional character of the divine act is conspicuous. We are no longer in the sphere of God's existence and attributes but in the realm of changing events which are the product of will.

God's intervention in the affairs of men is another characteristic of Revelation that differentiates it from Creation. Creation is an attribute of God inherent in His very nature and without it existence would remain static and unchanged. Revelation is not an attribute but an act, an event;[116] and the content of Revelation, love, is also an event that takes place in the relationship between God and man.[117] Hence, the intervention of God in the affairs of man is not to be interpreted as mere Providence but as an act which makes God's presence manifest to man so that he could enter into a direct, dialogic relation with Him.[118] In this relationship God meets man here and now, a temporal relationship that serves as a bolt or latch between the past and the future, between the dim past of Creation and the beckoning future of Redemption.[119] God is now seen not as a mere *anima mundi* but as an Indwelling Personality with whom we can commune and enter into divine fellowship. This belief enhances man's inner worth, for he looks into his own experience for the disclosure of divine truth. Heaven begins on earth and we can lay hold of immortality in our temporal life. Revelation to Rosenzweig means that God is no longer solitary and insulated, but linked to man to whom He is closer than breathing, and nearer than hands and feet.

We here touch upon the inner dialectic in Rosenzweig's concept of Revelation, a dialectic that flows from the intimate connection between Revelation and the present moment. Rosenzweig now and then directs some sharp words against the theology of experience that rejects objective criteria for religion and finds the guarantee of faith in the subjective sentiments of the human heart.[120] He holds to both aspects of Revelation, experience and event; it is a true experience only insofar as it may ever recur as an event. The event is not further from God than experience; nature is not further removed from His comprehension than the soul.[121] Rosenzweig would make Revelation a link to connect the subjective element with the objective in the divine act of Revelation. This dual aspect is implied in its very definition; if Revelation means that God reveals Himself to man, then the accusative case represents objective reality and the dative case subjective experience. Furthermore, Rosenzweig seeks to ascertain the historical aspect in Revelation,[122] since this aspect expresses the dependence of experience on the past. The unique, historical act of Revelation, however, does not occupy a central place in Rosenzweig's system; his interpretations revolve not around the Ten Commandments but around the Song of Songs. It is clear that in this point of faith Rosenzweig, who regarded himself as an opponent of mystical ideas, had recourse to a mystical solution. He looked upon Revelation as an ever-recurrent event in the inner life of man, not an event maintained by the authority of an outward organization or embodied in a code of ecclesiastical law but an activity that miraculously takes possession of the human heart;[123] not an objective, historical event in the past but a constant reaffirmation of such an event in man's subjective experience.[124] The subjective element in this interpretation is evident in the two factors of confirmation and recapitulation that have been introduced into the concept of Revelation, for it is only by emphasizing the unceasing activity of Revelation in the present that Rosenzweig could impart a dialogic character to this cardinal concept of his religious philosophy.

Rosenzweig is indebted for this concept of Revelation, which fitted so well into his system, to his friend, Eugen Rosenstock. Revelation strengthens and supports the net of relationships in existence, providing a basis for what is above and below, the continents of the world, on the one hand; and what is before and after, the past and the future, on the other hand.[125] Since Revelation takes place in time between the past and the present, it may be regarded as a point of support in spatial and temporal orientation in reality whose primary function is to reveal the relations existing within this reality. The world prior to the relationships is the world of paganism in which the three elements of experience—God, man, and the world—appear independently. In this world, then, there is no discernible principle of order, since order is necessarily inherent in relations. Temporality is an integral part of the articulated structure of an orderly world. Here Revelation bursts the narrow confines of the concept of faith and we can say, in the language of Kant, that Revelation is the highest condition of experience, for it lies in the very nature of experience to create relations among the elements.

The relation between Revelation and time becomes clearer when we consider the role that language plays in this conception. The very fact that Revelation is interpreted as a dialogic form indicates the prominent position assigned to speech and language within this system. Revelation is not a visible phenomenon of forms and images but an auditory experience[126] in which words are addressed to the human ear. Thus, language is its instrument and vehicle.[127] Rosenzweig makes a distinction between the pre-religious and the religious world. The former is the self-contained world of thought and knowledge that comprises the past; the latter is expressed in human speech, which is a living occurrence giving *expression* to ideas, without freezing them as thought does. The role assigned to language by Rosenzweig is similar to that assigned to intuition by Bergson, and the sharp distinction drawn between thought and language is parallel to Bergson's distinction between the completed and the dynamic content.

In contrast to the transition from Creation in the distant past to Revelation derived from the relation between subject and object, we find in Rosenzweig the transition from inarticulate content to expressive speech.[128] Expression is not a quality associated with the origin of things, but arises in the second stage of development in conjunction with the acts that take place in time. The divine

Word is the second step that follows upon Creation; although Creation inheres in the very essence of God, it is the Word that gives expression to the esssence. Unexpressed essence is a transitory stage to the temporal occurrence; expression applies to essence embedded within the temporal structure. All speech can thus be regarded as translation[129] or the transference of the inexpressible to the realm of expression, of the inarticulate to the articulate. Speech is the organon of Revelation in that it discloses and reveals its content by means of dialogue, which endows events with dramatic form by verbally conveying to man the divine imperative to love, and, finally, through the temporal event which serves as a transition from dark, mute content to revealed expression, thus bridging the gap between the remote and the indwelling God. This helps us understand the role of language in Rosenzweig's philosophical system. The name, he insists, stands at the beginning and at the end of all cognition; the concept is to be found only in the middle. The first thing we know about someone is the name by which he is called, and only later do we learn general things about him that may or may not be correct; finally, we go beyond these generalities which fail to describe the entire man and go back to his name. But what is the meaning of the name and how does it differ from the concept? I *comprehend* a concept, but I *am called* by a name; I receive my name. There is a path that leads from the concept to the sentence, from the name to the word—that is, from the ear to the tongue. I speak only when I perceive that I am the one to whom the word has been addressed.[130] It is evident that for Rosenzweig the concept is not a primary instrument of cognition, since it occupies an intermediate place between the Alpha and Omega of speech; the spoken word does not break forth spontaneously, but is always inseparable from the dialogic form; at the outset man is passive, hears his name, but does not speak it himself. This act of passive listening is one of the characteristics of Revelation, a dialogic form that is inherent within it.

In this problem of the transition from Creation to Revelation we find in Rosenzweig's system still another category of faith—miracle. He regards miracle as the materialization of something shapeless and unformed that is completed and brought to light by Revelation, the expression of something that was latent in Creation[131]—that is, Revelation in its primary sense of *manifestatio*. A miracle is hence a fact that emerges from obscurity and breaks forth as an event in time, an occurrence that imbues a definite moment in time with significance. Miracle, as Revelation, is not simply an event that occurs at some time and in some place, but an event that is significant in and of itself and for those who witness it. The waters of the Red Sea had been stirred by an east wind countless times, but the one time that it blew and saved the hard-pressed Israelites constitutes a miracle.[132] Miracles are wrought for moral and not physical purposes and imply a manifestation of God different in kind from that exhibited in the ordinary course of natural events. Where natural, objective events in the invariable order of the physical world coincide with a human occurrence we have the setting for a miracle. This notion of the nature of miracles is to be found in S. H. Bergmann's dialogue, *Science and Miracle*, except that he is inclined to a strict line separating the spheres of science and faith, saying that there is room left for faith to revive the humdrum world of daily existence with the revelation of miracle.[133]

Rosenzweig is careful to distinguish between miracles and magic. The worker of miracles is not interested in adjusting the machinery of the natural world by imposing his will on God, but in anticipating and predicting future events. The prophet, he says, discloses the designs of Providence by looking into the future.[134] His aim is to predict and not to violate or adjust the invariable order found everywhere in the universe. Two temporal dimensions meet in miracle—one that proceeds from the past to the present, and one that proceeds from the present into the future. The future as a temporal dimension in which miracles are wrought is part of a process whose roots lie in Creation, its center in Revelation and its end in Redemption.

Revelation is interpreted as a dialogic encounter between God and man in which God is the active Speaker and man the passive listener. But the moment that man turns to hearken to God's voice, the soul is born within him and his role in the dialogue is not merely passive. He is drawn into the dialogue by God's love for him[135] and, although rooted in the world of experience to which he is confined,[136] he becomes a responsible partner in the eternal discourse, ready to respond to the authoritative Voice.

The response of man to God's love gives rise to the birth of the soul. The soul's activity is also one of love, except that this love is directed not to God but to one's fellow man, who is loved not for himself but as the representative of all humanity and of all things.[137] It is worth noting that Rosenzweig here introduces two thoughts that are also to be found in Cohen's system. We have already seen that in Cohen's first period ethical activity centered on generality whose realization is humanity. Later, however, it is the fellow man who becomes the object of ethical activity, and in this Cohen sees the transition from ethics to religion. Rosenzweig, no doubt unknowingly, combines these two thoughts of Cohen. He sees man's activity directed to man and things in general; that is, to the world which is the materialization of generality. But as man proceeds to this goal, he encounters other individuals around him engaged in the same pursuit. Rosenzweig refines this thought of the purely representative status of the fellow man by saying that he merits our love simply by virtue of his very presence and proximity.

This activity of man assumes a religious character when it is conceived as a progressive materialization towards the Kingdom of Heaven. We must regard this as an additional motif in Rosenzweig's conception, one that is not necessarily derived from the fundamental notion of the love of one's fellow man based on generality. We shall have to examine this connection between ethical activity and Redemption in order to see how successful Rosenzweig was in uniting the two, and this will also enable us to understand Scholem's observation that Rosenzweig's interpretation of Redemption adheres to the Christian point of view.

The transition between human activity and the beckoning goal of Redemption is grounded in the inner connection between the deed and the future. The deed as an activity is directed towards an unseen goal in the future. Just as Revelation bridges the gap between the past and the present, the deed bridges the gap between the present and the future. The practical world of man is thus conceived of as ever growing and dynamic, jubilantly reaching out to the highest ideals; it is not closed and self-contained,[138] but an unfolding world of infinite progression.[139] Two basic elements are thus involved in Rosenzweig's conception: progress towards the future and the hope of reaching the end of time, a hope that imparts redemptive significance to man's activities. In other words, this world to which we aspire dwells beyond our existence, but is also immersed in it; it dwells beyond the present world at the end of time in the future, but it is also ever present to us who hope for it.[140]

From the process of materialization directed to the end of time Rosenzweig takes a leap to the end of time itself. This end is not only a distant goal; it also negates the existence of man and the world: With Redemption man and the world disappear, and God alone perfects Himself. God becomes in Redemption only what vain, human thought has always sought—the All and the One.[141] Redemption at the end of time is existence within God himself, the condition itself, and not the progress towards it; it thus negates all the elements involved in this progression; man and the world, and everything is subsumed by an all-embracing pantheistic God. We may say that Redemption as a condition redeems God himself; all relationships are canceled and He alone remains: Redemption liberates Him from the work of Creation, it grants Him a day of rest, His Sabbath.[142] This God is One and His name is One. He is emancipated from speech and has become silent.[143] Redemption thus completes the flowing circle of reality—a reality, however, bereft of its initial attributes and swallowed up by the one absolute God. We cannot help noting the difference between Rosenzweig's conception, which begins with cowering man separated from God and ends in the harmonious union of the two, and Rav Kook's conception which begins with harmonious man. Rosenzweig's redemptive goal, which may be called in Rudolf Otto's phrase *theopanism*, sees God as the object of religious faith, which alone produces the harmony that thought, even existentialist thought, seeks in vain. Rosenzweig, who attacks Hegelian idealism as the attempt to evade disharmony by fleeing to the closed realm of abstract thought, himself escapes this disharmony by the flight to faith. It is a case of the pot calling the kettle black. Both idealism and existentialism seek to escape the real world, the one to the ideal realm of abstract thought and the other to the insulated realm of faith.

Rosenzweig sees an unbroken transition between man's progress towards the end of time and the end of time itself that lies beyond man. Furthermore, this union swallows up man and negates his existence. Rosenzweig failed to show, as Scholem points out in his criticism, how man's activism leads to God's redemption. Rosenzweig censures mysticism for lacking this active element[144] and for binding man to God so securely that he is unable to devote his energy to the world and to his fellow man. But Rosenzweig himself was unable to explain how this transition from human activity to God is effected. He believed that the transition constituted a forward movement and that there was a point at which the path and the end of time intersected, but he failed to explain how this meeting ceased to be a dialogue and became a monologue of God with Himself.

D. THE ETERNALITY OF BLOOD AND OF THE WAY

Cohen makes a distinction between Judaism as a historical religion and the religion of reason derived from Jewish sources. Judaism is the best example of a religion that has incorporated philosophical principles. Rosenzweig refrains from identifying his fundamental conception of faith with Judaism and insists that his *Star of Redemption* is a book of a Jew but not a Jewish book, an attempt to erect a philosophical system, not a philosophical system of Judaism.[145] He goes on to say that his purpose was not to discuss Jewish content, but simply use it to illustrate his method.[146] Rosenzweig's claim, however, is not to be taken uncritically and we have good reason to assume that the basic notions derived from his analysis of faith are also to be found in Judaism as he understood it. Although Judaism is not a historical *source* of faith as set forth in a philosophical system, it is nevertheless the historical crystallization of this faith.

The leap from the deed to the goal, which is the essential feature of Rosenzweig's conception of Redemption, is also found in Judaism. The two basic facts of Jewish consciousness, according to Rosenzweig, are: The Messiah has not yet come and the Kingdom of Heaven is already here and now.[147] This is the paradox of Rosenzweig's conception of Judaism: Redemption has not yet come to man and the world and yet the Kingdom of Heaven has been ushered in and has become a reality. The Jew lives his life in the reality of the Kingdom of Heaven.[148] The individual Jew lives his life at the beginning of the way and, according to the Jewish conception, the people as a whole have reached the end of the way as well as the world itself.[149] But for the Jew there is no such separation between the desired goal and reality, between his individual ideals and the people of whom he is a part.[150]

Rosenzweig sees this contradiction within the Jew as the result of the division between the Kingdom of Heaven and the Messiah that has not yet come, between the people that is beloved of God and the people who nevertheless look forward to the coming of the Redeemer.[151] It is interesting to note the solutions proposed by Rosenzweig to this vexing question, solutions that he put forward from the standpoint of the Liberal Jew. It was his opinion that these contradictions arise only when the elements that constitute the Jewish consciousness are viewed from a static point of view— that is, from an abstract, speculative standpoint. In real life, however, these contradictions disappear, since real life does not ask questions about essence.[152] It follows, then, that the unity of the contradictory ideas does not rest on a speculative basis, but is a fact. Rosenzweig is thus able to define the relation of Judaism to history and to give a description of the closed, self-contained circle of life.

The discrepancy between external existence as it is and the existence of Redemption in the Kingdom of Heaven cannot be reconciled to the objective facts that contradict the Jewish conception. In the spirit of "so much the worse for the facts," Rosenzweig answers that the Jew as the possessor of the real truth need not take account of reality.[153] Such an obvious disregard of reality could only take place by ignoring the basic existentialist element of time. Judaism is a self-contained system because it is assured of eternal life and immune against the ravages of time. It is not subject to time,[154] since it creates its own time in consonance with its own internal rhythm and the eternal rhythm of the Kingdom of Heaven imbedded in the heart of time. This separation from external reality is expressed by the fact that the people possesses the internal strength to insure its existence and sufficient inner power to resist the buffetings of temporal reality: "the people remain a people only by being one.[155] The real historical expression for this self-contained life within the closed circle untouched by time is found by Rosenzweig to reside in the consciousness of the successive Jewish generations. The Jewish tribe did not owe its unity to its attachment to the soil or to any factor outside itself, but to some vital impulse within it. The period subsequent to the destruction of the Temple, the period in which the people were left without any external support, is the one which is of central significance in Jewish history. Only after losing their country and national sovereignty[156] did the people regain their real life and become a vital factor in history—a view that is reflected in the works of the most prominent Jewish historians, especially H. Graetz (1817–1891).

Jewish life is not governed by commonly articulated time that proceeds in linear progression, but has created for itself its own circular time based on the division of the year into Sabbaths. The Sabbath is the means and the occasion of regeneration when the heart and mind return to God. On the Sabbath the community feels as if Redemption were already present and the leap from the Kingdom of Heaven to the Kingdom of the Messiah already consummated. The Sabbath is the recurrent festival of Creation, a Creation that took place for the sake of Redemption.[157] When existence as it is reaches the stage of Redemption, however, it is negated and ceases to exist. Rosenzweig here exhibits both the strength and the weakness of Liberal Judaism: He agrees with Liberal Judaism that the Kingdom of Heaven is already established on earth, but differs from it in that he regards the Kingdom as established in the inner world of the Jew, not in the world of objective history, or in the sphere where Jews come in contact with the nations of the world—that is, in the State based on law.

In his attitude to questions of faith and religion Rosenzweig was faced with the choice of following the mystics who desire to return to the beginning of the world, or those who look forward to the end of time and are eager to hasten its coming, a choice which Scholem designates as the alternative of Cabalist speculation. By adopting some of the ideas of Liberal Judaism, Rosenzweig was able to forgo making this choice. It was impossible to return to the beginning of Creation, since reality is inflexibly directed towards the future in a progressive movement that is a result of the tension between Creation and Redemption; and the eschatological expectation of the end is impossible because the end of time is a temporal concept and implies the introduction of Redemption in historical time. Rosenzweig places Redemption wholly within the *present*, the dimension which swallows up the end of time. The notion of Liberal Judaism that it is living at the terminal point of history stems from its inveterate belief in the infinite progress of man and the world. Rosenzweig's conception of the end of time, however, is a-historical. This penetration of eternity into real existence receives its most trenchant formulation in Rosenzweig's dictum: The Jew does not believe in anything, since he himself is belief.[158] Rosenzweig's category of Redemption is the category of Incarnation; eternity is incarnated in the present and the end of time is incarnated in Judaism.

But this principle, which is so central to Liberal Judaism, also weakens its foundations. The withdrawal of Judaism from the stream of history, its self-sufficiency and self-containment, do not apply to the abstract, theoretical-dogmatic sphere. On the contrary, it is clear that Rosenzweig transfers the resolution of theoretical problems to the practical sphere, so that he virtually effaces the distinction between Judaism and Jews—a cardinal distinction in the philosophy of Liberal Judaism. The reality of an enduring Israel is thus an indispensable element in this self-contained circle that is removed from time and history. Rosenzweig is therefore constrained to renounce the principal tenet of Liberal Judaism, its universalism and implied assimilationist-tendencies. Israel, according to Rosenzweig, is a people because it is a confession and it is a confession because it is a people.[159] He thus defines the relation between the dogmatic aspect of Judaism and its existential aspect. Like Liberal Judaism, however, he insists on the separation of Israel from objective, vital elements, such as soil, language and state; unlike Liberal Judaism, however, he regards Judaism as a biological phenomenon rooted in a common blood origin that links the successive generations to one another and ensures the eternality of Israel.[160] This strong assurance of eternality is hidden and its obscure origin[161] sets its seal upon the generations. A Jew is born a Jew[162] and does not become one. Rosenzweig, however, does not emphasize this biological factor in Jewish reality in order to find a basis for its racial or national existence but: a) to define its area of real existence over against its temporal, historical existence; b) to give prominence to life itself as a religious category over against dogmatic abstractions; c) to stress the vital, self-sufficient factor of actual Jewish existence, the biological factor of birth.

These two aspects of Jewish existence—the withdrawal from history and the eternality of man—are in reality one. Jewish existence does not take place in time but in a suprahistorical sphere it has created for itself, the sphere of holiness, to which it transferred the objective, time-bound, historical institutions, such as land and language. Land, language, customs, law were removed long ago from the vital center in life and raised to the level of holiness.[163] The language of the people is not the everyday speech contaminated by life's staining dyes and subject to the corrosions of time, but a language that moves in a fugitive realm, immune to the ravages of practical existence. It keeps the people whose religious life is conducted in the holy tongue from completely identifying itself with the temporal life of the secular world.[164] The holy language is not a dead language; it is simply not alive in the sense that it is not subject to death,[165] for, like all the expressions of Israel's existence, it operates in a realm that is removed from time. Israel cannot arrive at the end of time, where God alone dwells, for if it did, it would cease to exist, as does any other element of reality that is outside of God. Israel, however, lives in a sphere that is beyond time. We may say—and here the mystical strain in Rosenzweig's philosophy is most evident—that just as the Sabbath is a symbol of Redemption when seen against the background of the week and the year (*i.e.*, against the background of time and history), so is Israel the symbol of eternity within time itself.

Jewish law also falls within this sacred realm of timelessness where it is immune to change. This separation, which is the essential quality of holiness, is here meant not as a separation of law from the things and activities of the world, but as a separation from the temporal medium in which they all move and have their being, the separation from time. Two meanings thus adhere to Rosenzweig's conception of the eternality of Israel: a) eternality inherent in birth and transmitted by blood; b) eternality that comes from the conquest of time. This brings us back to the original difficulty in Rosenzweig's conception: He begins with the assumption of man's temporal existence and immersion in time, and he ends with the existence of the Jew in a realm removed from time. At first he regards faith as the supereminent end, the only safe haven for existentialist man; then he assigns this privileged position to Judaism and its enduring beliefs. We might say that when Rosenzweig speaks as an existentialist philosopher he does not speak as a Jew, and when he speaks as a Jew he does not speak as an existentialist philosopher.

Rosenzweig's understanding of the meaning of the God-concept is intimately related to his conception of Judaism. The essential point of Judaism is the identification of the one God with the indwelling God, the complete identification of God with our God.[166] The concept of unity is in itself not an exclusively Jewish idea; as we have seen, Cohen was mainly concerned with interpreting this unity as the Oneness of God and making it the cardinal doctrine of Judaism. Rosenzweig, however, starting with the category of faith and not of cognition or logic, emphasized the relationship between God's unity on the one hand, and man and the world on the other, rather than the special meaning attached to the concept of unity. The impersonal, circular concept of unity was thus invested with faith and the remote Creator brought close to man. Rosenzweig interpreted Judaism as a religious system which revealed the inner unity of God and His relation to man and the world.

This central point in Judaism is also apparent in Rosenzweig's conception of *faith* and *trust*. Faith is the mutual relation between God and man[167] and is expressed in their dialogic meeting, which is the essential feature of Rosenzweig's conception of Revelation. He does not identify the concept of Revelation with his ethical concept of Judaism, but emphasizes the basic feature of Judaism that might serve to support the systematic expression of his conception.

This basic notion concerning the identity in nature between the remote and the indwelling God is illumined by two historical observations which indicate the place that Judaism occupies among the religions. Rosenzweig points out how Judaism escaped from the two extreme positions—from Neoplatonism (which he calls Judeo-Grecian, alluding to Philo of Alexandria) on the one hand, and from Christianity (which he calls Judeo-Christian) on the other. These two movements introduce a dichotomy into the God-concept and negate the tension within it. Neoplatonism makes God a Spirit completely removed from the lives of men and the affairs of the world, an impersonal *rex tremendae majestatis*. In Christianity, on the other hand, God assumes human form and forfeits His transcendence.[168] Judaism is a kind of a middle ground between these two extremes, not in the sense of a mechanical fusion of the two but as the original seed-plot from which they arose. To emphasize the historical origin of these two extreme movements in Judaism, Rosenzweig calls them *Judeo*-Grecian and *Judeo*-Christian, *Judeo* being the original element in time and in content. In Jewish prayer this synthesis is expressed as: Our God, King of the Universe.[169]

The union of these two aspects is from another point of view the union of the subjective and objective aspect. The aspect of the indwelling God is interpreted as the God who reveals Himself as the lover of man. The God who loves is not to be identified with God as a whole, for love is but one of His manifestations. God, as viewed by Rosenzweig, is the God of Truth; love is His attribute. The truth here represents the objective aspect in God's existence, the aspect piror to Revelation or His transcendent aspect. Love represents the subjective aspect that is within Revelation. Christianity ignores the objective aspect of truth in the God-concept since the object of Christian faith is solely the God of love.

These two basic aspects in the nature of Judaism, viz. the with-

drawal from time and the concept of the perfect God, who is both
far removed from man and close to him, also represent an essential
weakness in Judaism. A religion like Judaism that is removed
from historical time and the vital currents of life loses contact with
the world.[170] This withdrawal to the dizzy edge of things between
the glory and the dark, to the timeless point where it can catch a
glimpse of eternity, removes Judaism from the endless agitation
of the empirical world.[171] While listening to the authentic tidings
from an invisible world, however, Judaism runs the danger of
forgetting man and the world. Active man, suspended between the
present and the future, no longer occupies a central position; if
the Kingdom of Heaven and Redemption are here and now, man
with his utopian plans and redeeming schemes can be ignored. We
can therefore say that this other aspect of Redemption means a
repudiation of this world and all its works, an a-cosmism and
a-anthropism.

If we examine these vulnerable points in Judaism, we cannot fail
to note their symbolic character. It is clear that Rosenzweig looked
upon Redemption as the Sabbath of the Lord, the day on which
God severs His relations with man and the world and remains
alone. Judaism, which has such a high conception of the perfect
God, has as a result an imperfect conception of the world and man.
It lives its life on the farther side of reality, beyond the world of
constant change and decay.

Eternal life in Judaism is turned in upon itself, in Christianity
it faces outward; Judaism may be compared to the burning coals
of a fire and Christianity to its leaping flames. The essential difference between the two religions, in other words, is that between
the infinity of the point and the infinity of the line.[172] Christianity
is the faith of a living religious community that exists within time,
borne along the stream of time towards an overarching goal.[173]
The Christian community is always en route between the beginning
and the end of time,[174] between the coming of the Messiah in the
past and his advent in the future. The Jew has already reached his
destination and lives his life at the end of the Way; the Christian
must begin his work every day anew in order to possess it.
Judaism remains fixed[175] with a strong assurance of its eternality

But R's interpretation of Judaism is absurd!

written in its blood. A Jew is born into the faith, the Christian must acquire it as he treads the path towards Christianity.[176]

The circumstance that Christianity is immersed in time and is involved in a constant struggle with it accounts for its missionary zeal and expansive impulse. Judaism lives beyond time, neither making claims upon it nor submitting to it. Christianity is impelled to move forward like a straight line into boundless infinity[177] and hence, unlike Judaism, sets no bounds between itself and the world, between itself and other peoples. Christianity has no need to forgo or relinquish anything;[178] it feels only the need to send forth missionaries to spread its message to the world and this missionary activity is the very substance of its faith.[179] The mission of Israel, which is a basic doctrine of Liberal Judaism, is transferred completely by Rosenzweig to the realm of Christianity.

It is obvious that Rosenzweig took Cohen's idealistic conception of the progressive illumination of knowledge, which considers the unending struggle towards the truth to be more important than the goal, and identified it with the dynamic aspect of Christianity. Moreover, in contrasting the infinity of the compressed point with the infinity of the expanding line he seems to be referring to Hegel's "bad infinity," which is characterized by its endless extension towards a distant, ever-receding goal. Even when Rosenzweig is not expressly criticizing Christianity, as in his *Star of Redemption*, he regards the basic element of Christianity as its dynamic idealism which, as we have seen, is the constant object of his criticism.

The most marked contrast between Judaism and Christianity, however, stems from their different conceptions of God. The Jewish God-concept is distinguished by its union of the remote and the indwelling God, by the fusion of the objective and the subjective aspects of the Godhead, whereas Christianity identifies God the Father with God the Son. The mediation between God and man, which constitutes the very essence of Christianity, expresses a division that applies to God himself.[180] This division impairs God's internal unity and impugns the essential nature of Judaism or, at least, relegates religion to its pre-Jewish state. This aspect of Christianity has in recent times been stressed in the dialectical theology of Barth and Gogarten[181] wherein God is prominent only as the incarnation of the Son.[182] Both the monotheistic faith and idolatry see God as a living Being; but the former also regards the living God as the Creator of life. Christianity, however, makes a distinction between the Creator and the living God: The remote God is the Creator who is not the living God; the living God is the indwelling God who appears as the Son of Man, but who is not the Creator. A change is thus effected in the Divine attributes of the Christian God. The remote God who is the Creator becomes in Judaism the God of Truth, and love is an aspect of God's Revelation, being a manifestation and not an essence of divine Being. The Christian Messiah, however, arrogates to himself the Truth and leaves to the transcendent God only the attribute of love.[183] This difference in the divine attributes causes a profound change in religious outlook. Christianity does not identify the God of Truth with biblical righteousness; it makes of the biblical God the God of love, thus contracting the essence of God and splitting it in two.

In extolling the infinite perfection of God as an eternal, independent, and self-existent Being whose purposes and actions spring from Himself, Judaism runs the danger of neglecting man and the world. It tends to glorify God and His righteous government to the detriment of His sentient creatures. Christianity, on the other hand, teaches that God may be apprehended in the incarnate Son and in Him alone. This is the root of Christianity and the source of its perennial revelation, viz. that indestructible life can be found only in Man Incarnate—and this at the same time is the ground of pantheism, dualism, polytheism, and all false religions (as Hermann Cohen has pointed out). Christianity bestows upon a historical Person the Truth that belongs to God alone, who is both spiritualized (as in Neoplatonism) and deprived of His role as the Creator and Governor of the universe.[184]

Rosenzweig describes Judaism and Christianity as two distinct but equally cogent conceptions, each with its peculiar excellencies and defects. He places them on an equal footing and refrains from judging them. Neither is within the sphere of the real truth; both are on the way to the Truth. The God-concept is needed by both the religion that turns its back on time and the one that marches towards it. From the standpoint of God, they are co-workers in a common cause.[185]

Despite the tolerance Rosenzweig evinces for the shortcomings of both Judaism and Christianity, his preference seems to be for the former. When he speaks of the two religions with respect to their attitude to time, he puts them both on the same plane, but Judaism fares better than Christianity because of its God-concept. Even Judaism's neglect of the world and man is but an aspect of the perfect God who, in redeeming Himself from time, perforce ignores the world He created and its sentient creatures. But this apparent shortcoming in Judaism turns out to be a gain, although not expressly acknowledged by Rosenzweig; the last word does not lie in defendings but in judging.[186] In this matter of the two religions it seems that he did judge, although modestly and not openly.[187]

E. THE TRUTH AND THE STRUGGLES FOR THE TRUTH

Rosenzweig's decision in favor of Judaism does not exempt the Jew from striving towards the truth which lies beyond him. God remains the transcendent even for Judaism, which regards the people and its history as having already reached the end of the way. To understand the nature of this transcendence we must first examine the meaning that Rosenzweig attaches to the concept of truth and determine the place it occupies in his system.

There are two basic principles of idealism with which Rosenzweig found himself in agreement: a) the truth is self-sufficient and does not depend on anything outside itself;[188] b) the truth is at the end of the way, the goal towards which we strive;[189] it is not found ready-made, but must be earned by ceaseless struggle.

Rosenzweig needed these two principles for his concept of the truth in order to include them in the sphere that is beyond cognition. The sphere of truth is that of reality, the sphere of God. The first principle, that the truth is self-sufficient, is identified by Rosenzweig with God, and included in the closed circle in which God the Redeemer dwells. Truth that is self-contained and applies to nothing outside itself is a characteristic of God in whom the elements of experience have been swallowed up. The second principle concerning the nature of truth, namely, that it is at the end of the way and not at the beginning, is also made part of God by Rosenzweig in order to emphasize the difference between the God of Redemption who is the object of faith and the God who reigned before Redemption. The God of truth, or the God whose seal is the truth, is the Creator, the perfect God who returns to Himself at the end of the way where also dwells the Truth towards which man strives.

The difference between Rosenzweig and the idealistic conception of truth revolves around the question of the relation between God and the truth. Rosenzweig takes the truth to be an attribute of God, but he does not *identify* God with the truth, for God is more than the truth. Just as the subject contains more than its predicate which expresses but one of its qualities, so does God contain more than the truth that inheres in Him.[190] Here we see a basic difference between Rosenzweig's conception and that of Hegel. In Hegelian idealism the subject is swallowed up by the predicates, that is, the entire content of the subject is expressed in the predicates without which there is no content whatever. Hegel was therefore able to see the nature of the divine process in his logical theory, which deals with the various predicates. Rosenzweig here draws a sharp distinction between God as subject and the truth as His attribute or predicate. God is Being and His truth is an attribute of Being. God's transcendence is thus assured in that no one attribute, not even the highest among them, exhausts the full content of God's being. Thus, if we say that the truth is found at the end of the way, it does not mean that God is the end of the way. The perfect God, the God of Truth, *i.e.*, the God, one of whose attributes is truth, is also beyond this end. Rosenzweig bases God's transcendence on the ultimate irrationality of the God-concept, the content that is not exhausted in its predicates.

Two layers of transcendence can be distinguished in Rosenzweig's conception. The essential feature of the first layer is the distance that separates man from the ultimate truth which is not a given fact found in the human sphere but an attribute of God. Truth is not a cognitive concept but an ontological fact. The essential feature of the second layer is the distinction between the truth and God in His perfection. There is a transcendence within transcendence—that of God in relation to truth. God remains hidden to the world, but His truth illumines it.

What then remains for man in the face of this double separation? The long journey towards the beckoning goal, the inflexible pursuit of the truth, and sacrifice! The truth that is sought by the believer is not to be found within the confines of a theoretical system, for it consists in the fulfillment of an imperative. What Rosenzweig calls "the law of messianic knowledge" is nothing more than the attempt to find a nontheoretical and noncognitive criterion that might serve as a guide. This messianic knowledge evaluates the truths (the plural is deliberately used, since we are still within the human sphere) in accordance with the price that man pays in attaining them and in accordance with the unifying ties that they succeed in creating among men.[191] This is the sphere in which Rosenzweig assigns a place for human deeds, since these are but the expression of distance that divides man from transcendence. The truth that man seeks is not isolated and self-contained but always related to something outside itself. It is man's destiny to grope towards truths, to complete and unify them in the light of a higher command in order to give form to his imperfect life.

Faith is the attempt to bridge the chasms between the three separate entities: God-man-world. Such a faith gives rise to the concept of God as He who redeems Himself and negates man and the world, who in the process of Redemption swallows up man within Himself instead of redeeming him. What then is man to do in the meantime and to what end is he to direct his insurgent energies? There is nothing left for him but to tread the way until he completes his probation on earth, animated by the desire for the fuller life which Rosenzweig designates by his motto: *Towards Life*. Faith seeks to redeem man from his finitude, but man is never fully redeemed, since he never attains the goal. He is destined to remain on the way, spurred on by the assurance of faith, *fiducia*, and sustained by the truths of Revelation. To maintain his existence in reality and resist being swallowed up, he must pay a price; that is, he must forgo Redemption. Rosenzweig's motto, *Towards Life*, is that of existential man and not that of man redeemed. In this motto Rosenzweig was able to find support for some doctrines he adopted after he had written the *Star of Redemption*, among them a more sympathetic attitude towards Zionism.

If we are to determine Rosenzweig's historical position in the development of Jewish thought in recent generations, we must keep in mind that Rosenzweig, like Steinheim (although he was unaware of the connection), emphasizes the factual elements of human experience and existence, which constitute the basis of faith, rather than the ratiocinative logic of idealism, which disregards the fallibility of human reasoning. Like Cohen in his later period, he also interprets the God-concept as Being, but he removes this concept from the sphere of cognition and places it within the stream of real time. The idealistic dynamism that is beyond time is replaced by a temporal dynamism. Rosenzweig seeks to find a road between the real existence of man as man and God as authentic Being—the road which is called the Star of Redemption—by means of faith that lifts us above the crushing weight of the world and its disharmonies. It may be that the disharmony of the world is overcome, but not the distance and the tension which are elements of this disharmony. Transcendence still remains.

It is an interesting and significant fact that the deepest principle of harmony developed in modern Jewish thought was not borrowed from other disciplines but sprang from the heart of traditional Judaism itself.[192]

7

Harmony and Return

RAV KOOK

Judaic thought in recent times presents a varied picture. In idealistic philosophy it was conceived as the religion of the spirit, while paganism was the religion of nature; it comprehends the world not in its totality but only as a reflection of the spirit. To Steinheim, however, Judaism was something more firm and assured than philosophic conviction that is produced by logical demonstration or other evidence of the understanding. Judaism is not dependent on logical evidence or the elements of cognition; its cogency rests solely on knowledge derived from Revelation. At the basis of Rosenzweig's religious thinking there is a dismemberment of elements, which he calls the "breaking of the vessels." The world lacks an inner principle of harmony and is bereft of all intrinsic relations and connections, and all we find are layers spread over the initial layer of Creation to which man has been given insight. This empirical insight is for Rosenzweig the beginning of religious insight in man, who resists being swallowed up in the totality of things. The world is not grounded in a principle of harmony but is fundamentally disharmonious.

Orthodox Judaism was spared all these theoretical speculations, for it is founded on the laws of halakah. These laws do not admit of fundamental change and need no theory to support them, deriving their indisputable cogency from the ready acceptance of the faithful. The purpose of the halakah is to safeguard the separate nature of the Jew in a world where separatism is frowned upon. This Judaism which builds its world on Law does not require harmony, but insists on establishing its own unique elements as bulwarks against the world without.

There is within orthodox Judaism a conception that looks upon existence as a unified whole and seeks to bridge its disparate realms—this is the philosophical conception of Rav Abraham Isaac Hakohen Kook, who was born in Lithuania in 1861, became Chief Rabbi of Palestine, and died in 1935. An analysis of his thought is rendered difficult by the circumstance that it has no orderly arrangement but consists of innumerable aphorisms and sayings that appear unrelated. Nevertheless, it is clear that for Kook the beginning of religious and philosophical insight into the world as it is, the world without and the world within man, is to see all existence in the light of the Shekinah; to look within the lights themselves.[1] To look upon the world as it is, reveals its true nature and its unity. The purpose of religious insight is not to see the world piecemeal and then set aside for itself a special sphere of faith, but rather to see the world in its given diversity. Religion also finds support by having a place in the inner life of man. The process of knowledge of the mysterious tends to develop the powers of the soul to a point where it needs no outside support or intermediary aid and thus all experience gets to know itself; by virtue of this independent, inner self-knowledge, the stream of life, especially the understanding and the will, continues in its uninterrupted flow.[2] Religious insight depends on the inner power of man to plumb the depths of his being and discover the abundant life within himself and the world. By means of this insight, religious truth reveals the world and man's own inner life; for the religious truth is the empirical truth, the inner and outer empirical truth of man. There is no breach here that cuts through the spheres of the given and overflows into the content beyond it. We might say that the beginning of religious insight in this sphere expresses the mystic ingredient within it. The religious truth does not depend on a unique, historical Revelation in the past, but on a continuous revelation that comes to man when he confronts himself and the world. Religious subjectivism, which can be detected in Rav Kook's conception, has its roots in this attitude towards religious experience. The highest holiness, he says, the ground of the greatest spiritual righteousness, is a genial power or talent. There is, of course, room to develop this talent by means of free will, but it is at bottom a talent and not simply a matter of the will.[3] The emergence of religious truth in the given world depends on man's experience and this experience is based on religious talent, whether of the individual or of the community.

In addition to this religious insight directed to the world there is also a unifying activity, a harmony in the world which Rav Kook calls an "equilibrium." The universe is but a revelation of unity which manifests itself in various sparks.[4] The world seen through faith is a unified world, an organic entity and not a haphazard world of shreds and patches;[5] it is an organism[6] with definite, articulated parts.[7] Religious insight concentrates on no special object, nor does it create a new content not found in the world, nor does it condense some given content; the entire world is the object of this insight, the world that is in "general harmony and accord with reality."[8] This basic religious insight is not confined to any fragment of experience and does not regard religion as a separate, independent sphere of consciousness or existence. Since religious thought applies to all reality, all things fall within its purview and nothing is exempt from its scrutiny. The harmony that is revealed by religious insight is nothing more than the expression of a general, all-inclusive view of things.

This aspect of religious thought is sometimes expressed as the nature of cognition and not of the object alone. The quality of *spiritual insight* consists in seeing all things in their unity.[9] The perfection of the understanding does not depend on the multiplicity of the concepts but on the *unity* inherent within them; it is evident that the greater the diversity of concepts the greater the unity that is revealed.[10] The truth is not revealed to man piecemeal but all at once as a general phenomenon.[11] The movement of cognition, then, is towards generalization and its tendency to subsume all particulars in a unified framework. The religious talent mentioned above is characterized by this impulse towards unity: He who feels this inner urge towards unity is one of the great men of the world, whose basic spiritual concern is the general unification of all reality and enduring true peace.[12]

Kook's approach applies not only to the unity of the Godhead but to the whole world. He emphasizes the unity that pervades the objective sphere of the world by discussing the relation between matter and spirit, the holy and the profane, or the cognitive process and the faculties of the soul.

Rav Kook is not intent upon spiritualizing matter out of existence. His view acknowledges the indestructibility of matter: Spiritual Revelation has no need to efface the material world and its manifestations, but only to refine and liberate them and make them clearer to us.[13] This involves the clarification of the relation between matter and spirit, even raising matter to the level of spirit in order to achieve harmony. The greatness of wisdom, the study of truth and authentic Judaism is that in the abundant spirit of holiness it elevates all materiality to the level of spirituality.[14] Materiality is neither obliterated nor abolished; it merely emerges from its unrelated, isolated state and becomes a part of the harmonious structure of the world. This harmony produced by the spirit as it penetrates matter is an important element in the understanding of Rav Kook's conception of nationalism: Spirituality can be attained in our generation only through a *material* fulfillment.[15] Materialization is the necessary basis in the world's order; hence spirit that is unrelated to materiality is defective, just as matter is defective when unrelated to spirit. The national Jewish movement in recent times was an attempt to establish a Jewish world in the sphere of reality and this required a supernatural, spiritual basis of holiness (as we proceed from the ontological to the axiological realm) which, in turn, calls for materialization. The impulse towards materialization is not rooted in materiality, but springs from the dictates of the spirit. The secret of the present-day movements lies in the fact that holiness itself, the light of the world—that is beyond nature and society, demands from the world in general—and from Israel, broken and dispersed, in particular— a replica of nature: simplicity, and normal well-being, in life, feeling, understanding, and action.[16]

But, as has already been stated, this unity that is within harmony is found not only in the sphere of the world in the two aspects of the object (matter and spirit) but also within the subject in the sphere of cognition and the faculties of the soul. Every thought that proceeds from man is part of a well-ordered system. All thoughts are logically and systematically connected; even a casual, fleeting thought, if examined more closely, will disclose a logical core, for this is the nature of thought. And we know that no thought is lost in the entire world and that every thing has its place. And if there are empty, vain thoughts, they appear so only outwardly, but if we enter into them more deeply we find in them an element of life, since wisdom is the source of life.[17] The dictum "everything has its place" was here taken from the ontological realm of things and transferred to the realm of thought to show that every thought is part of a well-defined, harmonious arrangement and not an isolated fragment. Every thought, no matter what its quality, has its place and independent position within the unified whole; and this fixed place occupied by the thought in the general scheme is of more enduring significance than its defective sensible content.

Whether the objective or the subjective aspect of this conception is the subject of our inquiry, it is plain that it points to what is now called the modern world and its multidimensional aspects. The modern element in Rav Kook's conception is that it does not relinquish any of the basic ingredients of given existence, but embraces the world of man in all its fullness and variety. The religious man is not required to forgo anything; his task is to illumine everything in the light of the harmonious whole. We find here no chiliastic visions or eschatological hopes of the final denouement of all terrestrial affairs. The world is as it is and it is only necessary that it be properly *understood*. The modernity of this idea is evident in the subjective element. The defects that exist are not in the world but in ourselves and in our faulty vision, our limited comprehension. The idea of the proximity of distant worlds is the foundation of the spiritual world and its perfection; it is the scarlet thread that runs through all of life's manifestations and always needs to be given a more adequate form. The analytical quality must make room for the synthetic quality.[18] The task of the specific "religious talent" is to surmount the differences that are rooted in our subjective nature.[19] The improvement of the world depends on the manner in which it is comprehended by man and not on actual changes in the external world outside of him. In short, the religious conception is based on a *point of view* and not on the *elements* themselves as they actually are.

Harmony in the sphere of the subject means the unity of the psychological faculties—the imagination and the understanding on the one hand, the will and the speculative power on the other. In the course of time, Rav Kook says, some of the imaginative parts will become hypothetical and the hypothetical parts will be clarified by knowledge and cognition.[20] The imagination and the understanding, however, are not distinct and separate but differ only in degree.[21] This is true of all the different parts of existence, the difference between them being gradual and not absolute, including the subjective realm with its various faculties. The ideal of religious knowledge is based on the reactions of the imagination and the understanding, as well as on the reactions of the faculties of the soul in general, the speculative faculties and volition, the union of the practical will with the theoretical understanding.[22] The perfect man is the one who has developed these faculties of the soul to the highest degree and thus achieved an inner harmony.

This harmony is not confined to the faculties of the soul, but also applies to the various cognitive spheres. The most inclusive unity is that in which divine knowledge is united with scientific knowledge. These two forms of knowledge appear to be distinct and separate only when seen subjectively: When looked at more deeply, the content of divine knowledge and the scientific analysis of reality are only subjectively contradictory, but are united objectively.[23] It is only from *our* point of view that things appear separate, but not from the standpoint of the thing itself. This union of science and divine knowledge is based on the actual union in the world of objects as we have already indicated above. It follows that the object of religious knowledge is not separated from the world but is the world itself in all its variety, and it is this same world that is the object of scientific knowledge. Theology and science, then, are not two different spheres. The unity of the world is the genuine concern of all speculation and is the guarantee for the unity of the various spheres of speculation. Since this unity of the world is the specific task of religious knowledge, we may say that the religious conception has also infiltrated scientific knowledge. There is no dimension of reality that is exempt from this religious penetration and this includes the secular sphere of science. Rav Kook therefore makes no attempt to justify this inclusion or to explain the nature of the science that forms a part of the religious knowledge (Rosenzweig's "true science"). The union of these two speculative paths is effected in their very inclusion within the same framework and there is no need for a third path to connect them.

This unity also applies to the historical and literary manifestations of knowledge and to the religious life of Israel. The spirit of prophecy is filled with glorious ideals and the spirit of the halakah is filled with the power and energy of practical life. The world will have its remedy to the degree that these two spiritual forces unite and mutually influence each other.[24] The oral tradition is from heaven but is manifested on earth, and it is necessary that the land of Israel be built and the orders of priesthood, prophecy, judges, and rulers be restored; then the Oral Law will shine forth resplendent and be united to the Written Law. In the Diaspora the two had been severed and the Written Law raised to the level of holiness while the Oral Law was relegated to an inferior station.[25] The distinction between prophecy (the Written Law) and the halakah (the Oral Law) is only a historical distinction and does not refer to their respective contents.[26] The religious conception bridges the gap between them by placing them both on the same plane.

Similarly, the difference between revealed and hidden wisdom is purely subjective: The content that divides the revealed from the hidden in the Torah and in all wisdom in general depends on the different qualities of those who pursue these studies.[27] But this subjective difference that is the result of the varying powers or proclivities of the soul should not affect the inner relation between these two spheres: Every mysterious thought needs a host of patent thoughts as props and supports to sustain it, so that it may not succumb to the imagination and untruth and be destroyed; and every revealed thought needs mysterious sparks to refine it and keep it from degrading.[28] Here we meet with a new expression bestowed by Rav Kook on the relation between the holy and the profane. The open or revealed thought is a support (a prop and a staff) for the secret thought, which in turn is the spark that causes the latter to rise. The relationship between the two is of mutual benefit: Just as the highest virtue is to attain a state of peace where the light of the soul is not dimmed by corporeality, so also is there a high virtue in the fact that the power of hidden knowledge grows in proportion to the power of revealed illumination.[29] And the writings of the Torah and of wise men are not for the purpose of perfecting some defective power but of making new connections and associations.[30] The highest cognitive function is to effect such connections for purposes of unification and harmony.

The tendency of cognition to achieve harmony reaches its high point in determining the relationship between faith and atheism. For the light of infinity all things are equal; atheism is also the revelation of a life force which contains a vital spark of a higher illumination.[31] The difference between faith and the denial of God is not absolute, as faith itself does not attain the perfect truth and falls short of the highest knowledge of the Divine. Since neither faith nor the denial of God arrive at the truth, the only difference between them,[32] is that the one strives towards the truth, and the other tends to fall into error. Each proceeds in a different direction, but they are both rooted in a common soil of an undifferentiated life force. In this principle of a life force as well as in the principle of harmony we have a clear indication of the affinity between Rav Kook's conceptions and Bergson's ideas of dynamic religion. Rav Kook's principle of harmony, however, contains more "sympathy with all things" than that of Bergson. Bergson's world is a dualistic one, although the dualism is not radical: Matter is the product of the lax spirit; the impetus of life has evolved the intellect that the latter might know the inert world of matter; the essence of life is intuition and one of its forms is the intellect, which directs man's activity. In Rav Kook's religious conception, however, the harmony is all-embracing, uniting all the manifestations of existence and knowledge.

It is of interest to examine Rav Kook's concept of harmony in the light of the cabalistic thoughts of Isaac Luria which dominated the mystical literature of Judaism for centuries. In Rav Kook we do not find the notions of condensation and contraction, the breaking of the vessels and the repairing of defects in the sense that they are used in the Kabbala. He was faced, however, with the same religious problem—the unity of the world with the Creator and the return to the Oneness that reigned at the beginning. But the world is here not described from the standpoint of historical acts and events that take place in time; the dimension of time is discarded and events are viewed not as occurring in succession but simultaneously. The world as it is must be accepted as given and regarded in the light of religious insight which discloses its essential unity. The unity of the world is not achieved by a fragmentary view of the successive historical events in the cosmic drama that takes place in real time; the solid moorings of faith are in the harbor of subjective cognition.

Harmony is not achieved by mere religious speculation but must be raised to the level of holiness, which is the knowledge of innermost things[33] whose essential feature is the negation of "the truncated thought,"[34] the thought that is discrete, isolated, and particular. The fundamental character of holiness, Rav Kook says, is that Revelation is inherent in all the faculties: All the manifestations of life—action, sentiment, imagination and understanding —constitute one unified Whole.[35] Harmonious existence is raised to the order of holiness and becomes one with it.

The removal of harmony to the realm of value brings to the fore some aspects of its nature which were obscured when the world was seen only from a speculative and ontological standpoint. There is no exaggeration of existence in holiness: Whatever is or could be pictured and imagined exists in truth. Holiness imparts to thought its creative character. The relation between holiness and creative thought, however, is not sufficiently clarified by Rav Kook, but it seems that this relation is inherent in the view of the highest religious subject, God, not only as an object of knowledge or of religious feeling but also as the subject of thought and, being a holy subject possessing creative power, His thought also will be creative. In this conception man's creative power is bound to his imaginative faculty. In the storehouse of the imagination is to be found all truth and greatness which gradually come to light through a number of channels of the understanding. Our rational understanding reflects only a small part of the intense light that streams from our imagination.[36] The importance that Rav Kook attached to the imagination is related to the conception, prevalent in medieval Jewish philosophy, of prophecy as a revelation of the imaginative faculty. The imagination as a creative faculty is raised to the same level as the principal power in the concept of holiness.

To endow speculative knowledge with value also gives it an active, didactic function. The knowing of holiness is not merely a passive intuition of the world but a kind of active knowledge superior to other forms of knowledge in that it is able to change the will and the inner character of its disciples.[37] It adds an ethical value to contemplative knowledge. Placing no restrictions on science, it animates all things with an impulse of righteousness, goodness, and humility.[38] The principle of harmony within holiness is also evident, since ethical and volitional powers as well as the speculative and imaginative are emphasized. Holiness inspires man to perfect all his powers to the utmost to the end of a unified and harmonious structure of knowledge.

The distinction between the holy and the profane occupies a significant place in Rav Kook's conception of religion. His principle of harmony is not confined to the ontological realm; that is, to the difference between the various parts of reality, such as matter and spirit, and their ascent to the level of generality. It also applies to the realm of values: Raising the various parts of reality to the same plane effaces the differences between the holy and the profane. To raise all things to the level of holiness, love, and harmony, he says, is the enduring and all-embracing thought of existence.[39]

The difference between the holy and the profane, like the differences between the various parts of existence, is only subjective. There is a profane world and a holy world, and the two contradict each other; man's finite understanding cannot reconcile the two, for they can only be reconciled in a higher world, in the Holy of Holies.[40] It is precisely the value of holiness that requires the comprehensive view which effaces the absolute distinction between the holy and the profane. One of the attestations of the revelation of the secrets of the Torah in the world is to view the profane also in the light of the holy, to know in truth that there is no absolute profane. In this way the two worlds unite and their unity is made apparent.[41] In short, the impulse to obliterate the differences between the holy and the profane does not originate beyond the confines of the holy or the sphere of faith. It is faith itself, the highest religious value, the element of holiness that provides the impulse to bridge the gaps between these apparently disparate values and to create unity. The sphere of faith is not broken in two and does not depend on impulses outside itself. The impulse that reaches out to include the profane in the world of faith is an inner impulse within this world itself.

The profane can find a place within the sphere of the holy because it serves as a means in the edifice of the holy. On the basis of the Aristotelian distinction between matter and form we might say that the profane is the matter and that the holy is the form. The holy must perforce build on the solid basis of the profane; the profane provides the matter for holiness which is its form; and the more solid the matter the more significant is the form.[42] This conception abolishes the separate character of the sphere of holiness; holiness needs the profane because a spiritual value needs a material basis. But in this teleological or Aristotelian formulation there is a limit to the obliteration of differences between the two spheres. The profane does not take the place of the holy and the two cannot be interchanged. A line of demarcation is preserved between the two spheres. The introduction of the profane in the sphere of the holy is then, from the teleological point of view, a hospitable juxtaposition of two interrelated forces.

It is interesting to note how the original meaning of the concept of holiness as something separate or set apart here acquires an opposite signification of a creative, all-embracing sphere. Rav Kook makes a distinction, however, between the "holy" and the "most holy" or the "holy of holies," the former being the part that is attached to the profane and the latter the combination of the holy and the profane,[43] the intimate union of the two as one entity.[44]

The holy of holies is the ground of all things.[45] Just as there is an ultimate ground in the realm of existence, a "life-giving force" behind all its manifestations, so also do we find in the realm of values an ultimate ground of "the most holy" which is the root principle common to both the holy and the profane. The union of the holy and the profane is not merely a reciprocal relationship of two contiguous realms but a union that forms an integral part of "the most holy," proceeding harmoniously from a common root. The subjectivism implicit in this conception is apparent. Just as religious truth is rooted in the knowledge that the differences in the sphere of reality are subjective, so also do we find the differences in the realm of values to be merely subjective, except that here the question arises concerning the ultimate *source* of the content.

The harmony that is revealed to religious insight is not derived from the combination of the various fragments of existence in one frame but from the relation of existence to one source, the divine source of all reality.[46] The concept of "the most holy" in the realm of values is at once the highest value and the highest source, and the knowledge that is derived from it is the knowledge of all from the source of all.[47] In this sphere of true religious knowledge in which reality is understood as all-inclusive and all-holy human knowledge and thought flow from one divine source.[48] Thought must then be regarded not as an autonomous human activity but a supernatural force that proceeds from a source beyond man. Thought is here seen to take two directions; one towards existence and one that leaves existence to return to its source. Rav Kook sees this fertilizing activity of thought shuttling back and forth from existence to source: The sturdy, spiritual root filled with the sap of life and existence ceaselessly sends forth shoots without number; and sometimes when the soul is weary of these interminable shoots it would fain lay hold of the root at its source and then all is renewed and it rejoices once more together with all the rejuvenated shoots and sprouts new buds and fruit that never before saw the light of the world.[49]

Here in the realm of knowledge we approach the religious vision of the return of everything to its source and this return of all things to God is the highest perfection in existence.[50] It is this aspiration towards the source that accounts for the movement in existence.[51] The return is here one of knowledge essentially and not one of objective existence, and this again emphasizes the subjective aspect of Rav Kook's religious conception which is chiefly concerned with the inner life of man. The religious aspiration to return to the source is not the last stage in the life of faith; it is not swallowed up in the depths of nothingness, but returns from the source to the world of reality, which is not a complete, self-contained world but an open world characterized by this dynamic movement to and from the source.

Three principal concepts of religious thought are to be found in this harmonious structure—sin, repentance, and piety.

Sin consists in the separation and estrangement of man from the world. Sin obscures the light of the highest wisdom, which comes from the perfect relation of harmony of the soul that knows the laws of all existence and the highest source.[52] This shutting out of the light of the highest wisdom—that is, the isolation of man from reality—is expressed in the human sphere by man's hatred of his fellow man and the absence of human sympathy. Every sin, even the lightest, implies some hatred within man towards the created world and repentance causes love to shine forth again.[53] Sin is not a defect in the world of reality, but the product of a human act whereby man cuts himself off from the world. Existence in general is free of sin which is found only in connection with particulars; in the general scheme of things eternal harmony reigns.[54] All sin causes the heart grief, for it negates the unity that binds individuals to all existence and this grief is assuaged only by repentance.[55] The moment that man sins he is aware of his isolation. When he is touched by love, he at once feels the unity that flows through all things, secular and divine, wherein no evil exists, since evil is only an ingredient to season the good and enhance its value; real merit thus accrues to evil.[56] This identification of sin and evil with the destruction of harmony is the other aspect of the conception that sees its religious ideal in harmony.

Repentance overcomes sin by bringing man back into the circle of universal harmony. It is achieved as a result of the sinner's own efforts and desire to improve, but it is also an objective, metaphysical law. Repentance is the common ground where the human and the universal wills meet.[57] Repentance is then not only a religious and ethical concept, but also a fact of the natural world where its function is to preserve the laws of nature and the prevailing harmony.[58] In the human sphere repentance is a religious vision of a twofold return, a return to the world and to its source. Sin isolates man from a world that is essentially harmonious and unified throughout and repentance re-establishes the fraternal union,[59] and illumines the dark recesses of the penitent heart.[60] In repentance, which is an event that takes place in the human sphere, the ontological aspect of harmony converges with the axiological aspect of holiness: Through repentance all things return to God and by dint of the power that resides in it all thoughts, feelings, sentiments, and desires revert to their essential qualities.[61]

Sin and repentance are concepts that apply to the human sphere. Through repentance man corrects his errors and thus draws closer to God. Piety, however, is a contemplative and not a practical ideal. It concerns the direct relationship between man and God. But even this constant yearning of man and this "greatest bliss in life"[62] are not isolated phenomena but the expression of a general cosmic law, the law of harmony: The need of communing with God is the source of general unity throughout life.[63] Communion with God is one of the manifestations of the unity of the world; man's striving to be one with God is an integral part of cosmic unity. The changes that have taken place in this concept are worth examining. The subjective aspect of this religious conception in all that concerns religious insight has already been touched upon. The very essence of this insight consists in the ability to see existence differently from what it at first appears to be by looking at it in the light of ontological harmony or holiness. Here in the realm of those ideals related to religious aspiration, the ideals of repentance and fellowship with God, a change takes place in the ideals themselves. Repentance resides in the deep recesses of reality, for it is prior to the world; the repentance for sin is already in existence before the sin itself.[64] The harmonious Whole is the true reality and is antecedent to all forms of separation, to sin and evil. Man's aspiration for fellowship with God is, therefore, rooted in this reality or, in other words, repentance and communion with God find their objective guarantees in reality itself and depend on cosmic laws and not on man's will alone. The harmony that is revealed to man through his religious conception is the guarantee of his religious aspirations.

What is the special place assigned to God within this harmonious Whole? God is not beyond this harmony: He reveals his unity in the world, in man, among the nations, and in the content of existence.[65] Since this unity is all embracing, it contains more than only God and the question thus arises whether God is included in the unity of the world or whether He is apart from it. That God is said to be "the true existence"[66] might refer to God alone and not to the world, which may be only an illusion, similar to Hermann Cohen's distinction between *Sein* and *Dasein*. God is here conceived as a unified plurality, somewhat in the cabalistic sense of mystical emanations, and this concept is also applied to the world. The question that confronts us, therefore, is that of the relation between God as a unified plurality and the world as a unified plurality. This leads us to a consideration of the aspect of *source* in the concept of "true existence": the attribute of originality or primal source adheres to God alone and not to the world. The world is a unified plurality that is dependent on the Source from which all things flow; God is a unified plurality in the sense of the Source itself. This distinction brings us close to Spinoza's distinction between *natura naturans*, the divine substance or extended Deity considered as the whole of modification, and *natura naturata*, the results of this divine essence. It is precisely this distinction which leaves unanswered the question as to whether there is an ontological difference between God and the world in the sense that God dwells beyond the world and distinct from it.

This brings us to the question of creation and emanation in Rav Kook's conception and the question of pantheism that is bound up with it. In his *Oroth Israel* he says that the world-view that is peculiar to Judaism . . . is the view that is rooted in the renewal of the world in accordance with the first verse of the Bible: "In the beginning God created heaven and earth."[67] The concept of renewal is necessarily followed by the volitional element in the

world: The universal will that has fashioned all things and preserves them from destruction and sends its impulse through the
world—[68] but this will, as far as we can determine from the author's
vague language, is not the highest principle in the development of
the world but only an intermediary between the effulgent light
from the sources on high and the world. Rav Kook states explicitly:
There is no harm in removing the will from God because it is a
limited attribute, but necessity is certainly more limited than the
will, so that instead of the will and necessity a third attribute must
be found that is superior to both, an attribute that we have no
means of characterizing. Similarly, there is no harm in removing
the attribute of intention, but contingency is even more dis-
pensable, since it is in essence inferior and weaker than intention,
and we must hence find an attribute that is higher than these two,
one that is a prime cause of activity in the world and a necessary
manifestation of God.[69] This principle is not far removed from
that of the negative attributes—necessity and contingency are
dispensed with, but the limited attributes of will and intention are
not part of God's essence. The tendency is to find an attribute with
an element of spontaneity inherent in an unlimited will and intention.

But now we find that *emanation* is superior to *creation*: Divine
emanation as the source of all existence is above creation.[70] The
volitional factor is not prominent in emanation nor is the negative
attribute derived from the negation of the will. This refers to the in-
herence of the world in a higher reality: The finite content is included within the infinite substance.[71] Moreover, the difference
between individual finite existence and infinite existence is not
ontological; it is a result of our limited understanding and defective vision that recognizes only particulars.[72] Man's finite existence
is unreal because it is fragmentary, but becomes real when looked
at in the light of a more comprehensive and unified Whole, that is,
God.

This view tends to approach the philosophical doctrine of
pantheism, the belief that God and the universe are of the same
substance and man's soul but a modification of that divine substance. The difference between God and the world, writes Rav

Kook, depends on thought and comprehension and way of life; as thought increases, man and the world rise to divine heights of perfect thought where man discovers that the understanding is part of God's wisdom and that all existence is but a revelation of God which manifests itself in multitudinous particular forms; and because of this divine happiness is the happiness of all.[73] This pantheistic doctrine that there is nothing outside of God and that all things are absorbed in God[74] is called by Rav Kook "the monotheistic view," but is in reality *acosmism*, since it holds that God is the world and not that the world is God. God absorbs all being: The infinite passes into the finite, the absolute into the relative, the necessary into the contingent, the one into the many— all existences are only so many modes or forms of its manifestation and swallowed up in the aggressive expansion of the extended Deity, the *natura naturans* of Spinoza.

It is instructive to note the mystical strain in this conception as set forth by Rav Kook, the element of humility and the negation of being.[75] As man and the world rise to God, they gradually forfeit their particular essence. The religious sentiment here undergoes a marked change—man's recognition of his finitude does not make him conscious of his unworthiness, and the deep gulf between him and God only fills him with a sense of participation in the Spirit that rolls through all things great and small and makes the universe One. It is precisely the pantheistic view that now helps man overcome his insignificance in a vast universe and his abject terror before an implacable God.

Rav Kook stresses the pantheistic notion that the contemplative and the lyrical world of feeling keep increasing in power and in purity.[76] But this feeling cannot penetrate all areas of life and dominate them: At any rate the practical world cannot progress in conformity with this insight and here it is imperative that man should dim his light that he may better be able to adjust himself to the world of action.[77] It is only in the practical world[78] of inescapable facts that we refrain from acting in accordance with the lofty truths of pantheism. In the practical world of experience man's recognition of his insignificance in the universe would bring his active life to a standstill and he must therefore regard himself as unique. Hence his practical activity is governed by *pragmatic* considerations and his purely speculative life by the higher illumination that comes from the unity and harmony of the universe.

The pantheistic aspect of this system is also evident when we investigate the place that the concept of time occupies in the world order. Time exists only for us and not for God. This is the theme of Rav Kook's comment on the poem-prayer *Yigdal*: Our feeling of existence is bound up with our feeling of time and the psychological reason for this union is the circumstance that time appears to us as an incessant, never-ending flow and it is this aspect of time that characterizes the ever-changing face of existence itself in all its manifestations. We cannot escape from this current of time, but we know that there is an existence that is not subject to its ravages, that rises above all the vicissitudes of change and decay. This is the true existence and the source of all existence . . . an existence untouched by time.[79]

We have seen how pantheism expresses the astonishment of reason at the nothingness of man and the insignificance of existence. The soul cannot reconcile the turmoil of life with the unbroken mystery of the Unchangeable and, as it sighs for eternal Unity, it tends to deny to objective existence the quality of time. We must realize that time does not belong to eternity, and all existence that takes place in time is involved in a higher, more-inclusive eternity. There are no changes and all existences are equal and permanent.[80] That is, all protensive events or events that have duration disappear in a realm that is beyond time and change where the past, present, and future are a *totum simul* and what was will be and what has been done will be done and what has occurred in the past and in the future is being enacted in the present and all things live and perfect themselves in the light of the Source that unites and sustains all living things.[81] Thus seen, the world is one harmonious Whole and the changes in time are merely the experiences of the finite subject; the man who is imbued with this religious harmony lives beyond change and time. Naturally, the religious existentialist holds the exact opposite point of view, since for him man is essentially a temporal creature and time the very substance of his life.

The attitude of religion to pantheistic doctrines is the criterion that Rav Kook uses to establish the superiority of Judaism. Paganism, like pantheism, deifies man and by the same token lowers God.[82] Negating the distinction between the essence of absolute Being and the attributes of sentient creatures, it considers God and Nature as two different but inseparable aspects of universal existence. Christianity is pagan to the extent that it seeks to measure God with the yardstick of human ideals, so that instead of raising man to God it only succeeds in humanizing the *Deus opifex* and reducing Him to the level of man.[83] There is in Christianity a pantheistic strain that tends towards the belief in the consubstantiality of God and man and the necessary co-existence of the finite and the infinite.[84] In Islam there is a similar tendency to make God's wisdom and power accessible to man by obliterating the distinction between the human and the divine, between the perishing universe and its unchanging Author.[85] Paganism adheres to a cosmic conception which emphasizes the world and the forces of nature; Rav Kook's belief (which he identifies with the Jewish approach) is in an absolute, unlimited God; the things of this world are never co-eternal with Him, but are His creatures and His handiwork.

We find here a combination of three elements: a) the pantheistic element that identifies God with the universe; b) the doctrine of negative attributes, which denies that God can be known as a "positive Absolute"[86]; c) the mystical element that lifts God above human comprehension and makes him Unknowable.[87]

The religious feeling that inspires this conception is not one of man's nothingness, but his yearning to enter into fellowship with God and the strong assurance of his power to do so. For it is only his finite comprehension that separates him from God. In reality there is no world, but only God who is present in all things and in whom all things live and move. This world is harmonious because God is Harmony; in it there is no distinction between the sacred and profane, for God is the Holy of Holies; it is a world of repentance because man is not removed from his origin, but is immersed in the Source of all being. The world is filled with God, who is engaged in an eternal monologue: "His welfare is the welfare of all."[88] He does not come forth to hold converse with man, for He never underwent contraction for the sake of the world. In the reflection of His radiance man fixes his gaze on the unchanging scene beyond the passing pageant and by his desire for fellowship with God discovers the road back to his unified self.

8

Between Man and Nature

A. D. GORDON

A. THE YEARNING TO BE AT ONE WITH THE WORLD

In his lecture on philosophical intuition given at the Philosophical Congress in Bologna in 1911, Bergson set forth the root principle of his thinking: "In this point there is something simple, infinitely simple, so extraordinarily simple that the philosopher has never succeeded in saying it. And that is why he went on talking all his life. He could not formulate properly what he had in mind, and he felt obliged to correct his original formulation and then to correct his correction . . . thus proceeding from theory to theory *ad infinitum* only to convey with increasing approximation the simplicity of the original intuition. . . . All the complexity of his doctrine therefore is only the incommensurability between his simple intuition and the means at his disposal for expressing it."[1]

This basic perception, which Bergson calls "philosophical intuition," is to be found throughout the works of A. D. Gordon (1856–1922) and this thought, variously expressed, is one to which he constantly returns. The highest life to which man aspires is the cosmic life of the world.[2] Man's life, although rooted in the world, is not restricted to its particularity, to the individual self or the social group, but reaches out into the world and its infinite

[239]

expanses.[3] The expressions Gordon uses to describe this life, as when he speaks of the world's expanses as "abundance from on high,"[4] often remind us of the mystical language of the cabalists. The fundamental problem of man in general and of the Jew in particular concerns the gulf that separates finite man from this heavenly abundance. Man's yearning to reach out beyond himself and enter into communion with the world implies the concept of work which, as Gordon understood it, requires the creation of a new culture, neither urban nor rural, but indigenous to cosmic man, a culture that lives and has its being in nature, in which human life and culture is fused with that of the world. All being would be sustained and nourished, incessantly and without mediation, by this original source.[5]

B. BEING ONE WITH THE WORLD AND ITS EXPRESSION

The idea of man's oneness with the world is related to Gordon's conception of the nature of Judaism, which he sees under the double aspect of religion and of the people who created it.

Religion is taken as the expression of man's relation to the world and his place in it. The religious feeling, which is the most profound and vital of all human feelings is the feeling of unity experienced by the soul when it merges with the world and its pulsating life.[6] It seems that in evaluating the religious nature of man's relation to the world Gordon emphasizes man's efforts to rise above his limited existence. Religion is the expression of the human yearning for fellowship that is at the root of man's nature. The element of faith in religion, that is, the dependence of creation on the Creator and of all sentient creatures on their Maker, is ignored by Gordon, especially toward the end of his days. Thus he says that it is precisely deep and noble religions, such as Buddhism that do not rest on faith, and even deny the belief in God.[7] On a number of occasions Gordon alludes to the religion of Buddha, whose basic principle he seems to have understood to be the redemption of man from his finitude and his becoming one with all reality. The religious conception of which Gordon speaks is closer to the pantheistic notion of general harmony than man's dependence on faith. He also attaches little importance to the doctrinal aspect of religion and he opposes the view that sees religion as faith in divine Revelation, eternal truths and the divine origin of laws. It is, rather, something that flows from human nature, from the point where man and nature meet.[8]

As an expression of yearning of the human soul, religion is a creative activity of the community or, more precisely, of the national community. In Gordon's conception the nation serves as a connecting link between man and the existent world. Religion does not come from without; its source lies deep in national life and its forms express the corporate soul of the nation in its process of self-development towards its highest ideals. The nations of the world may be compared to the various instruments of an orchestra, each preserving its peculiar character and at the same time contributing to the universal harmony.[9] It is interesting to note the difference in this respect between Gordon and Ahad Haam. The latter regarded religion, at least the religion of Israel, as a creation of the people and not as a gift from heaven, as a reflection of the national spirit of the community. But he understood this creation as a *historical* process within the nation itself. For Gordon, however, religion derives its inspiration and vitality from a source outside and beyond the community. The people constitutes an entity within the world and not within history.[10] Religion is a *cosmic* and not a historical phenomenon. Although it is an expression of the soul of the nation's people, it bursts the narrow confines of the community and includes the world and nature. Religion is a national manifestation, but is at the same time an all-inclusive phenomenon.

Within this sphere of religion Gordon assigns a special place to Jewish monotheism. The highest unity, he says, between man and himself, between man and his countryman, between one nation and another, and among the different nations, as well as between man and the whole world of living nature is achieved by religion when it arrives at the conception of an absolutely unique and only God. Only a religion that attains this highest unity can understand such thoughts as: "Thou shalt love thy neighbor as thyself"; and "one nation shall not lift up the sword against another nation"; and "the wolf shall lie down with the lamb"; "the earth shall be filled with the knowledge of the Lord as the waters cover the sea"; or, from the standpoint of the nation and its responsibility: "Be ye holy for the Lord your God is holy."[11] In other words, Gordon took the moral imperatives that make for harmony among men throughout the world and attached them to the concept of monotheism. Although he himself does not explain the nature of this attachment, we may understand it as follows: Monotheism is the highest expression of the concept that regards the world as one unified whole, that redeems God from His parochial loyalties and makes Him the universal God of all mankind and the God that unites man with the cosmos. Jewish monotheism, therefore, contains the two elements which constitute the essence of religion: It stems from the people and is a product of its creative genius on the one hand and it expresses man unity with the world and the cosmos on the other.

C. THE IMAGE OF GOD

In Judaism we find, according to Gordon, the best illustration of the specific nature of religion as the unity of man with the world mediated by the national soul. Unlike the religions of the European nations, Judaism did not come from without but is the creation of national spirit, and the two have been absorbed to such an extent that one may say that the Jewish religion is the outer form of a people's national spirit from time immemorial.[12] This close relationship of the individual and the people to the world, which has been interpreted as the principal characteristic of religion in general, is best illustrated in Judaism: The strength of the Jewish religion does not lie essentially in its peculiar world view but in the peculiar relationship it has established between man and all that is outside him: "Ye shall be holy for I your God am holy" is not a new world view with respect to the time in which these words were spoken, but a new relationship of man to man and to himself.[13]

Nevertheless, Gordon concentrates on the *content* of Judaism, which he regards on the one hand as the creation of man and on the other as the expression of the all-inclusive world. He bases his conception of the content of Judaism on the idea of "the image of God" which he interprets in the light of his general system: If

we examine Judaism from within, we cannot help being struck by
the fact that everything—the entire system of ethics and religion,
the entire world of man—rests upon the image of God in man,
and if we translate this idea into the living language of our day, we
find the central thought to be that everything rests on its essential
self, on the human ego, both the personal and the national; that is,
the ultimate goal that man desires to attain, knowingly or unknowingly, is the perfection of his essential self; to be pure and
faithful to it, to achieve harmony between the active, vital powers
of his body and soul on the one hand and his wide-ranging, all-
inclusive spirit on the other, so that man might develop in the
image of the living God, in the image of the life of nature in its
highest sense.[14]

We shall now examine how Gordon employs his conception of
God. Apparently, it is to be understood as the universal spirit of
life that comprehends all, the life of nature in its highest sense.
The pantheistic identity of God with nature is obvious in this
formulation except that here nature is not swallowed up in God,
but God is swallowed up in nature.

Of the various meanings attached to the idea of "the image of
God" Gordon stresses that of the relation between the Original
and the replica. That man was created in the image of God means
that he was created after the pattern of an Archetype found in
the nature of the Godhead. In this relationship between the
Original and the replica Gordon emphasizes the harmonious relation between man and the world. The concept of "the image of
God" expresses the two aspects of Gordon's system: the power of
man on the one hand and his inclusion in the world on the other.
In proportion as man develops his native power he can rise above
the narrow confines of his finite existence and find his place in the
world without. In other words, instead of the relationship of dependence between the Creator and His creatures, the original idea
expressed in the concept of the "image of God," Gordon emphasizes
the relationship between the part and the whole. Man's aspiration to
live up to the image of God within him or to the demands of the
higher Will does not require that he transform himself into another
or efface himself before this higher Will. On the contrary, he has

to enter deeply into the life of the world not to aspire to live for the sake of the other, for the sake of the nation, for the sake of mankind or for the sake of God but to live more fully, to develop his natural powers, to live within himself, within all men and all the things of the created world. The concept of the image of God means, according to Gordon, the development of man's powers, a development which automatically identifies him with all existence. This totality of existence is conceived not only as an all-inclusive system but also as the source of existence and this accounts for the mystical strain in Gordon's language: "The highest relationship in Judaism is that of the image of God to the highest image, of the drop of life to the source of life, of the rays to the hidden light of reality, to the secret of reality."[15]

The basic principle of Judaism then expresses man's yearning to rise above himself and enter into communion with the world and all that is therein. According to Judaism man lives within the world as an *individual*, but he is at the same time a part of the *world*.

This idea that equates man with the world helps us to understand the meaning of two of Gordon's aphorisms concerning the place occupied in Judaism by the concept of truth: Jewish ethics rests entirely on truth, and Christian ethics on love; the truth necessarily leads to all virtues, including love, which is nothing but the root and the fruit of the tree.[16] And in another place: The beauty of truth is the highest beauty and corresponds to the thought: "And you shall see my back, but my face you shall not see." The nations of the world speak of beauty and the truth that resides in beauty; Israel speaks of the truth and the beauty that resides in the truth.[17] Gordon does not adequately explain how the concept of truth finds a place within his system, but we may understand its purpose to be that of indicating the correspondence between the knower and the known. The truth by its very nature lifts the knower out of his confined and isolated state and makes him dependent on something outside himself. The truth serves as a bridge between man and the world and expresses the harmonious relation between the two. We thus see how the rational concept of truth is made by Gordon the expression of inner harmony, the root and the compass of Jewish ethics. In Judaism man's relation to his fellow man is assured from the very beginning and has no need of external sentiments such as love and pity to bolster this relation as does Christianity. It is interesting in this respect to compare Gordon's conception with that of Ahad Haam. Whereas Gordon emphasizes the concept of truth, which includes the relation of man to his fellow man as well as to the world, Ahad Haam emphasizes the narrower concept of justice as the essence of Judaism. He describes justice as "truth in action"—that is, he confines the truth to the social sphere. In sum, Gordon regards the essence of Judaism as truth, and Ahad Haam, as justice, but neither takes the Christian sentiments of love and pity as the chief pillars of ethics.[18]

D. MAN THE WORKER

Man's power is a creative, dynamic force that flows from the "cosmic life" in which it is rooted. Man is constantly testing this power throughout his life, trying to complete that which cannot be completed.[19] Work itself and not the things produced by it constitutes man's essential task,[20] and man's highest ideal is bound up with the effort he expends in attaining it.[21] In this comprehensive view Gordon sees man as part of the family, the family as part of the nation, and the nation as part of the world—all these interrelated areas of human life moving in harmony, a harmony which is not only a fact but, for man at any rate, also a goal. It is therefore incumbent on man to confront the world as a worker. In other words, the dynamic nature of existence is reflected in man's dynamism—that is, in his work. Gordon thus interprets the concept of man's participation in the work of Creation, viz. a vital, human activity that is neither passive nor purely speculative.

Gordon was aware of the ethical content of Judaism, but he wished to extend its meaning. Ethics requires of man that he labor to fashion his life in accordance with the ethical imperative. Gordon's concept of human activity is not dependent on ethics; ethical activity is for him but one aspect of man's nature as a worker whose activity is directed towards one end: the fellowship with all existence. These then are the two aspects of Gordon's system—the theoretical element of harmony and the practical element of activity which strives towards and is nourished by the harmony that pervades all being.

The dynamic character of Judaism also appears in the concept that Gordon calls by the abbreviated name of "the educational step." Judaism regards man as one who actively seeks to embody ethical values. Man is not confronted directly with the highest ethical value nor is it immediately placed within his reach; he will approach this value gradually by intermediate stages. For Gordon, Judaism presents man with light that is concealed in many lamps placed within one another; and man's task is to bring forth light from these lamps. At first he sees these fragmentary lights from his own limited point of view, but in time he realizes that the light is hidden and that he must study and develop one lamp after another. Judaism supplies him with well-known general rules of procedure, but these are essentially propaedeutic and of a negative character, concerned with cleansing and the removal of filth and mire, for the labor is very delicate and requires that the tools—thought, feeling, will and all the implements used in the work—be kept absolutely clean.[22] Judaism thus guards itself against the danger of too hasty an encounter with the highest value. The commandment "Thou shalt love thy neighbor as thyself" is not the first rule of Judaism, but is added as a kind of affirmative conclusion to the negative admonitions that precede it, "thou shalt not steal" and "thou shalt not hate thy brother in thine heart, nor take vengeance nor bear a grudge." This is the same process the soul undergoes, since it is illumined by light only after being cleansed of the filth of finite existence.[23]

It seems that Gordon wished to explain, indirectly and by allusion, the well-known fact that has been the subject of extensive commentaries—Judaism has no formulated dogmas. He pointed out that dogma was absent not only from the speculative sphere of Judaism but also from its practical sphere. The commandments that are enjoined in Judaism are only preparatory stages on the road to the highest goal, auxiliary imperatives to help man liberate himself from his narrow confinement to follow the road that stretches out before him into infinity.

In this spirit Gordon interpreted Hillel's precept: "What is hateful to thee, do not unto thy fellow man; this is the whole Law: the rest is mere commentary—go and complete it." Gordon takes the last part of the precept to be as ethically significant as the first: *Go and complete it* means go and perfect it; study, develop yourself. In the last analysis, to Hillel the most important thing is the free, independent labor of man, which renews his life and is its very essence—and hence the essence of the teaching of life.[24] Gordon proceeds with his homiletical interpretation of the phrase "Go and complete it" and takes it as referring to activity and not to study. The original conception of Judaism requires man to undergo a course in self-discipline and ultimate self-conquest. A basic difference here becomes apparent in the views of Ahad Haam and Gordon. Ahad Haam stresses the negative aspect of Hillel's precept[25] and points out that Jewish ethics does not teach the superiority of one's fellow man but the equality of all men and that even the positive formulation of R. Akiba, "Thou shalt love thy neighbor as thyself," has a negative meaning: If you love your neighbor as yourself, you love him not more or less than yourself, but both equally, and this is what the Torah means: Do not permit your self-love to decide matters in your favor, but if you love your fellow man as yourself justice will decide between you and him, nor will you permit him to wrong you.[26] Ahad Haam seizes upon the aspect of objective justice expressed in Hillel's dictum whereas Gordon emphasizes its nondogmatic character ("the rest is mere commentary: go and complete it") in order to show the intimate connection in Judaism between active work and fellowship with all existence. For Ahad Haam the highest value is social justice, whereas for Gordon it is the totality of the world.

Gordon's interpretation of Hillel's precept is deliberately homiletical and not philological. This method is derived from his general attitude to the problem of interpretation. When he elucidates a text from the Talmud or from the Bible, Gordon does not mean to say that the present form of his thought is that which the original author had in mind. The expression is altered, extended, and deepened to the same degree that the idea within it continues to develop, but the inner core is always one and constitutes its essential significance; that is the difference between sayings of this kind and those from the sphere of abstract thought or even lyrical creations. The former are vital, all-inclusive and filled with a seed-bearing power. In his interpretations, Gordon always seeks to understand and illumine the essential kernel in Judaism and the hidden light within it, as far as this can be done.[27] Gordon sees Judaism as a dynamic movement whose inner core expresses a vital relation to the world that is not bound to any specific period in time.

E. THE OPPOSITE POLE

The peculiar nature of Judaism is seen more clearly when it is contrasted with Christianity. In speaking of the two religions Gordon says that Christianity runs counter to his Jewish views as well as to his world views, not only against the Jew, but also against the man in him.[28] These two views, however, of the Jew and the man are in this case identical, since they both rest on the principle of man's fusion with nature through active work. It may be worth while to examine some of the tendencies in Christianity mentioned by Gordon.

We must first note the historical fact that Christianity had its birth within Judaism and that whatever there is of truth in Christian ethics is of Jewish origin.[29] But Christianity then left the circle of Judaism and was adopted by people not born within it, so that it lacks the most important characteristic that, according to Gordon, is the peculiar mark of religion, namely, that it is the purest form of national existence and the deepest expression of the collective soul in its aspirations towards self-revelation. Christianity was given to the world and the world received it ready-made.

The world was able to accept Christianity as a finished product because of its dogmatic character and because it made salvation dependent on belief in formulated dogmas. Judaism prepares man for the ultimate goal; Christianity places man as he is, in his unfinished and wretched condition, at the goal itself. Christianity was given to the nations of the world ready-made and they accepted it as a bright and shining light and not as lamps concealed within lamps. Christianity went forth like a stamped coin from the mint and circulated from hand to hand among those willing to receive it, whereas Judaism remains concealed to the eye and can be determined by every man in his own way, dwells in his heart as something to be fashioned and wrought—unto eternity.[30]

In Judaism the Author of all things remains illimitable in his immensity, inconceivable in his mode of existence and indescribable in his essence; in Christianity the *Deus ineffabilis* assumes human form and takes upon Himself the sins of the world.[31] It is characteristic of Jewish monotheism to place God outside of the world and this permits man to open a window on infinity and on a limitless view of the world and all existence; Christianity limits the absolute unity of God[32] and at the same time man's vision of the universe.

This limitation of God's unity and the universal vision of man is reflected in the idea of mediation between God and man, in the idea that "God is in need of a helper." In other words, the meeting between man and God is obstructed by a mediator and thus the essential characteristic of religion, the direct communion of man with his Maker, is vitiated.

The idea of mediation also produces a profound change in the life of man. Christianity reduces man's power and efficacy. God is in need of a helper and man becomes an intermediary between himself and his Maker, between himself and the world, an intermediary unto himself. Man is thus reduced to a kind of wretched being, who is unable to help himself, improve his condition, or rise to a higher life; the higher life is offered to him ready-made and he need only accept it as it is.[33] Man casts his burden on Him who has been sent into the world to expiate its sins, for man by dint of his own power is unable to redeem himself. In Christianity man forfeits his chief prerogative, the ability to rise above himself, and instead of an active agent in his own dedemption becomes a passive creature patiently awaiting grace and election.

Devoid of all social aspiration to employ the resources of the world to improve the condition of man on earth, Christianity directs its gaze to the Kingdom of Heaven on the further side of reality.[34] In Christianity, in other words, man is removed from the active functions which constitute the meaning of his life on earth.

He transfers the burden of his redemption to a Redeemer from without and his hopes of salvation to a world beyond the one that he inhabits.

In short, Christianity appears to be the opposite pole of Judaism. The latter is a manifestation of the Jewish people, whereas Christianity is not a manifestation of the peoples that have adopted it. Again, Judaism does not erect a partition between man and the world; for Christianity, however, such a partition is essential and expresses itself in the concept of the Son of God. Finally, Judaism stresses the concept of man as an active worker, the active agent of his own redemption, in Christianity man appears as one who is in need of help from without.

F. INFLUENCES

The details of Gordon's spiritual biography are still extremely vague and it is therefore difficult to determine his place in the intellectual development of his time. It is reasonable to suppose, however, that his conceptions were not born *in vacuo* but were deeply influenced by contemporary opinion and the temper of the period in which he lived.

Let us turn to the last stage in the development of Bergson's thought, a stage which Bergson reached after Gordon's death and which could not, therefore, have directly affected Gordon's thinking. In *The Two Sources of Morality and Religion*, Bergson distinguishes between two types of morality and religion, between the religion that he calls static, whose function is to preserve the public peace and welfare against the dangers that threaten them from without, and the religion that he calls dynamic, which is not concerned with maintaining peace, but which is informed by a vital movement that impels man to burst the narrow confines of his parochial existence (including that of the nation and the community) and face the sources that gives rise to life. Static religion is intent on preservation; dynamic religion is the religion of renewal.[35]

In terms of this distinction, Gordon regarded Judaism as a dynamic religion, since it is principally concerned with redeeming man from his confined state and lifting him above finite existence.

Bergson, on the other hand, regarded Judaism as a static religion and Christianity as a dynamic religion, since the latter strives to lift man above the bounds of nationality. But if we consider the distinction between a religion that is the manifestation of a people and a religion that is transmitted to a people from without, the problem does not fall within the national sphere of religion, but concerns the nature of the relationship between the religion and the people.

One distinction made by Bergson is directly opposed by Gordon, viz. that static religion develops its ethical content without reference to the personality or morality of its promulgator, while dynamic religion from the very outset bears the imprint of a great personality who incorporates in his own person the ethical imperatives of the religion. For Gordon, however, religion is not dependent on any one great personality—a thought that he once expressed in the dictum that the only education is self-education. Gordon believed that every man had within him a deep content that could be developed through self-education. Here Gordon touched on ideas already expressed by Hirsch and H. Cohen.

There is a speculative trend in Gordon's thinking that stresses the harmony between man and the world—that is, the close relationship between man and the source of life; this is a mystical strain whose ideal is the redemption of man through union with God. This ideal, however, is not realized by speculation concerning existence and man's place in it (which leads to a negation of the world), but by human action directed towards the world.

As against what has sometimes been called "biologism" the view held by Gordon may be called "cosmism," for it bases ethics on man's relation to external nature and not on man's biological constitution. Gordon was able to identify his conception with ethical Judaism only by virtue of the fact that it contains the two poles—Unity and Action.

There are some instructive points of similarity between Gordon and Moses Hess (1812–1875). The three elements that constitute the basis of Judaism are, according to Hess: unity, action, and historical dynamism. Judaism conceives the world as being ruled by one Law. This Hess calls "the genetic view." Action refers to human events whereby unity is realized within the social order. This conjunction of unity and action is also found in Gordon except that he—and this is the basic difference between Gordon's conception and Hess's socialism—places action in the sphere of the relation between man and nature, whereas European socialism regards action as the builder of society and the instigator of revolution; that is, it places action within the historical sphere.

It is surprising that Gordon was not aware of his identification of Judaism with the concept of nature or with the concept of history.[36]

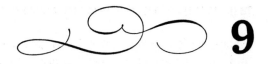

9

Conclusion—Between Two
Historical Views

The question that arises as we approach the end of our study is that of the relationship between Israel's historical existence and the speculations concerning the preordained essence of Judaism considered as a historical product or as a divine revelation. How can the historical and sociological aspect be reconciled with the dogmatic and theoretical? Are these two distinct provinces juxtaposed without any significant principle of unity? Is there no middle-ground between the reality of Israel's existence and the dogmatic principles of Judaism; and if there is such a common ground, what is its nature?

We have considered two systematic attempts designed to elucidate the meaning of the "eternality of Israel" and to bridge the gap between dogmatic Judaism and the historical phenomenon of Israel. The first sought to demonstrate that the attachment to the "absolute spiritual" requires infinite time and that this infinite time is the historical expression of the absolute infinite in the spiritual realm. The leading exponent of this system is Krochmal, who conceived Israel's historical existence from the standpoint of its religious principles; the most prominent thinker of the second view is Franz Rosenzweig, who argued that the eternality of Israel meant its separation from time and the negation of its historical experience.

[253]

The Jewish generation of today is confronted by problems that are even more acute; for good or ill, we have consciously entered the stream of history. This fact was clearly seen by the leaders of the Jewish Reform Movement in the last century, who were convinced that this entrance into history necessarily entailed a loss of national identity. Those of us who strove for national revival, however, entered into history in order to establish the Jewish people within it; to live, move, and have our being within it. The trust in the eternality of man and in the eternal principles of Judaism had been shaken by fate and Jews were resolved to enter history to preserve the people and sustain their faith. The historic consciousness of our generation was confronted not only with problems that demanded study and reflection but by the poignant experiences of living reality.

The basic question that confronts Jews in the present era concerns the relation between these two historical views of Jewish existence. Has a revealed, preordained Judaism any meaning for a generation at a time when it is caught up in the stream of events and swept along on its strong current? On the other hand, is there any meaning to a historical continuity that is devoid of Jewish content, however it may be interpreted? It is no longer a question as to which interpretation of Judaism enlists the sympathy and allegiance; the validity of the very concept of interpretation has been rendered doubtful.

These questions admit of no theoretical solutions prior to those claimed by the exigencies of existence itself. It may be repeated in this connection that the owl of Minerva, the goddess of wisdom, flies by night. It is difficult to imagine that there can flourish in our day a Judaism whose principles are not related to historical reality and whose basic concern is not directed to the preservation of the individual Jew struggling with his daily destiny. A modern metaphysics of Jewish history will not survey the temporal course of events from afar, but will hearken to their inner rhythm that they may prove wise guides to our steps. In the meantime one may look to the past for an authentic recovery of the mighty armory of ancient wealth and walk towards the future in a spirit of bold adventure.

Notes

N.B. In referring to sources that exist only in Hebrew, English titles have been given, and the notation "Hebrew" is made at the end of the citation.

INTRODUCTION

1. On the nature of Jewish philosophy in the Middle Ages, consult J. Guttmann, *Philosophies of Judaism: The History of Jewish Philosophy from Biblical Times to Franz Rosenzweig*, trans. D. W. Silverman (New York: Holt, Rinehart and Winston, 1964).
2. The ideas of articulation and justification are explained in my earlier book, *The Recurring Pattern: Studies in Anti-Judaism in Modern Thought* (New York: Horizon Press, 1963), pp. 9 ff.

CHAPTER 1

1. On Jewish thought, in addition to Guttmann's *Philosophies of Judaism*, see Max Wiener, *Jüdische Religion im Zeitalter der Emanzipation* (Berlin: Philo Verlag, 1933); S. H. Bergman, *Faith and Reason: An Introduction to Modern Jewish Thought*, trans. and ed. by A. Jospe (New York: Schocken Books, 1963). M. Mendelssohn, *Jerusalem: Oder über religiöse Macht und Judentum* (Berlin: Welt-Verlag, 1919), pp. 69-70; in English, *Jerusalem: A Treatise on Religious Power and Judaism*, trans. I. Lesser (Philadelphia: C. Sherman, 1852), pp. 59-60.
2. C. Garve, "Über den Charakter der Bauern und ihr Verhältnis gegen die Gutsherren und gegen die Regierung," *Vermischte Aufsätze* (Breslau: W. G. Korn, 1796), p. 225.
3. Mendelssohn, "Gegenbetrachtungen über Bonnets Palingenesie," *Gesammelte Schriften; Jubilaumsausgabe* (Berlin: Akademie-Verlag, 1929-32), VII, 65 ff.

4. *Ibid.*
5. *Ibid.*, pp. 75 ff.
6. *Ibid.*, p. 89.
7. See J. Guttmann, "An Enquiry into the Sources of the Book of Fundamental Principles," *Studies in Memory of Asher Gulak and Samuel Klein* (Jerusalem: The Hebrew University Press Association, 1942), p. 66 (Hebrew).
8. Guttmann has also pointed out the relation between Mendelssohn and Spinoza in his essay, "Mendelssohn's *Jerusalem* und Spinoza's *Theologisch-politischer Traktat*," in *Achtundvierzigster Bericht der Hochschule für die Wissenschaft des Judentums* (Berlin, 1931).
9. Mendelssohn, *Jerusalem*, pp. 111-113 (trans., pp. 100-102).
10. In particular see Mendelssohn, "Einleitung zur Übersetzung der Schrift des Menasse ben Israel 'Rettung der Juden,'" *Schriften zur Philosophie, Aesthetik und Apologetik*, ed. M. Brasch (2d ed.; Breslau: W. Jacobsohn, 1892), II, pp. 492 ff (henceforth = Schriften).
11. Mendelssohn, *Jerusalem*, p. 16 (trans., pp. 9-10).
12. *Ibid.*, p. 114 (trans., p. 103).
13. Mendelssohn, "Briefe über die Empfindungen," *Schriften*, II, 91.
14. Mendelssohn, *Jerusalem*, p. 11 (trans., pp. 4-5).
15. Mendelssohn, "Über den Selbstmord," *Schriften*, II, 265.
16. Mendelssohn, "Gegenbetrachtungen über Bonnets Paligenesie," *Gesammelte Schriften; Jubiläumsausgabe*, VII, 76.
17. Mendelssohn, "Rhaphsodie oder Zusätze zu den Briefen über die Empfindungen," *Schriften*, II, 102.
18. Mendelssohn, "Briefe über die Empfindungen," *Schriften*, II, 63.
19. Mendelssohn, "Über das sittlich und physisch Gute," *Schriften*, II, 251.
20. *Ibid.*
21. Mendelssohn, *Jerusalem*, p. 52 (trans., pp. 43-44); p. 20 (trans., p. 14).
22. Mendelssohn, *Schriften*, II, 492.
23. R. Hönigswald, *Hobbes und die Staatsphilosophie* (Munich: E. Reinhardt, 1924), p. 198.
24. See the enlightening discussion of this development in E. Zeller, *Geschichte der deutschen Philosophie seit Leibnitz* (2nd ed.; Munich: R. Oldenbourg, 1875), pp. 121 ff., 179 ff.
25. Mendelssohn, *Jerusalem*, p. 51 (trans., p. 43).
26. *Ibid.*
27. Mendelssohn, *Schriften*, II, 492.
28. This idea of the symbolic character of *Mitzvoth* recurs in the thought of Rabbi Samson Raphael Hirsch (b. Hamburg, 1808; d. Frankfort a. M., 1888) as well as Jehiel Michael Pines (b. Rozhany, Russia, 1842; d. Jerusalem, 1912), doubtless under Mendelssohn's direct influence.
29. Mendelssohn, "Von der Evidenz in den Anfangsgründen der Sittenlehre," *Schriften*, II, 92.
30. See S. L. Steinheim, *Moses Mendelssohn und seine Schule in ihrer Beziehung zur Aufgabe des neuen Jahrhundrets der alten Zeitzrechnung* (Hamburg: Hoffman, 1840).
31. Z. Jawitz, *Collected Essays*, ed. B. Klar (Jerusalem: Mosad ha-Rav Kook, 1943), p. 143 (Hebrew).
32. J. Gutmann, "Moses Mendelssohn's *Jerusalem* und Spinoza's *Theologisch-polit-*

ischer Traktat," in *Achtundvierzigster Bericht der Hochschule für die Wissenschaft des Judentums* (Berlin, 1931).

33. On these streams of thought, see H. Hettner, "Das Zeitalter Friedrichs des Grossen," in *Literaturgeschichte des achtzehnten Jahnhundreds* (3rd ed; Braunschweig: Friedrich Vieweg und Sohn, 1879), Dritter Teil, Zweites Buch, pp. 179 ff.

34. On Mendelssohn's *Jerusalem*, see S. Rawidowicz, "The Philosophy of *Jerusalem*," in *Bialik*, ed. J. Fichman (Tel Aviv: The Anniversary Committee and Omanuth Press, 1934), Sec. C, pp. 99-140 (Hebrew).

CHAPTER 2

1. S. D. Luzzatto, *Studies in Judaism* (Warsaw: Ha-Tzefira, 1913), I, Part 1, 22.
2. *Ibid.*, p. 39.
3. Luzzatto, *Lezioni di teologia morale israelitica* (Padova: A. Bianchi, 1862), § XLVI, 42, n. 1 a.
4. Luzzatto, *The Epistles of Shadal*, ed. E. Gräber (Przemyśl: Żupnik and Knoller, 1882-1891), V, 661 (Hebrew).
5. Luzzatto, *Studies in Judaism*, I, Part 2, 208.
6. Luzzatto, *Lezioni . . .* , § IV.
7. *Ibid.*, § V.
8. *Ibid*, vii.
9. Luzzatto, *Studies in Judaism*, I, Part 1, 11 ff.
10. A. Schopenhauer, *The Basis of Morality*, trans. A. B. Bullock (London: Swan Sonnenschein and Co., 1903), p. 170.
11. Luzzatto, *Studies in Judaism*, I, Part 1, 21.
12. *Ibid.*, p. 30.
13. *Ibid.*, p. 11.
14. *Ibid.*
15. This idea can also be found in the writings of Rabbi Isaac Samuel Reggio the scholar from Göritz, Illyria (1784-1855).
16. Luzzatto, *Lezioni . . .* , § XXI.
17. Luzzatto, *Studies in Judaism*, I, Part 1, 76.
18. "Die Verfolgung Luzzattos," in *Israelitische Annalen* (1839), pp. 25-27, 33-35, 41-45.
19. Luzzatto, *The Epistles of Shadal*, VI, 780.
20. *Ibid.*, III, 367.
21. Luzzatto, *Epistles to Letteris*, ed. Y. Zmora (Tel Aviv: Mahbaroth le-Sifruth, 1943), pp. 8, 16 (Hebrew).
22. Luzzatto, *Studies in Judaism*, I, 24.
23. Luzzatto, *Highlights in Shadal*, ed. E. Gräber (Przemyśl: Żupnik, Knoller and Hammerschmidt, 1888), p. 441 (Hebrew).
24. Luzzatto, *Lezioni . . .* , p. v.
25. *Ibid.*, § XLIII.
26. *Ibid.*, § XXIII.
27. Luzzatto, *Studies in Judaism*, I, 364.
28. *Ibid.*, p. 71.
29. *Ibid.*, p. 76.
30. *Ibid.*, p. 77.

31. I. Kant, *Critique of Pure Reason*, B648 ff.
32. *Ibid.*, B655.
33. Luzzatto, *Studies in Judaism*, I, 207.
34. For further information on Luzzatto, see J. Klausner, *A History of Modern Hebrew Literature* (2nd ed.; Tel Aviv: Ahiasaf 1952), II, 47-127 (Hebrew); and his paper, "Samuel David Luzzatto," in *Philosophers and Thinkers* (Tel Aviv-Jerusalem: Dvir, 1941), pp. 79-116 (Hebrew).

CHAPTER 3

1. M. Lazarus, *The Ethics of Judaism*, trans. H. Szold (Philadelphia: The Jewish Publication Society of America, 1900), I, 3.
2. *Ibid.*
3. *Ibid.*, I, 2.
4. *Ibid.*, I, 41.
5. M. Lazarus, *Die Ethik des Judentums*, Vol. II, ed. J. Winter and A. Wünsche (Frankfurt a.M.: J. Kauffmann, 1911), p. 42.
6. *Ibid.*, I, 127 ff.
7. *Ibid.*, I, 150.
8. *Ibid.*, I, 109-110.
9. *Ibid.*, I, 118.
10. *Ibid.*, I, 119.
11. *Ibid.*, I, 111 ff.
12. *Ibid.*, I, 135 ff.
13. *Ibid.*, I, 24 ff.
14. *Ibid.*, I, 131 ff.
15. Lazarus, *Die Ethik* . . . , II, xxvii ff.
16. I. Kant, *Fundamental Principles of the Metaphysic of Ethics*, Chap. 2.
17. *Ibid.*
18. Lazarus, *The Ethics* . . . , II, 4 ff.
19. *Ibid.*, II, 153.
20. *Ibid.*, II, 40 ff.
21. *Ibid.*, II, 45.
22. *Ibid.*, II, 84.
23. *Ibid.*, II, 185, 176.
24. Cf. N. Rotenstreich, *The Problem of Substance in Philosophy from Kant to Hegel* (Jerusalem: Rubin Mass, 1939), pp. 127 ff. (Hebrew).
25. Lazarus, *Die Ethik* . . . , II, 364.
26. Lazarus, *The Ethics* . . . , II, p. 2-3.
27. *Ibid.*, p. 54-55.

CHAPTER 4

1. H. Cohen, *Ethik des Reinen Willens* (3d ed.; Berlin: Bruno Cassirer, 1921), p. 64.
2. Cohen, *Die Religion der Vernunft aus den Quellen des Judentums* (Leipzig: Gustav Falk, 1919), p. 278.
3. Cohen, *Ethik* . . . , p. 477.
4. *Ibid.*

5. *Ibid.*, p. 469.
6. *Ibid.*, p. 427.
7. *Ibid.*, p. 424.
8. *Ibid.*, p. 93.
9. *Ibid.*, p. 442.
10. *Ibid.*, p. 449.
11. *Ibid.*, p. 450.
12. *Ibid.*, p. 445.
13. *Ibid.*, p. 91.
14. *Ibid.*, p. 459.
15. Cohen, *Jüdische Schriften* (Berlin: Bruno Strauss, 1924), III, 147.
16. Cohen, *Ethik* . . . , p. 470.
17. *Ibid.*, p. 469.
18. Cohen, *Jüdische Schriften*, I, 21.
19. *Ibid.*, III, 44 ff.
20. *Ibid.*, pp. 1-35.
21. *Ibid.*, p. 138.
22. *Ibid.*, p. 133.
23. *Ibid.*, I, 293.
24. *Ibid.*, III, 135.
25. *Ibid.*, I, 31 ff.
26. *Ibid.*, p. 30.
27. Cohen, *Die Religion* . . . , p. 292-293.
28. *Ibid.*, p. 340.
29. *Ibid.*, p. 344.
30. Cohen, *Jüdische Schriften*, I, 116.
31. Cohen, *Ethik* . . . , p. 31.
32. Cohen, *Jüdische Schriften*, I, 19.
33. *Ibid.*, III, 112.
34. Cohen: *Die Religion* . . . , pp. 278 ff.
35. Cohen, *Logik der reinen Erkenntnis* (3d ed.; Berlin: Bruno Cassirer, 1914), p. 473.
36. *Ibid.*, p. 472.
37. Cohen, *Die Religion* . . . , pp. 15 ff.
38. *Ibid.*, p. 38.
39. Cohen, *Der Begriff der Religion im System der Philosophie* (Giessen: Alfred Töpelmann, 1915). p. 10 ff., 59.
40. *Ibid.*, p. 11.
41. *Ibid.*, p. 2.
42. See S. H. Bergman, "The Late Work of Cohen," in *Thinkers of the Generation* (Tel Aviv: Mitzpeh, 1934-1935), pp. 219-243 (Hebrew).
43. Cohen, *Der Begriff* . . . , p. 52.
44. *Ibid.*, p. 55.
45. *Ibid.*, pp. 52-58.
46. Cohen, *Die Religion* . . . , p. 470.
47. Cohen, *Der Begriff* . . . , p. 51.
48. *Ibid.*, p. 48.
49. Cohen, *Die Religion* . . . , p. 209.
50. Cohen, *Der Begriff* . . . , p. 116.

51. *Ibid.*, p. 32.
52. Cohen, *Die Religion* . . . , pp. 193 ff.
53. Cohen, *Der Begriff* . . . , p. 134.
54. Cohen, *Die Religion* . . . , p. 197.
55. *Ibid.*, p. 278.
56. *Ibid.*, p. 25.
57. *Ibid.*, p. 250.
58. *Ibid.*, pp. 189 ff.
59. *Ibid.*, p. 118.
60. *Ibid.*, p. 161.
61. Cohen, *Jüdische Schriften*, III, 78.
62. Cohen, *Die Religion* . . . , pp. 197 ff.
63. *Ibid.*, p. 217.
64. *Ibid.*, p. 227.
65. *Loc. cit.*
66. Cohen, *Der Begriff* . . . , p. 66.
67. Cohen, *Die Religion* . . . , p. 222.
68. Cohen, *Jüdische Schriften*, I, 22.
69. Cohen, *Ethik* . . . , p. 211.
70. *Ibid.*, p. 214.
71. *Loc. cit.*
72. *Loc. cit.*
73. *Ibid.*, p. 213.
74. *Ibid.*, p. 215.
75. Cohen, *Die Religion* . . . , p. 130.
76. *Ibid.*, p. 132.
77. *Ibid.*, p. 19.
78. Cohen, *Der Begriff* . . , pp. 76-79.
79. Cohen, *Die Religion* . . . , p. 511.
80. *Ibid.*, p. 171.
81. *Loc. cit.*
82. Cohen, *Jüdische Schriften*, III, 57.
83. Cohen, *Die Religion* . . . , pp. 158 ff.
84. *Ibid.*, p. 169.
85. *Ibid.*, p. 170.
86. *Ibid.*, p. 165.
87. *Ibid.*, pp. 477 ff.
88. *Ibid.*, p. 168.
89. *Ibid.*, p. 171.
90. *Ibid.*, p. 22.
91. *Ibid.*, p. 172.
92. *Ibid.*
93. *Ibid.*, p. 188.
94. *Ibid.*, p. 187.
95. *Loc. cit.*
96. *Ibid.*, p. 191.
97. Cohen, *Die Religion* . . . , p. 58.
98. *Ibid.*, p. 859.
99. *Loc. cit.*

100. *Ibid.*, p. 187.
101. Cohen, *Der Begriff* . . . , pp. 18-20.
102. *Ibid.*, pp. 20 ff.
103. Cohen, *Die Religion* . . . , p. 51.
104. *Ibid.*
105. Cohen, *Der Begriff* . . . , p. 23.
106. Cohen, *Die Religion* . . . , p. 48.
107. Cohen, *J. Schriften*, I, 20.
108. Cohen, *Die Religion* . . . , pp. 41-42.
109. *Ibid.*, p. 51 ff.
110. *Ibid.*, pp. 62, 66.
111. Cohen, *Jüdische Schriften*, I, 89.
112. *Ibid.*, p. 24.
113. Cohen, *Die Religion* . . . , p. 263.
114. *Ibid.*, p. 51.
115. Cohen, *Jüdische Schriften*, I, 91.
116. Cohen, *Der Begriff* . . . , p. 17.
117. Cohen, *J. Schriften*, I, 21.
118. *Ibid.*, III, 64.
119. Cohen, *Die Religion* . . . , p. 488.
120. *Loc. cit.*
121. *Loc. cit.*
122. *Ibid.*, p. 68.
123. *Loc. cit.*
124. *Ibid.*, p. 69.
125. *Loc. cit.*
126. S. H. Bergman, "The Principle of Origin in the Philosophy of Hermann Cohen," *Knesseth*, 1943-44, Sec. C, pp. 143-153 (Hebrew).
127. *Ibid.*, p. 152.
128. Cohen, *Die Religion* . . . , p. 76.
129. *Loc. cit.*
130. *Loc. cit.*
131. *Loc. cit.*
132. *Loc. cit.*
133. *Ibid.*, p. 75.
134. Cohen, *Jüdische Schriften*, III, 179.
135. Cohen, *Die Religion* . . . , p. 79.
136. Cohen, *Jüdische Schriften*, III, 179.
137. Cohen, *Die Religion* . . . , p. 82.
138. *Ibid.*, p. 83.
139. *Ibid.*, p. 82.
140. *Ibid.*, pp. 82, 84.
141. *Ibid.*, p. 95.
142. *Ibid.*, p. 101.
143. *Ibid.*, p. 103.
144. *Ibid.*, p. 122.
145. *Ibid.*, p. 236.
146. *Ibid.*, p. 258.
147. *Ibid.*, p. 92.

148. *Ibid.*, p. 82.
149. *Ibid.*, p. 123.
150. *Ibid.*, p. 119.
151. *Ibid.*, p. 116.
152. *Ibid.*, p. 121; *Jüdische Schriften*, III, 191.
153. Cohen, *Die Religion* . . . , p. 129.
154. Cohen, *Jüdische Schriften*, III, 189.
155. Cohen, *Die Religion* . . . , p. 243.
156. *Ibid.*, p. 359.
157. *Ibid.*, p. 358.
158. Cohen, *Jüdische Schriften*, I, 143.
159. *Ibid.*, III, 157.
160. *Loc. cit.*
161. *Loc. cit.*
162. *Ibid.*, p. 241.
163. *Loc. cit.*
164. Cohen, *Jüdische Schriften*, I, 140.
165. Cohen, *Die Religion* . . . , p. 243.
166. *Ibid.*, p. 241.
167. Cohen, *Jüdische Schriften*, I, 140.
168. *Ibid.*, p. 136.
169. *Loc. cit.*
170. Cohen, *Die Religion* . . . , p. 243.
171. *Ibid.*, p. 245.
172. Cohen, *Jüdische Schriften*, I, 125.
173. Cohen, *Die Religion* . . . , pp. 356 ff., 409.
174. *Ibid.*, p. 441.
175. *Ibid.*, p. 443.
176. Cohen, *Die Religion* . . . , pp. 438 ff.
177. *Loc. cit.*
178. *Ibid.*, p. 52.
179. *Ibid.*, p. 76.
180. Cohen, *Die Religion* . . . , p. 399.
181. *Ibid.*, p. 405.
182. *Ibid.*, p. 406.
183. *Ibid.*, p. 382.
184. *Ibid.*, p. 3.
185. *Ibid.*, p. 1.
186. *Ibid.*, p. 5.
187. Cf. S. H. Bergman, "The Historical Place of Hermann Cohen's Theory in Philosophy," *Moznayim*, XV (1942-1943), pp. 102-106 (Hebrew).
188. Cohen, *Die Religion* . . . , p. 8.
189. *Ibid.*, pp. 10, 40.
190. *Ibid.*, pp. 174, 275.
191. *Ibid.*, p. 175.
192. Cohen, *Jüdische Schriften*, II, 257 ff. For further reading see Y. Klatzkin, *Hermann Cohen* (Berlin & London: Rimon, 1923) (Hebrew), and S. H. Bergman, "A Late Work of Hermann Cohen," *op. cit.*, pp. 219-243. Cf. also M. Buber, "The Love of God and the Idea of God," *Knesseth*, 1943-1944, Sec. C,

pp. 154-159 (Hebrew). Here, as in the rest of this book, the reader is referred to J. Guttmann, *Philosophies of Judaism: The History of Jewish Philosophy from Biblical Times to Franz Rosenzweig*, trans. D. W. Silverman (New York: Holt, Rinehart and Winston, 1964).

CHAPTER 5

1. S. Formstecher: *Die Religion des Geistes, eine wissenschaftliche Darstellung des Judentums nach seinem Character, Entwicklungsgange und Berufe in der Menschheit* (Frankfurt a.M.: John. Chr. Hermann' sche Buchhand lung, 1941) (henceforth = *Religion*).
For this and also some of the following chapters see M. Wiener, *Die Jüdische Religion im Zeitalter der Emanzipation* (Berlin: Philo Verlag und Buchhandlung, 1933); H. J. Schoeps, *Geschichte der judischen Religionsphilosophie der Neuzeit* (Berlin: Vortrupp Verlag, 1935), I; J. Fleischmann, *The Problem of Christianity in Modern Jewish Thought* (Jerusalem: The Magnes Press, 1964), (Hebrew).
2. *Religion*, p. 18.
3. F. W. J. v. Schelling, "Bruno, oder uber das göttliche und natürliche Prinzip der Dinge," *Schellings Werke*, ed. O. Weiss (Leipzig: Fritz Eckardt Verlag, 1907), p. 446.
4. *Ibid.*, p. 443.
5. *Religion*, p. 21.
6. *Ibid.*, p. 119.
7. *Ibid.*, p. 111.
8. *Ibid.*, p. 25, 153.
9. *Ibid.*, p. 29.
10. *Ibid.*, p. 20.
11. I. Maybaum, "Samuel Formstecher, Ein Beitrag zur Geschichte der jüdischen Religionsphilosophie im neuazehntein Jahrhundert," *Monatschrift für Geschichte und Wissenschaft des Judentums* (Frankfurt a.M.: J. Kaufmann Verlag, 1927), pp. 88 ff.
12. *Religion*, p. 63.
13. *Ibid.*, p. 100.
14. *Ibid.*, p. 60.
15. *Ibid.*, p. 116.
16. *Ibid.*, p. 29, pp. 66-67.
17. *Ibid.*, p. 69.
18. At this point there is a clear affinity between Formstecher's view and some of the ideas of H. Cohen discussed before.
19. *Religion*, p. 360.
20. On the relation to Hegel's philosophy see J. Guttmann's *Philosophies of Judaism*.
21. *Religion*, pp. 48, 49, 52.
22. *Ibid.*, p. 44.
23. *Ibid.*, p. 156.
24. *Ibid.*, p. 195.
25. *Ibid.*, p. 31.
26. *Ibid.*, p. 33.
27. *Ibid.*

28. *Ibid.*, p. 125.
29. *Ibid.*, p. 158.
30. S. Hirsch: *Das System der religiösen Anschauungen der Juden und sein Ver-hältniss zum Heidentum, Christentum und zur absoluten Philosophie, I, Die Religionsphilosophie der Juden* (Leipzig: Hunger, 1942), (henceforth = *Religionsphilosophie*). This is the only published volume of Hirsch's opus.
31. *Religionsphilosophie*, p. xxxviii.
32. *Ibid.*, p. 11.
33. *Ibid.*
34. *Ibid.*
35. *Ibid.*, p. 12-13.
36. The present author dealt with this question in his essay on Hegel and the roots of evil, included in *Norm* (Tel Aviv, Am Oved, 1958), (Hebrew).
37. *Religionsphilosophie*, p. 25.
38. *Ibid.*, p. 26.
39. *Ibid.*, p. 28.
40. *Ibid.*, p. 621.
41. *Ibid.*
42. *Ibid.*, p. 33.
43. S. Hirsch: *Das Judentum der christliche Staat und die moderne Kritik. Briefe fur Beleuchtung der Judenfrage an Bruno Bauer* (Leipzig: Hunger, 1843), p. 40.
   On Hirsch's involvement in the Bruno Bauer controversy, see my essay, "For and against Emancipation, The Bruno Bauer Controversy," in *Publications of The Leo Baeck Institute of Jews from Germany*, IV (1959), p. 11 ff.
44. *Religionsphilosophie*, p. 547.
45. *Ibid.*, p. 615.
46. *Ibid.*, p. 29.
47. *Ibid.*, p. 30.
48. *Ibid.*, p. 521.
49. S. L. Steinheim: *Die Offenbarung nach dem Lehrbegriffe der Synagoge*, Dritter Teil, *Die Polemik, der Kampf der Offenbarung mit dem Heidenthume, ihre Synthese und Analyse* (Leipzig: 1863), p. 396. Verlag von Okar Leiner.
50. *Religionsphilosophie*, p. xvi.
51. *Ibid.*, p. xvii.
52. *Ibid.*, p. 141.
53. *Ibid.*, pp. 41, 42.
54. *Ibid.*
55. *Ibid.*, p. 449.
56. *Ibid.*, p. 569.
57. *Ibid.*
58. *Ibid.*, p. xxix.
59. *Ibid.*, p. 529.
60. *Ibid.*, p. 97.
61. *Ibid.*, p. 615.
62. *Ibid.*, p. 622.
63. *Ibid.*, p. 750.
64. *Ibid.*, p. 775.
65. *Ibid.*, p. 745.

66. *Ibid.*
67. See E. Fackenheim, "Samuel Hirsch and Hegel," in *Studies in Nineteenth-Century Jewish Intellectual History,* ed. A. Altmann (Cambridge, Mass.: Harvard University Press, 1964), pp. 171-199.
68. On Krochmal's relation to Schelling (and not only to Hegel, as it was generally assumed), see J. Guttmann, *Philosophies of Judaism, op. cit.* pp. 365 ff.
69. Krochmal, who wrote Hebrew, is known in the abbreviated form of his name: HARENAK (= Rabbi Nachman Krochmal). Our references to his major work (*Guide to the Perplexed of This Time*) are to the edition of S. Rawidowitz, *The Works of Rabbi Nachman Krochmal* (Berlin: Ayyanot Publishers, 1924) (henceforth = *Krochmal*). *Ibid.,* p. 25.
70. *Ibid.,* p. 31.
71. *Ibid.,* pp. 37-38.
72. *Ibid.,* pp. 11, 13.
73. *Ibid.,* p. 24.
74. *Ibid.,* p. 272; also pp. 29, 31.
75. *Ibid.,* p. 38.
76. *Ibid.,* p. 11.
77. *Ibid.,* p. 12.
78. Here we notice Krochmal's affinity to the rationalistic trend in medieval philosophy, and especially his relation to Maimonides.
79. *Krochmal,* p. 17.
80. *Ibid.,* p. 272.
81. *Encylopädie der philosophischen Wissenschaften,* ed. G. J. P. J. Bolland, (Leiden: A. H. Adriani, 1906), p. 736 (Zusatz).
82. C. L. Michelet, *Entwickélúngsgeschichte der neuesten deutschen Philosophie mit besondered Rücksicht auf den gegenwärtigen Kampf Schellings mit der Hegelschen Schule* (Berlin: Duncker-Humbolt, 1843), I, 300, 318.
83. *Religionsphilosophie,* pp. xvii-xviii.
84. *Krochmal,* p. 24.
85. *Ibid.,* p. 29.
86. *Ibid.*
87. *Ibid.,* p. 38.
88. *Ibid.,* p. 37.
89. *Ibid.,* p. 38.
90. I deal with the problem of reality and history in modern Jewish thought in my forthcoming book, *Tradition and Reality.*
91. Krochmal's opus appeared posthumously and was published by the famous historian of Hebrew literature, L. Zunz. He gave it the title, *Guide to the Perplexed of This Time,* wanting to indicate clearly the relation of the work to the tradition of Maimonides. Krochmal himself wished to call his work *Sharey Emunah Tserufah (Gates of Pure Faith).*

CHAPTER 6

1. Our references are to the following editions of Steinheim's opus:
   Die Offenbarung nach dem Lehrbegriffe der Synagoge, ein Schiboleth (Frankfurt a.M.: S. Schmerber, 1835) (henceforth = *Offenbarung* I).
   Die Glaubenslehre der Synagoge als exacte Wissenschaft (Leipzig: L. Schnauss, 1856) (henceforth = *Offenbarung* II).

Die Polemik, Der Kampf der Offenbarung mit dem Heidenthume, ihre Synthese und Analyse (Leipzig: O. Leiner, 1863) (henceforth = *Offenbarung* III).

Funf Monomachieen (Altona: G. Bonn, 1865) (Henceforth = *Offenbarung* IV).

It has to be observed that Steinheim uses the term *Synagoge* as connoting Judaism. It is clearly a parallel term to *Church*.

2. *Von Bleibenden und Vergänglichen im Judentum* (Berlin: Vortrupp-Verlag, 1935), p. 28. It should be observed in this context that in his polemic against Mendelssohn, Steinheim stresses that the latter brought about an emancipation of Jewry—mainly of Western Jewry—from the superstitions of traditional Judaism as represented by Eastern—especially Polish—Jewry. The point is interesting from the angle of modern Jewish history, but is beyond the scope of the present analysis. While speaking about the superstitions of Eastern Jewry, Steinheim uses very strong words. For example, there is a hair disease called in German *Weichselzopf*, a kind of folded hair; the technical term is *plica polonica*. Steinheim says that Mendelssohn was the physician who released "the European Israel" from this disease. (*Moses Mendelssohn und seine Schule in ihrer Beziehung fur Aufgabe des neuen Jahrhundredts der alten Zeitrechnung* [Hamburg: Hoffmann und Campe, 1840], p. 43.)

3. *Offenbarung* II, 38, 205.
4. *Offenbarung* II, 172.
5. See J. Guttmann, *Philosophies of Judaism*, pp. 344 ff.
6. *Offenbarung* I, 5 ff.
7. *Offenbarung* III, 396; cf. I, 146.
8. *Offenbarung* I, 70, 71.
9. *Ibid.*, pp. 10-11.
10. *Ibid.*, p. 188.
11. *Ibid.*, pp. 355 ff.
12. *Offenbarung* III, 93.
13. *Offenbarung* II, 254, 285; also xiii.
14. S. L. Steinheim, *on Bleibenden und Vergänglichen im Judentum*, p. 21 and *passim*.
15. *Offenbarung* I, 267.
16. *Ibid.*, p. 283.
17. *Ibid.*, p. 351.
18. *Ibid.*
19. *Offenbarung* II, 245.
20. *Ibid.*, p. 4.
21. *Ibid.*, p. 245.
22. *Ibid.*, p. 246.
23. *Ibid.*
24. *Ibid.*, pp. 263, 246.
25. In German, *Einzig-Einer*.
26. *Ibid.*, p. 263.
27. *Ibid.*, p. 179.
28. *Ibid.*, p. 3.
29. *Ibid.*, p. 7. The view expressed here is close to Hegel's analysis of the relation between religion and Enlightenment in *Phenomenology of Mind*.

30. *Offenbarung* I, 38, 310; *Offenbarung* II, 7.
31. *Offenbarung* II, 11.
32. *Ibid.*
33. *Ibid.*
34. *Von Bleibenden und Vergäganglichen im Judentum*, p. 14.
35. *Offenbarung* II, 13.
36. *Ibid.*, pp. 162, 63, 76.
37. *Offenbarung* I, 248.
38. *Offenbarung* II, 54.
39. *Offenbarung* I, 283.
40. *Ibid.*, p. 253.
41. *Ibid.*
42. *Ibid.*
43. *Ibid.*, p. 234.
44. *Ibid.*, p. 18.
45. *Ibid.*, pp. 29-31.
46. *Ibid.*, p. 324.
47. *Ibid.*, p. 211.
48. *Ibid.*, p. 226.
49. "Abraham Geigers Briefe an J. Dérenbourg (1833-1842)," *Allgemeine Zeitung des Judenthums*, No. 11, 60. Jahrgang (Berlin, March 13, 1896), p. 130 (Letter XI, May 14, 1836). Professor G. Scholem called my attention to this letter.
50. He was the son of J. G. Fichte.
51. Our references are to the following editions of Rosenzweig's works:
    Der Stern der Erlösung (Frankfurt a.M.: J. Kauffmann Verlag, 1930), Part I, II, III (henceforth = *Stern* I, II, III).
    Briefe, ed. E. Rosenzweig and E. Simon (Berlin: Schocken Verlag, 1935) (henceforth = *Br.*).
    Kleinere Schreiten (Berlin: Schocken Verlag, 1937) (henceforth = *K.S.*).
    Understanding the Sick and the Healthy, ed. N. N. Glatzer (New York: The Noonday Press, 1953) (henceforth = *Un.*).
    Jehuda Halevi, Zweinndneunzig Hymnen und Gedichte Deutsch (Berlin: L. Schneider, n.d.) (henceforth = *J.H.*).
52. *K.S.*, p. 398.
53. *Ibid.*, p. 383.
54. *Br.*, p. 475. See my essay, "Common Sense and Theological Experience on the Basis of Franz Rosenzweig's Philosophy," *Journal of the History of Philosophy*, V/4 (1967), pp. 353-360.
55. *Br.*, p. 475.
56. *K.S.*, pp. 514-515.
57. *Ibid.*, p. 379.
58. *Stern*, I, 33.
59. *Br.*, pp. 53-54.
60. *Stern*, I, 109.
61. *K.S.*, p. 388.
62. *Ibid.*, p. 381.
63. *Br.*, p. 611.
64. *K.S.*, p. 528.
65. *J.H.*, p. 205.

66. *K.S.*, p. 528.
67. *Ibid.*, p. 532.
68. *Br.*, p. 264.
69. *K.S.*, p. 235.
70. *Ibid.*, pp. 357 ff.
71. *Stern*, I, 19 ff.
72. *K.S.*, p. 361.
73. *Stern*, I, 22.
74. *Ibid.*, p. 17.
75. *K.S.*, p. 359.
76. *Ibid.*, p. 27.
77. *Stern*, I, 7 ff.
78. E. Spranger, "Der Kampf gegen den Idealismus," *Sitzungsberichte der Preussischen Akademie der Wissenschaften*, philosophisch-historische Klasse (Berlin, 1931), p. 445.
79. Karl Löwith, "M. Heidegger and Franz Rosenzweig, or Temporality and Eternity," *Philosophy and Phenomenological Research* III (1943), pp. 53 ff.
80. Karl Jaspers, *Existenzphilosophie* (Berlin and Leipzig; Walter de Gruyter & Co., 1938), p. 17.
81. H. Barth, "Philosophie, Theologie und Existenzproblem," *Zwischen den Zeiten*, X (Munich, 1932), pp. 99-124.
82. *Ibid.*, p. 107.
83. *Ibid.*, pp. 106, 107.
84. E. Reisner, "Existenzphilosophie und existentielle philosophie," *Zwischen den Zeiten*, XI (1933), pp. 57-78.
85. "Finitum non est capax infiniti" (E. Brunner).
86. *Stern*, II, 31 ff.
87. *Ibid.*, p. 20.
88. *Stern*, III, 16.
89. *Stern*, II, 36.
90. *Ibid.*
91. *Ibid.*, pp. 46-47.
92. *Ibid.*, p. 33.
93. *Ibid.*, p. 43.
94. *Ibid.*, p. 42.
95. *Br.*, p. 81.
96. *Stern*, II, 20.
97. *Br.*, p. 210.
98. *Stern*, I, 81.
99. *J.H.*, p. 174.
100. *Stern*, II, 94.
101. *J.H.*, p. 188.
102. *Stern*, III, 156.
103. *Ibid.*, p. 158.
104. *J.H.*, p. 189.
105. *Stern*, II, 88 ff.
106. *Ibid.*, p. 126.
107. *K.S.*, p. 527.
108. *J.H.*, p. 180.

109. *Ibid.*
110. *Stern*, I, 112.
111. *Ibid.*
112. *K.S.*, p. 364.
113. *Stern*, II, 119.
114. *Ibid.*, p. 107.
115. *Ibid.*, p. 10.
116. *Ibid.*, p. 92.
117. *Ibid.*, p. 98.
118. *Ibid.*, p. 94.
119. *Stern*, III, 74.
120. For instance, *Stern*, II, 25.
121. *J.H.*, p. 174.
122. *Stern*, II, 12.
123. *Ibid.*, pp. 88 ff.
124. *Ibid.*
125. *Br.*, p. 211.
126. *K.S.*, p. 217.
127. *Stern*, II, 30.
128. *Ibid.*, p. 28.
129. *K.S.*, p. 141.
130. In German, *angeredet*. Cf. *Almanach des Schocken Verlags auf das Jahr 5699* (Berlin: Schocken Verlag, 1938), pp. 55-56.
131. *Stern*, II, 26.
132. *J.H.*, p. 194.
133. S. H. Bergman, "Science and Faith" *Machbarot le-Sifrut* (Tel Aviv, 1945), p. 106 (Hebrew).
134. *Stern*, II, 9-10.
135. *Ibid.*, pp. 102 ff.
136. *Ibid.*, p. 168.
137. *Ibid.*
138. *Ibid.*, pp. 169-170.
139. *Ibid.*
140. *J.H.*, p. 206.
141. *Stern*, II, 194-195.
142. *Stern*, III, 159.
143. *Ibid.*, p. 160.
144. *Stern*, II, 154.
145. *K.S.*, p. 374.
146. *Br.*, p. 407.
147. *Ibid.*, p. 316.
148. *Stern*, III, 19.
149. *Ibid.*, pp. 86-87.
150. *Ibid.*, p. 78.
151. *Ibid.*, p. 60.
152. *Ibid.*, p. 61.
153. *Ibid.*, p. 312.
154. *Ibid.*, p. 48.
155. *Ibid.*, p. 51.

156. *K.S.*, p. 18.
157. *Stern*, III, 69.
158. *Ibid.*, p. 105.
159. *K.S.*, p. 29.
160. *Stern*, III, 49.
161. *Ibid.*, p. 56.
162. *Ibid.*, pp. 190 ff.
163. *Ibid.*, p. 57.
164. *Ibid.*, p. 53.
165. *K.S.*, p. 22.
166. *Ibid.*, p. 192.
167. *J.H.*, p. 236.
168. *Stern*, III, 97 ff.
169. *Ibid.*, p. 59.
170. *Br.*, p. 78.
171. *Stern*, III, 185.
172. *Ibid.*, p. 103.
173. *Ibid.*, pp. 98, 110.
174. *Ibid.*, pp. 90, 101, 103.
175. *Ibid.*, p. 147.
176. *Ibid.*, p. 175.
177. *Ibid.*, p. 104.
178. *Ibid.*, pp. 97 ff.
179. *Ibid.*, p. 104.
180. *Ibid.*, p. 114.
181. *K.S.*, p. 192.
182. *Stern*, III, 115.
183. *Ibid.*, pp. 97 ff.
184. *Stern*, III, 183.
185. *Ibid.*, p. 200.
186. *K.S.*, p. 42.
187. See the above-mentioned book of J. Fleischmann, pp. 147 ff.
188. *Stern*, III, 104.
189. *Ibid.*, p. 179.
190. *Ibid.*, p. 162.
191. *K.S.*, p. 396.
192. Consult also: G. Scholem, *Franz Rosenzweig and his Book "The Star of Redemption"* (Hebrew) (Jerusalem: The Hebrew University Press, 1930); Else Freund, *Die Existenzphilosophie Franz Rosenzweigs*, (Leipzig: Felix Meiner, 1933); S. H. Bergman, *Thinkers of the Generation* (Tel Aviv: Mitzpeh, 1935), (Hebrew); N. Glatzer, *Franz Rosenzweig: His Life and Thought* (New York: Schocken, 1953); S. Schwarzchild, *Franz Rosenzweig (1896-1929)* (London: Hillel Foundation, n.d.).

CHAPTER 7

1. *The Lights of Holiness* ed. D. Cohen (Jerusalem: The Society for the Publication of the Writings of Rav Kook, 1935), p. 83 (Hebrew), (henceforth = *Holiness*).

2. *Ibid.*, p. 95.
3. *Ibid.*, p. 310.
4. *Ibid.*, p. 16.
5. *Ibid.*, p. 144.
6. *Ibid.*, p. 231.
7. *Ibid.*, p. 407.
8. *Lights of Return* (Jerusalem: Hegel Yerushalayim, 1936), p. 26 (Hebrew).
9. *Holiness*, p. 41.
10. *Ibid.*, p. 259.
11. *Ibid.*, p. 179.
12. *Clouds of Purity* (Tel Aviv, n.d.). This book has only appeared as a fragment.
13. *Holiness*, p. 109.
14. *Ibid.*, p. 102.
15. *Ibid.*, p. 146.
16. *Ibid.*, p. 327.
17. *Ibid.*, pp. 17, 25.
18. *Ibid.*, p. 25.
19. *Ibid.*, p. 48.
20. *Ibid.*, p. 221.
21. *Ibid.*, p. 237.
22. *Ibid.*, p. 56.
23. *Ibid.*, p. 47.
24. *Ibid.*, p. 24.
25. *Clouds of Purity*, p. 18.
26. *The Letters of Rav Kook* (Jerusalem: The Society for the Publication of the Writings of Rav Kook, 1923), pp. 75 ff. (Hebrew).
27. *Clouds of Purity*, p. 20.
28. *Holiness*, p. 112.
29. *Ibid.*, p. 65.
30. *Ibid.*, p. 63.
31. *Clouds of Purity*, p. 32.
32. *Ibid.*
33. *Holiness*, p. 63.
34. *Ibid.*, p. 297.
35. *The Lofty in Holiness*, p. 4.
36. *Holiness*, p. 225.
37. *Ibid.*, p. 1.
38. *Ibid.*, p. 3.
39. *Ibid.*, p. 322.
40. *Ibid.*, p. 321. See also *The Lofty in Holiness*, p. 3.
41. *Holiness*, p. 143.
42. *Ibid.*, p. 145.
43. *Ibid.*, p. 64.
44. *The Lofty in Holiness*, p. 12.
45. *Ibid.*, p. 15.
46. *Ibid.*, p. 3.
47. *Holiness*, p. 2.
48. *Ibid.*, p. 43.
49. *Ibid.*, pp. 52-53.

50. *Ibid.*, p. 210.
51. *Ibid.*, p. 388.
52. *Lights of Return*, p. 35.
53. *Ibid.*, p. 52.
54. *Ibid.*, pp. 1, 4.
55. *Ibid.*, p. 25.
56. *Ibid.*, p. 52.
57. *Clouds of Purity*, p. 15.
58. *Lights of Return*, p. 1.
59. *Ibid.*, p. 4.
60. *Ibid.*, p. 28.
61. *Ibid.*, p. 8.
62. *Ibid.*, p. 20.
63. *Holiness*, p. 353.
64. *Lights of Return*, p. 17.
65. *Holiness*, p. 225.
66. *Ibid.*, p. 210.
67. *Lights of Israel* (Jerusalem: Yerushalayim, 1942), p. 70
68. *Holiness*, p. 382.
69. *Clouds of Purity*, p. 22
70. *Holiness*, pp. 360-361.
71. *Ibid.*, p. 365.
72. *Ibid.*, p. 209.
73. *Ibid.*, p. 212.
74. *Ibid.*, p. 250.
75. *Ibid.*, p. 215.
76. *Ibid.*
77. *Ibid.*, p. 250.
78. *Ibid.*, p. 215.
79. *The Prayer Book with a Commentary by Rav Kook* (Jerusalem, 1939), I, 51 (Hebrew).
80. *Arpeley Tohar*, p. 37.
81. *Holiness*, p. 385.
82. *Ibid.*, p. 10.
83. *Lights of Israel*, p. 40.
84. *Ibid.*, p. 41.
85. *Ibid.*, pp. 41-42.
86. *Ibid.*, pp. 40-41.
87. *Ibid.*, p. 83.
88. *Holiness*, p. 412.

CHAPTER 8

1. Henri Bergson, *The Creative Mind* (New York: Philosophical Library, 1946), p. 128.
2. *The Writings of A. D. Gordon* (Tel Aviv: The Central Committee of Ha-Poel Ha-Tzair, 1926), III, 20 (Hebrew). References to Gordon's work will be made to the five volumes of this edition, and will be cited as *Gordon* I, II, III, IV, V,
3. *Gordon* III, p. 200.

4. *Ibid.*, p. 216.
5. *Gordon* II, 141.
6. *Ibid.*, 248.
7. *Gordon* V, 216.
8. *Gordon* IV, 87.
9. *Ibid.*, 135.
10. For Gordon's view of the nature of peoplehood, see my book *History and Reality* (Tel Aviv: Am Oved, 1945), pp. 243 ff. (Hebrew).
11. *Gordon* III, 129.
12. *Gordon* II, 125.
13. *Gordon* I, 125.
14. *Gordon* III, 200.
15. *Ibid.*, pp. 202-203, 228.
16. *Gordon* I, 125.
17. *Gordon* IV, 250.
18. Ahad Haam, *At the Crossroads* (Berlin: Judischer Verlag, 1930), IV, 38 ff., III, 210 ff. (Hebrew). [English translation, "Moses," in *Nationalism and the Jewish Ethic, Basic Writings of Ahad Haam*, edited and introduced by Hans Kohn (New York: Schocken Books, 1962).]
19. *Gordon* IV, 89.
20. *Gordon* III, 228.
21. *Ibid.*, 223.
22. *Ibid.*, pp. 225-226.
23. *Ibid.*, p. 223.
24. *Ibid.*, p. 224.
25. Ahad Haam, *At the Crossroads, op. cit.*, IV, 45 ff. (Hebrew).
26. *Ibid.*, pp. 48-49. (Included in *Nationalism and the Jewish Ethic., op. cit.*, pp. 300-301.)
27. *Ibid.*
28. *Gordon* III, 198.
29. *Ibid.*, p. 223.
30. *Ibid.*, p. 232.
31. *Ibid.*, pp. 222-223.
32. *Ibid.*, p. 223.
33. *Ibid.*
34. *Ibid.*, p. 135.
35. Henri Bergson, *The Two Sources of Morality and Religion* (London: Macmillan and Co., 1935), pp. 194 ff.
36. See S. H. Bergman's introduction to A. D. Gordon, *Man and Nature* (Jerusalem: The Zionist Library, 1951), p. 9 ff. (Hebrew).

Index